Globalization on the Ground

Globalization on the Ground

Postbellum Guatemalan Democracy and Development

Edited by Christopher Chase-Dunn, Susanne Jonas, and Nelson Amaro

ROWMAN & LITTLEFIELD PUBLISHERS, INC.
Lanham • Boulder • New York • Oxford

ROWMAN & LITTLEFIELD PUBLISHERS, INC.

Published in the United States of America
by Rowman & Littlefield Publishers, Inc.
4720 Boston Way, Lanham, Maryland 20706
http://www.rowmanlittlefield.com

12 Hid's Copse Road, Cumnor Hill, Oxford OX2 9JJ, England

Copyright © 2001 by Rowman & Littlefield Publishers, Inc.

Earlier versions of chapters 3, 4, 6, 12, and 13 appeared in a special issue of the *Journal of Interamerican Studies and World Affairs*, volume 42, no. 4 (Winter 2000). Chapter 9 is reprinted with permission from Princeton University Press.

All rights reserved. No part of this publication may be reproduced, stored in a retrieval system, or transmitted in any form or by any means, electronic, mechanical, photocopying, recording, or otherwise, without the prior permission of the publisher.

British Library Cataloguing in Publication Information Available

Library of Congress Cataloging-in-Publication Data

Globalization on the ground : postbellum Guatemalan democracy and development / edited by Christopher Chase-Dunn, Susanne Jonas, and Nelson Amaro.
    p. cm.
   Includes bibliographical references and index.
   ISBN 0-7425-0866-8 (alk. paper) — ISBN 0-7425-0867-6 (pbk. : alk. paper)
    1. Democratization—Guatemala. 2. Guatemala—Politics and government—1985-
3. Guatemala—Economic conditions—1985- I. Chase-Dunn, Christopher K. II. Jonas, Susanne, 1941- III. Amaro, Nelson, 1940-

JL1496 .G56 2001
972.8105'3—dc21

                                                                      00-045828

Printed in the United States of America

♾™ The paper used in this publication meets the minimum requirements of American National Standard for Information Sciences—Permanence of Paper for Printed Library Materials, ANSI/NISO Z39.48-1992.

Contents

List of Illustrations   vii

Part I: The Future of Guatemalan Development

1   Guatemalan Development and Democratization: 3
Past, Present, and Future
Susanne Jonas and Christopher Chase-Dunn

2   Development and Equity: 9
The Agenda for the Twenty-First Century
Gert Rosenthal

Part II: Democracy, Demilitarization, and the State

3   Global Forces and Regime Change: 21
Guatemala within the Central American Context
John A. Booth

4   Democratization through Peace   49
Susanne Jonas

5   Decentralization, Local Government, and Citizen Participation: 83
Unsolved Problems in the Guatemalan Democratization Process
Nelson Amaro

6   Demilitarization and Security in El Salvador and Guatemala: 101
Convergences of Success and Crisis
A. Douglas Kincaid

7   Democracy and the Market in Guatemala   119
Edelberto Torres Rivas

8   Coffee and the Guatemalan State   129
Stephen G. Bunker

Part III: Indigenous Movements and Social Change

9 Pan-Mayanism and the Guatemalan Peace Process   145
  Kay B. Warren

10 Development of Globalization in the Mayan Population   167
   of Guatemala
   José Serech

11 Linguistic Diversity, Interculturalism, and Democracy   177
   Michael Richards and Julia Richards

Part IV: Globalization on the Ground

12 Neoliberalism, the Global Elite, and the   189
   Guatemalan Transition: A Critical Macrosocial Analysis
   William I. Robinson

13 Globalization from Below in Guatemala   207
   Christopher Chase-Dunn and Susan Manning

14 Theories of Development and Their Application   229
   to Small Countries
   Alejandro Portes

Appendix: Summary of the Accord on Identity   241
and the Rights of Indigenous Peoples

Index   245

About the Contributors   251

Illustrations

Figures

11.1.	Present-Day Amerindian Language Boundaries	178
13.1.	Openness Trade Globalization, 1830-1992	210
13.2.	Portfolio Investment Dependence, 1975-1998	220
13.3.	Direct Investment Dependence, 1975-1998	220

Tables

3.1.	Central American Regime Type, 1970-1998	23
3.2.	Gross Domestic Product Per Capita, Central America, Selected Years, 1987-1996	33
3.3.	Selected Economic Data on Guatemala, 1987-1996	35
3.4.	Attitudes, Values, and Political Participation, Urban Central Americans, Early 1990s	37
5.1.	Guatemala: Criteria for the Distribution of Local Funds	94
14.1	Political Participation and Attitudes in the Caribbean Basin, 1992	235

Part I:

The Future of Guatemalan Development

1

Guatemalan Development and Democratization: Past, Present, and Future

Susanne Jonas and Christopher Chase-Dunn

"Looking back over the last twenty-five years, you can see a gigantic leap forward; but looking ahead, what stands out is uncertainty." These words, written in 1997 by El Salvador's Roberto Turcios, capture an essential dilemma of interpreting postwar transitions and provide an excellent starting point for understanding Guatemala in its current transitional moment.

With the December 29, 1996 signing of peace accords ending Latin America's longest and bloodiest civil war (lasting thirty-six years and costing more than 200,000 civilian lives, primarily highlands Mayas), Guatemala has entered a new stage in its history. The past half century—following the 1954 Central Intelligence Agency (CIA)-orchestrated overthrow of the ten-year national democratic Revolution of 1944 to 1954—was characterized by levels of state repression and violence, ethnic and racial discrimination, and exclusionary politics virtually unparalleled in Latin America. During the early 1980s, state-sponsored violence against Mayan communities took on the characteristics of genocide. The 1996 peace accords were designed to make a definitive break from the past. Even the prospect of becoming a "normal" country promised to open up a new era in Guatemalan history. This perceived new moment in Guatemalan history was also the inspiration for the 1998 conference that forms the basis for this book.

The peace process has created an important opening for Guatemalan society. Formerly excluded groups have been invited to participate in legal and institutional processes for formulating policies of development and democratization. The vision of creating a new multiethnic nation that recognizes the political, cultural, and socioeconomic rights of its poorest and least powerful citizens is more widespread now than it has been since the decade of 1944 to 1954. The turn toward societal normalization and democratization allowed Guatemalans the space to consider how a more inclusive—multiethnic, multicultural, and multilingual—national community could emerge; it also opened up discussion of what options could be available for socially equitable responses to economic, ideological, and geopolitical neoliberalism. In short, as a result of the peace accords, many Guatemalans have been organizing proactively and interacting on the basis of rising expectations rather than fear as the driving force—in itself a very significant advance, even though the realities of change lag far behind those rising expectations.

By 1998, the great hopes sparked by the peace process were already being tempered by the evident gap between the vision of peace and the realities of postwar Guatemala. For one thing, even if the peace accords as signed had been fully implemented, they would have brought meaningful participatory democracy to Guatemala, but not necessarily social justice. Furthermore, and far more serious, the post-1996 battles for gaining governmental compliance with what had been signed proved to be even more difficult than the six-year negotiation and struggle (1991 to 1996) to reach agreement on the terms of the accords. In these ongoing battles, pro-peace forces in Guatemalan civil society have continued to need all the support they can get from the international community. Worse yet, even after the signing of the accords, violence—some of it politically motivated—continued. The most brutal act of political violence in recent years, the April 26, 1998 assassination of Msgr. Juan Gerardi—two days after his Human Rights office issued a major report attributing more than 85 percent of the killings during the war to government security forces—was a postwar political crime. This crime dramatically highlighted the fact that "postwar" is not necessarily the same as peace.

From a broader perspective, postwar Guatemala exemplifies many of the problems that plague other regions of the Third World—widespread poverty, ethnic discrimination, and political exclusion, to mention only the most obvious. Guatemala is not among the world's poorest countries. Based on gross national product (GNP) per capita it falls within the category that the World Bank terms "low to middle income countries." But among countries in this category, Guatemala is one of those with the highest incidence of poverty (especially among the Mayan population and among women), and it is the third most unequal, that is, in terms of the disparity between rich and poor. Despite its abundant, valuable human and natural resources, Guatemala ranks among the worst on such indicators as unequal land tenure and unemployment/underemployment. The tax ratio relative to gross domestic product (GDP) is one of the lowest in the world, as is the rate of "social spending" on health and education.

Complicating the analysis of Guatemala at this transitional moment is a new international context. Many aspects of postwar Guatemala can best be illuminated in the light of the country's articulation with this changing world order. The end of the Cold War, the emergence of powerful global market forces, changing policies in the advanced industrial countries, the emergence of stronger multilateral agencies at the world level, and the current hegemony of neoliberal policy prescriptions emanating from powerful global agencies such as the World Bank and the International Monetary Fund—all of these broader contextual factors pose significant challenges as well as possible opportunities for Guatemalan democratization and development. Some international agencies, most notably the United Nations, have stimulated democratization, while others have imposed new constraints.

The situation of Guatemala as a developing country emerging from a long period of strife within a new global context suggests comparisons with other specific countries—most obviously, neighboring El Salvador, but also South Africa and the Middle East. Ultimately, these cases of armed conflict and partial political reconciliation need to be compared to one another and placed in the historical context of decolonization and national liberation movements. Our purpose here is to contribute to that eventual goal through a collection of in-depth analyses of the Guatemalan case. What we learn from this case may prove more broadly relevant. How the relationship between the developed and the developing countries is worked out in the next decades will be a major determinant of the nature of the twenty-first century world-system. Guatemala can be a nodal point for understanding these connections.

To take one example, ethnic conflict has long afflicted societies in both the periphery and the core. Indigenous peoples in all areas of the world are now demanding cultural, political, and economic recognition alongside social justice. The war in Guatemala was not per se an ethnic conflict; rather it was a Cold War civil war with important ethnic aspects because the majority of the Guatemalan population (60 percent) is an oppressed indigenous population and because the 1980s phase of the war took place mainly in the indigenous highlands. Guatemala's Accord on Identity and the Rights of Indigenous Peoples, one of the peace accords, is a conceptual breakthrough to be studied and emulated in many other countries that are experiencing ethnic conflicts or those with important ethnic aspects. In short, the Guatemalan case could potentially make an important contribution in the area of resolution of deep and longstanding conflicts with important ethnic dimensions.

Returning to the case at hand: Is it possible—against all odds—to build a new society in a country where such unspeakable horrors as modern-day genocide have occurred? Are we witnessing the growing pains of a "new democracy" or the tragedy of a unique historical opportunity about to be lost? These are among the troubling questions that frame the essays and analyses offered in this book.

This book presents research, analysis, and reflections on the major issues of Guatemalan development and democracy: the role of the military, the involvement of Mayan communities in national development, the possible emergence of more inclusive political institutions, and the roles of international forces and agencies in Guatemalan social change. The chapters in this book have been written by scholars and public policy experts from Guatemala and the United States. In Part I, Gert Rosenthal, himself an important actor in the Guatemalan drama, presents a vision for a more egalitarian form of development in the twenty-first century.

Part II contains six chapters that focus on democratization, demilitarization, and the state. In chapter 3 John Booth presents Guatemalan political trends in a comparative Central American framework and considers the effects of global forces on regime change. In chapter 4 Susanne Jonas discusses the contested nature of democracy and the contradictions and possibilities of the Guatemala peace process. In chapter 5 Nelson Amaro discusses recent changes and future prospects for political decentralization and increasing political participation in Guatemala. Chapter 6 contains A. Douglas Kincaid's comparative analysis of demilitarization and security problems in Guatemala and El Salvador. In chapter 7 Guatemala's dean of sociology, Edelberto Torres Rivas, presents his observations on the peace process and possibilities for democratization and development. Stephen Bunker discusses the past and possible future connections between coffee agriculture and state structures in Guatemala in chapter 8.

Part III focuses on indigenous movements, cultural differences, and democratization. Kay Warren discusses the pan-Mayan movement and the struggle for cultural rights in Guatemala. José Serech discusses the idea of including the Mayan majority in Guatemalan development projects, and the relevance of globalization processes and the global indigenous rights movement. Michael and Julia Richards discuss the complex relationship between linguistic differentiation and intercultural communication, competition and cooperation in Guatemala.

In Part IV global structures and pressures are described and the constraints and opportunities they present for Guatemalan development and democracy are considered. William Robinson analyzes the emergence of a global capitalist class, its ideology of neoliberalism, and its Guatemalan allies in Central American comparative perspective. Christopher Chase-Dunn discusses a structural approach to the global system and considers the historical trajectory of Guatemala in this larger context, as well as the possibilities for proactive popular strategies in the new age of globalization. Alejandro Portes considers the relevance of three different social science perspectives for understanding Guatemalan social change. He shows that increasingly dense transnational networks are playing a fundamentally new role in the Guatemalan drama.

Earlier versions of chapters 3, 4, 6, 12, and 13 appeared in a special issue of the *Journal of Interamerican Studies and World Affairs*, volume 42, no. 4 (winter 2000). Moreover, earlier versions of the chapters of this book were presented at a conference on Guatemalan development and democracy held at the Universidad del Valle in Guatemala City in March 1998.[1] We wish to thank the Division of International Programs of the National Science Foundation of the United States, the Universidad del Valle, and the United Nations Development Program for their support of this conference. We are also grateful for the helpful contributions of Richard Adams, Patricia Landolt, Claudia Scholz, Aura Aparicio, June Nash, John Ruthrauf, and Aonghas St-Hilaire. Thanks are due to William Robinson for his help in translating Edelberto Torres Rivas's chapter contribution into the English. Dean Birkenkamp and Matt Boullioun at Rowman & Littlefield were crucial to the publication of the book.

The conference was organized binationally and was pervaded by a sense of the transnational dimensions of Guatemala's future. We are convinced that reason, understanding, and goodwill on the part of the people of Guatemala and their friends abroad can contribute to a more democratic, sustainable, and just future. Susanne Jonas's opening words at the conference, on behalf of the U.S. conference organizers, convey our sense of the importance of the current transitional period:

> This is a very special event: Guatemala is not just one more country but a very special country; and this is a very special moment in its history. Guatemala is the most beautiful and dramatic country in the world (in my rather subjective view), and it is experiencing its most important process of transformation of the last half century, as a result of the signing of the Peace Accords. This opens up an historic opportunity for a "reinvention," that is, for the creation of a new "possible Guatemala"—although this possibility can be realized only through the efforts of many actors, both Guatemalans and friends of Guatemala from other countries.
>
> It is within this historical conjuncture or moment and this context that we had the idea of organizing this transnational conference, with both Guatemalan and international participants. For those of us who have come from outside Guatemala, it is a true privilege to have this opportunity to accompany the Guatemalan process at a moment that is so critical for its democratization and development. For us, the "accompaniment" is realized through reflections, ideas, interchanges, and intellectual work—all of which might appear somewhat distant from Guatemala's most immediate tasks, but which, in the long run, could contribute to the construction of a Guatemala that is as modern and civilized as it is beautiful and dramatic.

Note

1. Versions in Spanish of most of the conference papers are available at <http://www.jhu.edu/~soc/ladark.html>.

2

Development and Equity: The Agenda for the Twenty-First Century

Gert Rosenthal

This chapter was inspired by two simple ideas. First, Guatemala suffers tremendous lags in many areas: education, health and nutrition, physical infrastructure, exclusion (economic and ethnic), and institutional development (e.g., in the areas of administration of justice and security). These lags need to be addressed. Indeed, Guatemala is a country of extreme contrasts, with islands of modernity and progress in a sea of backwardness. The country reveals some of the highest levels of absolute poverty in Latin America; the same can be said for the pronounced inequality in income distribution (UNDP 1997). Furthermore, economic performance in the past few years (growth rates of from 3 percent to 4 percent per annum) has been mediocre (ECLAC 1998).

Second, having said all of the above, there is still ample room to come closer to meeting the country's potential for development. In other words, it would not be an unreasonable proposition to aspire to a much better performance to bridge the gap between reality and potential.

It would be pretentious to try to offer a blueprint on how to achieve the challenge of fostering Guatemala's development in the dawn of the twenty-first century. A less ambitious undertaking would be to explore some of the basic issues that the country will have to face in order to achieve greater growth, improved income distribution, and the defense of its natural capital, all within the context of democracy and respect for the fact that Guatemala is a multiethnic society. Some of the main parameters of the debate that surrounds those issues are also discussed.

Economic Activities for Growth

One of the first issues Guatemala will have to grapple with revolves around the question of what activities will promote growth. Will the country continue to rely on a few basic commodities to generate its foreign exchange, or will it be able to move into higher value-added activities? Will those activities be identified by private entrepreneurs as a result of market forces, or will their development require special incentives? Will they be internationally competitive? Will they be environmentally rational? These are all very central questions connected with the development agenda.

To be sure, growth does not equal development, but without sustained and dynamic expansion of the country's productive capacity, it is hard to imagine that the other crucial aspects of development—especially greater equity—can be achieved. What should be pursued is good quality growth, based on increasing levels of productivity (per person, or for all the factors of production).

Unfortunately, many enterprises in the country, even the larger and modern ones, have in the past and even in the present continued to guide their activities by short-term profit considerations, or by acquiring international competitiveness by the simple expedient of repressing real wages, as happened especially in 1985 to 1986 and again in 1990 to 1991 (Sistema de las Naciones Unidas en Guatemala 1998). This approach is at odds with assuring sustainability of growth through increasing levels of productivity. This is the only means of competing in today's global economy and, in turn, offering the possibility of a more equitable distribution of the benefits of growth through the creation of employment opportunities and the possibility of increased real wages.

Some specific points can be made in this regard. First, increasing productivity is not a function of the size of the firm; it is necessary in large as well as microenterprises, and even in peasant farming. Each type of enterprise, within its respective context, has the potential of improving productivity through the application of technology. Second, application of technology should not be synonymous with greater capital intensity. Guatemala should make an effort to foster international competitiveness by making use of its abundant and underutilized supply of labor. Third, the application of technology does not only include machinery and equipment ("hard technology") but improved management and organizational techniques, as well as enhanced labor proficiency ("soft technology").

Few would take issue with the desirability of growth based on greater efficiency. The main question is how to achieve this goal, or how to improve international competitiveness. The requirements that must be fulfilled form part of the agenda of development. These respond both to conditions that fall under the aegis of the firm and those of a more general nature that affect the whole economy, and which fall under the purview of public policy.

It is obvious, for example, that good macroeconomic management is necessary. This entails coherence in its different components (monetary, credit, fiscal, exchange, trade, and labor policies) in order to ensure financial stability and sustainability of macroeconomic equilibrium in the foreseeable future. Another goal of macropolicies would be to avoid serious distortions in the efficient allocation of resources in order to expand productive capacity, encourage savings and investment, and promote innovation.

The formulation and implementation of coherent policies is not so much a product of preferences or ideology, but a basic prerequisite to any economy open to transnational forces. It will no doubt be a constant in Guatemala's agenda for development in the future, as it is in the present. In this regard, there is no doubt that one of the traditional obstacles to ensuring financial stability lies in improving the country's tax system. This means that fiscal reform will have a privileged place in Guatemala's future development agenda (IMF 1997).

So far, the requisites outlined sound like the conventional wisdom being dispensed by most multilateral development organizations. However, especially in the case of Guatemala, where the market is plagued by imperfections and externalities, a coherent and stable macroeconomic management, while basic, is not enough. Complementary selective policies are also necessary, in order to promote enhanced productivity as well as to strengthen public and private institutions that support development. These include the educational system, the administration of justice, the legal system, the financial system, the development of modern enterprises, and many others, some of which are touched upon below.

Furthermore, growth does not only depend on the performance of individual firms, but on the whole system made up of these individual parts. Thus, increasing efficiency impacts areas such as the educational system, the technological and physical infrastructure (energy, transport, communications), the quality of labor relations, the quality of the financial system, the capacity of the public sector, and many more realms. Moreover, there are numerous links between each of these elements. For example, the efficiency of an individual firm could be annulled by high user chargers in inefficient ports, or deficient financial services. This is of particular relevance for Guatemala, which enters the next millennium with serious lags in physical infrastructure, weak institutions, and poorly trained human resources. The main point to be made is that acquiring international competitiveness—and the capacity for dynamic and sustained growth—requires advancing simultaneously on numerous fronts.

And what will constitute the "engine of growth" of the Guatemalan economy? Will it continue to be coffee, sugar, bananas, and other basic products? Or will there be a continuing expansion of recently opened niches in vegetables, flowers, fruits, the sale of services (especially tourism), subcontracting (especially in apparel and electronic components), and petroleum? These newer niches are all moving in the direction of clusters of interrelated industries espoused by Professor Michael Porter of the Harvard Business School, and they are being actively promoted in Central America by the Instituto Centroamericano de Administración de Empresas (INCAE) (Porter 1980; INCAE 1996). In fact, in general terms, this approach appears to be the obvious way to go for Guatemala, since it would be compatible with applying technology to the productive process, leading to increased levels of productivity as well as economic diversification. The country has already demonstrated a potential to move modestly in this direction; this potential can be very much enhanced.

Finally, growth should be environmentally rational; that is, it should not occur at the expense of future generations. Anyone who has witnessed the degradation of Guatemala's natural resources, in Petén, on the Pacific Coast, in the highlands, and in the transversal belt, will certainly share this concern (FLACSO and WWW 1997). For a country whose development essentially depends on the exploitation, transformation, and marketing of natural resources, good management of those resources is tantamount to improved standards of living. In addition, in a country where a growing proportion of the population lives in urban centers, the strains caused by uncontrolled physical expansion, on the one hand, and the finite character of the natural resources, on the other, bring pressure on the provision of services, contaminate the environment, and generate unmet demand for housing, to name just a few consequences. For this reason, incorporating environmental considerations into economic policy is not a matter of responding to the latest fads, but an essential element of the future development agenda (CCAD 1998).

The Question of Equity

A second major issue to be faced concerns greater equity for Guatemalans, for even if dynamic and sustained levels of economic growth are achieved, these will not necessarily translate into greater material welfare for all of the population. In academic circles, a lively debate has been taking place since the time of Adam Smith on the link between growth and equity. The Nobel laureate Simon Kuznets posited in the 1960s that during a protracted period of time in the process of development in now industrialized countries, income distribution tended to deteriorate. At some point, however, this trend peaked, and from then on income distribution improved as growth proceeded apace (Kuznets 1966). In more recent years, there is increasing evidence that suggests that, through appropriate policies, it is possible to overcome the above-described trajectory (Chenery et al. 1974; World Bank 1990). In other words, it is possible to simultaneously achieve growth and improved income distribution in the development process.

This topic is of singular importance, especially in a country such as Guatemala, marked by obvious inequalities that seem to grow more acute as the years go by. According to a recent World Bank study, 75 percent of Guatemala's population lives below the poverty line, and almost 58 percent lives in extreme poverty (World Bank 1995). Prospects for the future are not promising either, given the link between poverty and underemployment and unemployment. The fact that Guatemala still experiences one of the highest rates of population growth in the region (around 2.6 percent per annum) suggests that during many years a truly monumental effort will have to be made to generate enough jobs for the emerging economically active population (Funkhouser and Pérez Sáinz 1998). The main point, then, is that concern for equity must be at the center of Guatemala's development agenda.

In this regard, historical experience suggests that economic growth by itself is not enough to resolve inequality. A more promising approach would be to respond globally to the objectives of growth and equity, instead of dealing with them as separate, or even antagonistic goals. Indeed, the measures designed to respond to the two objectives can mutually reinforce each other (ECLAC 1992). In other words, policies pursuing growth and policies pursuing improved income distribution do not always entail trade-offs; many public policies, both in the economic and social domain, have an impact on growth *and* equity. For example, the dissemination of technology, especially at the level of microfirms in the rural areas; decentralization; and, most especially, investing in human resources are functional both to greater growth and improved income distribution.

Nevertheless, even with high levels of economic growth coupled with the right policies, it will surely take a long time for the benefits of growth to reach all Guatemalans, given the high levels of underemployment and other structural impediments to incorporate all segments of society to productive activities. For this reason, one must think of some complementary redistributive policies. Among these, the access to land, in accordance with the instruments created in the peace accords, should be highlighted.

Other redistributive policies that would be part of the development agenda of the country should include training for microentrepreneurs, subsistence farmers, and the self-employed; the elimination of red tape to create new microenterprises; adapting the delivery of social services so that they can benefit the poorest segments of society; decentralization of the decision-making process; and, especially, taking advantage of the redistributive potential of fiscal policy, both on the side of the structure of the tax system and, most notably, on the side of public expenditures. For the longer term, a more active role of public policy in promoting "responsible paternity" is also highly desirable.

The Multicultural and Multilingual Nature of Guatemala

A third major issue that Guatemala will face refers to fostering development in the context of a multiethnic, multicultural, and multilingual country. Historically, and from the point of view of development there has been a dominant culture, susceptible to transnationalization of lifestyles and social organization. In this context, Guatemala's indigenous people, and especially those descendants of the Maya civilization, have been strongly pressured to assimilate, or change their cultural identity, in order to be able to even have the opportunity to access the benefits of the development process (Cojtí Cuxil 1996).

This fact, in addition to violating the most elemental human rights, reflects a set of myths and prejudices that must be overcome in Guatemala's future development agenda. Today, the Accord on Identity and the Rights of Indigenous Peoples seeks to eliminate the image that two distinct cultures exist in the country: one that is open to modernization and development, and another that is moored to values and traditions thought to be inimical to modernization and progress. In nonindigenous circles, the view that indigenous communities constitute an obstacle to development is often heard.

This latter view is profoundly misguided. It is contrary to the fundamental right of being able to advance on the path of material and spiritual progress without obligating certain groups of the population to renounce to their cultural identity, that is, their forms of life, their philosophy and spirituality, their history, language and traditions. In addition, even more important, there is nothing in the worldview and culture that forms the basis of the Mayan identity (the majority of the country's indigenous population) that in any way runs counter to the modern concept of development. This is made clear in a recent publication on their values and philosophy (Salazar and Telón Sajcabún 1998). According to the authors, the social and family organization, as well as the moral basis of the Maya, is based, among other aspects, on the respect of elders, solidarity between persons, a sense of interdependence between nature, and valuing diligent and responsible work. The authors also mention the Mayan vocation for giving and receiving advice and help as a reflection of solidarity. Most of these values certainly sound compatible with the Weberian values so revered in the West. In fact, there should be no doubt that different cultures can live together in Guatemala; although characterized by differing beliefs, social organization, and languages, these groups are united in their desire for progress, greater well-being, and a commitment to democracy.

Moreover, a case can be made that different cultures not only can coexist, but that their presence can even become an important asset for the country. Certainly other societies have discovered the richness derived from diversity. In short, in addressing a Guatemalan agenda of development for the next century, the cultural dimension seems to be inescapable if one wishes to think of citizenship beyond the empty and rhetorical forms with which the subject has been treated historically.

The Political System

A fourth important issue that will emerge when discussing Guatemala's development agenda refers to the political system within which development would presumably take place. While it is not possible to neatly identify cause-and-effect relationships between political systems and development, Guatemala's peace accords seek the consolidation of democracy as an intrinsic value. Thus, the question that must be asked is how to promote development within democracy (World Bank 1996).

There are no blueprints to ensure that a democratic culture takes root. As is true for cultural identity, it involves, among other aspects, a change in values and attitudes. But it also involves the development of solid democratic institutions, including political parties, more effective mechanisms of information and participation, the separation of powers, a subsidiary and specific role for the military, and many other formal requirements that need not be mentioned here.

What is worth highlighting is that, in a democracy, a broad agreement is needed regarding the general thrust of a developmental process, including the actions and policies required, priority setting, and means and instruments to be used to further common policy goals. The media, universities, public and private institutions, and every citizen have a responsibility in making sure that the mechanisms of consensus building work.

Thus, creating or perfecting these institutions also forms part of Guatemala's development agenda for the future. It will cover such diverse aspects as consolidating the rule of law (which in turn will require substantial improvements in law enforcement and in the application of justice), developing stable and representative political parties, ensuring all civic and political freedoms, and striving for greater accountability and transparency in the acts of publicly elected or designated officials.

Other Developmental Issues

Finally, there are several specific issues that will appear in very prominent positions in Guatemala's development agenda in the following years, and they must be addressed. These include financing the country's development, public sector reform, and the central role of knowledge and education.

As to the first aspect, it is noteworthy that Guatemala's investment to GDP ratio barely reaches 10 percent, one of the lowest in the Western Hemisphere (ASIES 1998). It is therefore germane to ask how the economy's expansion will be financed in the future. Although modern growth theory puts a heavy emphasis on innovation as a causal factor of growth, as opposed to the neoclassical growth model that gives investment a crucial role, no one doubts that without increasing levels of investment in capital assets, infrastructure, and human resources, one cannot expect to attain dynamic levels of growth. In addition, higher levels of investment also require higher levels of domestic savings.

But how to go about increasing savings and investment? The conventional wisdom holds that financial stability and good macroeconomic management foster both. Some also hold that it is possible to foster a culture of savings and thrift, as opposed to a culture of consumerism. Moreover, strong financial institutions (banks, pension funds, capital markets, mortgage titles) certainly contribute to encourage savings. But here we have a "chicken and egg" dilemma: Do higher rates of saving favor these conditions, or do these conditions favor higher savings?

What can be said with certainty is that Guatemala cannot aspire to higher levels of growth with greater equity without significant increases in both domestic savings and productive investment. It is for this reason that financial reform, the development of private capital markets, pension fund reform, and—once again—tax reform will appear prominently in Guatemala's development agenda. Furthermore, these topics are linked to the whole issue of public sector reform, the second aspect of specific topics mentioned above.

Historical experience in Guatemala and in other developing countries amply shows that structural and institutional factors impede dynamic and sustained growth based exclusively on the signals of the market and on good macroeconomic management. The latter need to be complemented and enhanced by other measures in the domain of public policy. But this recognition provokes controversy, since it raises age-old dilemmas. Once the proposition is accepted that market forces do not resolve all problems, the next question refers to the selective intervention of public policy, with all its connotations. How much intervention? What type of intervention? What concrete form does interaction between the state and the market take?

A rather doctrinaire resistance against selective public policy interventions observed in the 1980s led to a point in which what was formally called sector policies (agriculture, industry) practically disappeared from Guatemala's policy agenda. Today, the idea of some sort of primacy of the market over the state, or vice versa, has been largely overcome. It is recognized in most circles that in a modern society, both are indispensable. What matters is how the public sector and private agents interact, and how each one carries out its respective role.

It is for this reason that it is important to pay attention to the reform of the state, in all its manifestations. This would involve the quality of public interventions, a redefinition of the border between public action and private enterprise, a reform of the legal, organizational, and financial underpinnings of the state, and the practical means in which public policies are applied.

Lastly, if there is one theme that is especially crucial in Guatemala's future development agenda, it refers to education. Suffice it to recall its significance for the imperatives of growth based on higher productivity, greater social equity, cultural plurality, and democratic governance. With this in mind, educational reform becomes a basic factor for the development of aptitudes and skills, as well as the capacity to innovate and adapt, all of which are indispensable to acquire competitiveness. Indeed, knowledge is a central element of the new productive paradigm.

At the same time, education is equally important as an element of social integration, solidarity, and social mobility. Numerous empirical studies reveal a close and direct link between more and better education and the reduction of poverty. Furthermore, education is an essential part of the democratic order. The material and symbolic basis of democracies does not depend exclusively on the type of economic and institutional organization, but also on the application of knowledge, information, and communication.

The breach that exists in Guatemala between what is needed and what is available in these domains is overwhelming. Guatemala is one of the few countries in Latin America that has not even resolved universal coverage at the primary level, not to mention middle-level education. If dramatic improvements are not forthcoming in education, it does not bode well for improving the more equitable distribution of opportunities or for obtaining growth based on increasing productivity. One would also have to rely on the educational system as a vehicle to instill values compatible with cultural plurality and political democracy in Guatemala's youth. The main point is that education must receive a much higher profile in Guatemala's development agenda than it has in the past.

Conclusion

As Guatemala approaches the twenty-first century, its development agenda is ample and complex. The main purpose of this article is to try to convey at least a sense of direction, or a vision, regarding how to approach development in the coming years, and to present some of the main issues that need to be addressed.

The country is far from reaching its full potential to achieve higher rates of growth, with greater equity, and within the democratic process. As in all human endeavors, this raises challenges and opportunities, as well as entails obstacles and risks. What perhaps is cause for at least cautious optimism today, in spite of renewed difficulties that plague the international economy (and that are beginning to affect Latin America in an adverse manner), is that in this new era of internal peace and the internationalization of the economy, Guatemala is better positioned than before to begin to overcome its situation of relative backwardness.

Note

This chapter is based on a keynote address that was prepared for the Conference on Development and Democracy in Guatemala, held in March 1998 in Guatemala City. The conference was organized in the context of the application of the peace accords that put an end to the thirty-six-year-old conflict that has afflicted the country.

Works Cited

Asociación de Investigación y Estudios Sociales (ASIES). 1998. *Evaluación de la Actividad Económica 1997 y Perspectivas 1998*. Guatemala City: ASIES.
Chenery, H., S. Ahluwalia, C. L. G. Bell, J. Duloy, and R. Jolly. 1974. *Redistribution with Growth*. New York: Oxford University Press.
Cojtí Cuxil, D. 1996. "The Politics of Maya Reivindication." In *Maya Cultural Activism in Guatemala*, edited by Edward F. Fischer and R. McKenna Brown. Austin: University of Texas Press.
Comisión Centroamericana de Ambiente y Desarrollo (CCAD). 1998. *Estado del ambiente y los recursos naturales en Centroamérica, 1998*. San José, Costa Rica: CCAD.

Economic Commission for Latin America and the Caribbean (ECLAC). 1992. *Social Equity and Changing Production Patterns: An Integrated Approach.* Santiago, Chile: ECLAC.
————. 1998. *Economic Survey of Latin America and the Caribbean, 1997-1998.* Santiago, Chile: ECLAC.
Facultad Latinoamericana de Ciencias Sociales and World Wide Fund for Nature. 1997. *Fortaleciendo las perspectivas para el desarrollo sostenible en Centroamérica. Evaluación de la Sostenibilidad: Caso de Guatemala.* Mimeographed. Guatemala: FLACSO.
Funkhouser, E., and J. P. Pérez Sáinz. 1998. "Mercado laboral y pobreza en Centroamérica," series: *Centroamérica en Reestructuración.* San José, Costa Rica: FLACSO.
INCAE (Instituto Centroamericano de Administración de Empresas). 1996. *Agenda Centroamericana para el Siglo XXI: Análisis de Competitividad de los Países Centroamericanos,* presented in five publications (one per country). San José, Costa Rica: INCAE.
International Monetary Fund (IMF). 1997. *Guatemala: Rompiendo la Barrera del 8 Por Ciento.* Mimeographed report prepared by Milka Casanegra de Jantscher, Patricio Castro, Alberto Ramos, and Osvaldo Schenone. Washington, D.C.: IMF.
Kuznets, S. 1966. *Modern Economic Growth.* New Haven: Yale University Press.
Porter, M. E. 1980. *Competitive Advantage.* New York: Free Press.
Salazar Tetzagüic, M., and Vicenta Telón Sajcabún. 1998. *Valores Mayas.* Guatemala: Ministerio de Educación.
Sistema de las Naciones Unidas en Guatemala. 1998. *Guatemala: Los contrastes del desarrollo humano.* Guatemala.
United Nations Development Program (UNDP). 1997. *Human Development Report, 1997.* New York: UNDP.
World Bank. 1990. *World Development Report 1990: Poverty.* Oxford: Oxford University Press.
————. 1995. *Guatemala: An Assessment of Poverty,* Report No. 12313-GU, Washington, D.C.: World Bank.
————. 1996. *Guatemala: Building Peace with Rapid and Equitable Growth,* Report No. 15352-GU. Washington, D.C.: World Bank.

Part II:

Democracy, Demilitarization, and the State

3

Global Forces and Regime Change: Guatemala within the Central American Context

John A. Booth

Central America's political regimes have changed enormously and repeatedly in the last two decades. It took the United States almost two centuries of war and gradual evolution to move from authoritarian rule by Britain to constitutional democracy with voting rights for the whole populace. In stark contrast, Guatemala, Honduras, Nicaragua, and El Salvador have traversed the great political distance from authoritarianism to civilian democracy at a vertiginous pace, although by divergent paths. That four countries have moved so far toward democracy so rapidly places into dramatic relief the region's regime change.

Just a decade ago social scientists struggled to explain why revolutionary insurrections occurred in Central America in the 1970s and 1980s while two neighboring countries escaped such violent turmoil (Booth and Walker 1993; Selbin 1993; Wickham-Crowley 1992). Since then, geopolitical change; the efforts and cooperation of Latin American powers, international institutions, and Central American governments; and the labors of domestic forces have ended the lengthy civil wars in Nicaragua (1990), El Salvador (1992), and Guatemala (1996), and the 1990 election in Nicaragua terminated the Sandinista revolution. Elections during the 1980s replaced the military regimes of Honduras, El Salvador, and Guatemala with civilian governments. Four of the region's five nations thus underwent dramatic, multiple regime changes from the military authoritarian status quo of the 1970s to civilian democracy by the 1990s.

This chapter seeks to account for such far reaching political transformation in the region and to examine Guatemala's place within it. It sets forth a theory that incorporates and seeks to account for disparate phenomena: political stability, guerrilla insurgency, military reformism, personalistic authoritarianism, socialist revolution, and civilian-led liberal democracy.

An Overview of Regime Change in Central America

Regimes are coherent systems of rule over mass publics established among a coalition of a nation's dominant political actors. The coherence of the system of rule refers to the existence of a persistent and identifiable set of political rules by which access to power and decision making occur.[1] Regimes are thus distinct from the separate governments or administrations that operate under the same general rules. For instance, Costa Rica has had a single civilian democratic regime since the 1950s, consisting of a series of constitutionally elected presidential administrations. Guatemala in the 1970s had a military authoritarian regime, subdivided into governments headed by various president-generals.

One regime may be differentiated from another when it changes both the fundamental rules of politics and the makeup of its coalition (a regime shift). Seven basic regime types encompass Central American experience between 1970 and 1998: *military authoritarian*, dominated by a corporate military establishment in coalition with a narrow range of civilian sectors; *personalistic military*, the only case of which is Nicaragua, dominated by the Somoza family and military in coalition with Liberal and Conservative Party and key financial sectors; *reformist military*, dominated by reformist military elements and intent upon a liberalizing or democratizing political transition; *civilian transitional*, with elected civilian rulers backed by a strong military and mainly incorporating center and rightist parties; *revolutionary*, in this case Nicaragua's Sandinista-led center-left coalition; *institutionalized revolutionary*, the Nicaraguan regime that established an electoral system in 1984 and new constitution in 1987; and *civilian democratic*, with elected civilian constitutional governments, broad coalitions, and political competition open to parties from left to right.[2]

Using this scheme, table 3.1 arrays Central America's regimes since 1970. Across these three decades only Costa Rica remained politically stable, that is, did not change regimes. Among the other four countries there occurred eleven regime shifts (changes between categories). Nicaragua's 1978 to 1979 insurrection led to a de facto Sandinista government from 1979 through 1984, followed by an institutionalized regime constructed through the 1984 election and new constitution. This institutionalization of the revolution permitted citizens to oust the revolutionary government in 1990. Honduras's military regime, anxiously eyeing neighboring El Salvador's and Nicaragua's revolutionary turmoil at the end of the 1970s, moved quickly toward civilian democratic rule. El Salvador and Guatemala traversed three similar stages after military authoritarian rule: in each a military-led reformist regime embroiled in civil war replaced itself with a transitional civilian regime. The settlement of each war eventually ushered in a much more inclusive civilian democratic government.[3]

How did these Central American regime shifts occur? What were the particular processes or instruments at play? One answer is that the processes and means were quite divergent across the cases. Military coups d'etat ushered in reformist military

Table 3.1. Central American Regime Types, 1970-1998
(with date of regime inception)[a]

Costa Rica	El Salvador	Guatemala	Honduras	Nicaragua
Cd[b]	MA	MA	MA	PM
	RM (1979)	RM (1982)	RM (1980)	Rev (1979)
	CT (1984)	CT (1985)	CD (1982)	IR (1984/87)
	CD (1992)	CD (1996)		

Source: Booth and Walker (1999).
[a]Explanation of regime type notation: CD = civilian democratic, MA = military authoritarian, PM = personalistic militatry, RM = reformist military, Rev = revolutionary, IR = institutionalized revolutionary, CT = civilian transitional, and CD = civilian democratic. See text for fuller explanation of types.
[b]Uninterrupted from 1949 to the present.

episodes in El Salvador, Guatemala, and Honduras. A widely based mass insurrection initiated the revolutionary regime in Nicaragua. Hoping to manage change and thus protect their interests, transitional military regimes voluntarily began holding fairer elections that eventually returned civilians to power in Honduras, El Salvador, and Guatemala. The first Nicaraguan revolutionary government established an election system and new constitutional rules that allowed citizens to oust the Sandinista Front for the Liberation of Nicaragua (FSLN) in 1990. Negotiated settlements of three civil wars admitted previously excluded actors into the political arena.

These multiple and complex regime changes necessitate a broad, widely encompassing explanation of how most of Central America has moved from authoritarian stasis through geopolitical crisis to emerge hugely transformed and unprecedentedly democratic. Of particular interest is whether the region's revolutionary turmoil and its democratizing steps were distinctive and unrelated processes, or similar products of a larger common process. We also need to understand why the ultimate outcomes in each Central American nation have been so apparently similar despite the distinctive paths of regime change illustrated in table 3.1.

Central America's small, neighboring nations have marked commonalities of history, global context, and political and economic development. These similarities in themselves suggest that much that affects Central America is likely to be part of a larger world dynamic (Chase-Dunn 1989, 1998; Robinson 1996). Just as common forces led to Central America's rebellions, many of the same forces shaped the overall process of regime change that eventually led from authoritarianism toward democracy. Indeed, the revolutionary movements themselves were key forces driving the multiple regime changes that led to the region's formal democratization.

A Theory of Regime Change in Central America

An explanatory argument integrating Central America's insurrections and democratization may be developed within a framework of regime change theory and drawing upon the political science literatures on democratization and revolution. Students of regime change have focused on causes, processes, and outcomes. Barrington Moore (1966) explored how the characteristics of several established regimes and the interaction of their various challengers led to the particular characteristics of new regimes. Guillermo O'Donnell (1973) examined the role of military/middle-class coalitions as bureaucratic authoritarianism replaced civilian governments in Argentina and Brazil. The contributors to Linz and Stepan's *The Breakdown of Democratic Regimes* examined the nature of democratic regimes and both the causes of and processes by which they collapsed to be replaced by authoritarian rule (1978). Some decades later, O'Donnell's *Transitions from Authoritarian Rule* performed a similar exercise for authoritarian goverments of southern Europe and Latin America (O'Donnell et al. 1986). Mark Gasiorowski (1995, 1996) has employed quantitative analysis to account for factors that contribute to regime change.

From the regime change literature we know that regimes are systems of rule over mass publics established among a coalition of a nation's dominant political actors. Regime coalition members benefit from inclusion in the regime. Social and economic change can generate and mobilize new political actors who may seek inclusion into the ruling coalition and its benefits, and who may or may not be admitted by those within the regime. Socioeconomic change can dramatically affect the resources available to the regime. Contented, indifferent, unorganized, or effectively repressed populations do not struggle for inclusion in the regime, nor do they violently rebel. Strong, flexible, resource-rich regimes with satisfied allies rarely collapse or wage war against their populations.

In a classic work, Charles Anderson (1967) explains that Latin American regimes have corporatist tendencies, one implication of which is that new actors are admitted to the regime coalition only when they prove themselves capable of destabilizing it. Regime transformations in the region are thus often highly conflictive because excluded forces have to fight for inclusion.[4] This theory accounts for the well-documented case of Costa Rica's last regime shift. The narrowly based and coffee-grower dominated quasi-democracy of the 1930s was disrupted by emergent working- and middle-class actors. Middle-class forces took the lead in forging a new regime after winning a brief but violent civil war in 1948. (See Peeler 1985, 1998, 50-53; Yashar 1997; Booth 1998; Wilson 1998, 28-36.)

A second relevant theoretical literature is that on political violence and revolution, part which perforce also examines regime change. For a rebellion or *national revolt* (Walton 1984, 13) to occur, there must be a fundamental basis of conflict that defines groups or categories of affected persons that provide "recruiting grounds for organizations" (Kriesberg 1982).[5] What bases of conflict are most likely to lead citizens to resort to a national revolt? Many scholars concur (see Olson 1963; Paige 1975; Skocpol 1979; Walton 1984; Foran 1997a) that rapid economic change and evolving class relations typically drive the mobilization required for a violent challenge to a regime.[6] For agrarian societies, their inclusion into the world capitalist economy through heavy reliance upon export agriculture may harm huge sectors of the peasantry, urban poor, and middle sectors, providing large numbers of agrieved citizens.

Once motivated, groups must organize and focus their struggle for change upon some target, most likely the state or the regime. Rod Aya (1979) and Charles Tilly (1978) have shown that effective organization for opposition requires the mobilization of resources, and they emphasize the key role of the state in shaping rebellion. The state or the ruling coalition are typically the targets of national revolts, but the state also reciprocally affects the rebellion as it both represses rebels and promotes change (Kriesberg 1982, 66-106; Tilly 1978; Aya 1979; Foran 1997a). Once a contest over sovereignty begins, political factors such as organization and resource mobilization by both sides eventually determine the outcome (Walton 1984; Skocpol 1979; Goldstone 1991; Gurr 1970). Goldstone (1991) and James DeFronzo (1991, 7-25) particularly emphasize the contribution to successful revolutionary movements of foreign actors, domestic interelite competition and alienation, and other factors that may weaken the state's capacity to act.

The third relevant literature is the rapidly growing body of scholarship on democratization. Here I will adopt a minimal procedural definition of democracy, Robinson's "polyarchy" (1996), as the criterion for a democratic regime.[7] There are four main explanations for democratization (the process of moving from an authoritarian to a democratic regime): political culture, political processes, social structures and forces (both domestic and external), and leaders and elites. The cultural approach argues that the ideal of political democracy may evolve within a society or spread among nations by cultural diffusion among elite and mass political actors (see Inglehart 1988; Seligson and Booth 1995; Muller and Seligson 1994; Diamond 1994a, 1994b). Elite and mass preference for democracy promote its adoption and help sustain a democratic regime. In contrast, process approaches examine the mechanics of and paths toward democratic transition (see Rustow 1970; Przeworski 1986; Huntington 1993; Seligson and Booth 1995; Casper and Taylor 1996). In these emphases process theories resemble and somewhat overlap the regime change literature.

Structural theories emphasize how shifts in the distribution of critical material and organizational resources among political actors can lead to democracy (see Lipset 1959; Vanhanen 1992; Rueschemeyer, Stephens, and Stephens 1992; Putnam 1993, 1996). Democratic regimes emerge when the distribution of political and economic resources and the mobilization of actors permit formerly excluded actors to disrupt the extant authoritarian coalition. Another structural approach involves the imposition of democracy by external actors (Whitehead 1991). The fourth approach examines the roles of leaders (see Peeler 1985; Diamond 1989; Higley and Gunther 1992; Huntington 1993). Key societal elites must engineer specific democratic arrangements (elite settlements) and agree to operate by them. The broader the coalition of political forces involved, the more stable and consolidated a democratic regime will be.

These three literatures have much in common. Each concerns the process of regime change, although the democratization literature emphasizes transition in one particular direction. Elements of all three envision a polity as having numerous actors whose makeup and roles may evolve. They jointly treat political regimes as coalitions of key actors that survive by successfully mobilizing resources in and around the state or governmental apparatus. All three recognize that regimes can enter into crisis, whether driven by challenges from without, deterioration from within, or the erosion of state capacity. All three have causal explanations for change, although there are divergent emphases and outright disagreements within and between fields over the importance of such factors as psychology, political culture, leaders and elites, masses, and social structures. However, the more sophisticated treatments in the revolution/violence and democratization literatures tend to view causality as both complex and multiple.

Finally, each of these fields and a substantial literature on foreign policy recognizes that international constraints affect regime change (see Lowenthal 1991; Carothers 1991; Huntington 1993, 85-106; Moreno 1995; Walker 1997; Robinson 1996; Prevost and Vanden 1997). Foreign governments may act as players in domestic politics, strengthening a prevailing regime by supporting it or weakening it through opposition or withheld support. External actors may supply resources to domestic actors, altering their relative strength and capacity to act. Key external actors may pressure domestic actors to adopt certain policies or regime types, employing as inducements such vital resources as money, trade, arms, and political cooperation. The international context may also constrain a nation's regime type by demonstration or contagion effects. For example, having mostly democratic neighbors makes it easier to adopt or retain a democratic regime.

Based upon these elements I propose the following outline of a theory of regime change: Political systems are nation states with defined populations and territorial boundaries. Political systems exist within an international context consisting of various types of actors and forces, including nation-states, formal and informal alliances among nations, the world political economy, international organizations, and political and ideological groupings. A political regime is a coherent system of rule over a nation's mass public established among a coalition of dominant political actors. Political actors within nations encompass individuals and (more importantly) organized groups, factions, ideological groupings, parties, interest sectors, or institutions. Each of these pursues objectives within the political system, and each employs its own resources. Actors may or may not constitute part of the regime coalition, the group of actors who dominate and benefit most from the state, its resources, and its policymaking capacity.

Political regimes persist based upon at least two things. They must constantly satisfy an endogenous objective of managing the state and economy so as to benefit coalition members enough to retain their loyalty. They must also continuously satisfy the exogenous objective of keeping actual and potential outside-the-regime actors (both domestic and external) content or indifferent or, if neither of these, keeping them disorganized, unmobilized, or otherwise effectively managed or repressed. Many factors can disrupt or destabilize a regime. International or domestic economic forces can undermine the political economy of a regime (harm a nation's established economic system or the security of regime coalition's members or other actors). Such forces may include very rapid economic growth, or a sharp economic downturn. Powerful external actors (a major regional power or hegemon, for instance) may withdraw active support and resources from a regime or may shift from tacit support to active opposition to it, thus creating a permissive external environment for internal actors to challenge a regime. Ideologies may suggest or other political systems may exemplify alternative political and economic rules (republicanism instead of monarchy, socialism instead of capitalism, or civilian democracy instead of military authoritarianism) to key actors within or outside the regime coalition.

A regime experiences a crisis or "critical juncture" (Casper and Taylor 1996; 23-24) when such forces (a) undermine the loyalty and cooperation of some or all of the coalition members, (b) undermine the resource base and capacity of the regime to respond to challenges or opponents, or (c) mobilize enough outside-the-regime actors against the regime. Regime crises may take various forms based upon the severity of the challenge and distribution of resources among actors: Regime coalition members may renegotiate the regime's political rules and benefits and deny significant adjustments to outside-the-regime actors. Regimes may make policy changes to mollify aggrieved outside actors. Regimes may initiate co-optative incorporation of new coalition members to quell a disruptive challenge to the regime; this will typically involve some reform of extant political rules and payoffs.[8] Outside-the-regime actors may initiate a violent challenge to the regime's sovereignty via a coup d'etat, insurrection, or even an external invasion. Inside-the-regime actors may also employ a coup to displace incumbents or, more interestingly, to initiate a new regime.

The evolution and outcome of the regime crisis will depend upon the ability of the regime and its challengers, if any, to mobilize and deploy their respective resources. The closer to parity of material, political, and human resources are the regime and its challengers, and the stronger both are, the longer and more violently they will struggle over power. The dominant actor (such as the military) in a weak to moderately strong regime confronted with a weak but potentially growing opposition might initiate a regime change (co-optative reform and the inclusion of new actors) in order to minimize expected damage to its interests. Other things equal, a strong, flexible, resource-rich regime will be most likely to reform and/or successfully repress or continue to exclude its opponents and to survive. A weak regime confronting a strong opposition coalition may be overthrown and replaced by a radically different, revolutionary regime that will subsequently exclude some or all of the old regime's coalition. A protracted regime crisis, especially a lengthy civil war, eventually increases the likelihood of a negotiated settlement and major regime transformation with new political rules, redistributed benefits, and the inclusion into the political game of both the challengers and key old-regime actors.

The consolidation of any new regime will derive from the eventual resolution of forces among the various political actors, which may in turn depend heavily upon the role of foreign actors. A single regime shift may not bring enough change to permit political stability. Military reformism, for instance, though intended to pacify a polity by including certain new actors and by policy reforms, may yet fail to satisfy violent opponents with antagonistic ideologies. Despite establishing a new coalition, new rules, and new policies, a revolutionary regime may quickly attract direct or indirect outside-the-regime opposition. To the extent that important actors (domestic or foreign) remain unsatisfied or unsuccessfully repressed, therefore, the consolidation of a new regime will fail. For a newly constituted regime, protracted instability increases the likelihood of its failure and further regime shifts.

Explaining Regime Change in Central America

Drawing upon the common elements of the theories examined above, the following propositions seek to account for the origin and development of regime change in Central America since the 1970s. The argument emphasizes the world economic and geopolitical and ideological context and its evolution, the regimes present in the 1970s and the causes of the crises that undermined them, regimes' and actors' responses to crisis, and the interplay of resources and foreign forces.

The Evolving Context

The U.S. View. The geopolitics of the Cold War predominated on the world scene in the 1970s and set the context for Central American geopolitics. U.S. policy was preoccupied with the threat of the Soviet Union and its perceived desire to expand its influence within the Western Hemisphere. The United States thus tended to regard most of the region's political and economic reformists and the opponents of Central America's friendly, anticommunist, authoritarian regimes as unacceptable potential allies of pro-Soviet/pro-Cuban communism. Civilian democracy, though an ideological preference of the United States, remained secondary to security concerns in this tense world environment.

Central America's authoritarian regimes thus usually enjoyed the political, military, and economic support of the United States. U.S. policy thus weakened and marginalized Central American moderates and ultimately encouraged many of them to ally with the radical left, which viewed civilian democracy and elections as tools by which an unjust capitalist political-economic system manipulated the lower classes of dependent nations.

U.S. thinking regarding the ideological geopolitics of Central America evolved in several stages. First, in the late 1970s Congress and the Carter administration came to view the inhumane anticommunist authoritarianism of Nicaragua, Guatemala, and El Salvador as unacceptable. This policy shift encouraged Central America's reformists and revolutionaries and briefly created a permissive international environment for regime change and encouraged an upsurge in opposition mobilization. After the Sandinistas' victory in 1979, the United States temporarily reverted to the previous Cold War hard line, but during the Reagan and Bush administrations Washington gradually moved toward accepting electoral democracy in two stages. First, in the mid 1980s elections per se were encouraged to promote limited reform that might strengthen the governments in El Salvador and Guatemala against their revolutionary challengers. Second, the end of the Cold War reduced the perceived geopolitical threat of communism in general and, therefore, the perceived danger of the Central American left. This permitted the longstanding U.S. second-order preference for civilian democracy to surface and become a vehicle for the promotion of peace settlements acceptable to U.S. policymakers.

Central American Viewpoints. Leftists had long regarded electoral democracy as a tool of capitalist domination. The 1970s ideological standoff between models of electoral democracy and revolutionary socialism began to evolve once Nicaragua's Sandinistas came to power in 1979. Once in power the FSLN began to view electoral democracy as an organizational arrangement compatible with the economic and participatory democracy it sought to construct. The FSLN also viewed electoral democracy as a stratagem that might enhance the acceptability of its revolution to the openly hostile United States and their Central American neighbors. Thus in 1984 the Sandinistas began the institutionalization of the revolution.

A second phase of the evolution of the ideological politics of democratization occurred in El Salvador and Guatemala during the late 1980s and early 1990s. Exhausted by long civil wars and with no prospect of victory, the Farabundo Martí National Liberation Front (FMLN) and the Guatemalan National Revolutionary Union (URNG) began to view electoral democracy as a minimally acceptable regime should they be allowed to participate freely and compete fairly for office. The armed forces of each nation, also exhausted, decided that they could accept electoral rules of the game with the leftists included in exchange for peace and their own institutional survival.

Other Actors' Views. European nations, other Latin American nations, and such international organizations as the United Nations and Organization of American States once largely deferred to U.S. influence in the region. However, during the 1980s they became increasingly fearful that the isthmian civil wars and U.S. intervention could escalate further. These external actors therefore embraced and promoted electoral democracy as a mechanism for promoting their interest through the pacification of Central America.

The Catholic Church in the isthmus was influenced by liberation theology in the 1960s and 1970s, a phenomenon that encouraged social mobilization and even some Catholic participation in insurgency. By the 1980s, however, the institutional Church had disavowed liberation theology but endorsed democratization and improved human rights as a means toward achieving social justice.

In summary, the geopolitical and ideological contexts within which Central America's regimes and actors operated evolved substantially from the early 1970s through the mid-1990s: (1) The powerfully influential United States initially obviated electoral democracy in Central America for security reasons, but eventually embraced it for instrumental reasons and an evolving perception of its security vis-à-vis the region. (2) Both left-wing and right-wing actors in Central America initially opposed electoral democracy, but tactical and ideological needs deriving from geopolitics and protracted civil wars led them to accept and pursue the model. (3) Other external actors, especially European and Latin American powers and international organizations, moved from effective indifference toward electoral democracy in Central America to embrace it on behalf of their own security interests.

The 1970s Regimes

In the early 1970s only Costa Rica among the region's nations had a broadly inclusive, constitutional, civilian-led democratic regime. The other four nations had military-dominated authoritarian governments: Nicaragua's personalistic military regime was dominated by the Somoza clan and a narrow coalition made up of key business interests and parts of the two major parties. Guatemala and El Salvador had military authoritarian regimes, allied with some business and large-scale agricultural interests and with the collaboration of weak political parties. Honduras had a military authoritarian regime, but it incorporated one of the two strong traditional political parties and tolerated a strong but anticommunist labor sector.

Causes of Regime Crises

A wave of economic problems afflicted all five Central American countries in the late 1970s and early 1980s. Rapidly escalating oil prices and resultant inflation, the deterioration of the Central American Common Market (in the mid- and late 1970s), and natural or economic catastrophes (e.g., the 1972 Managua earthquake, 1978 to 1979 Common Market trade disruptions) greatly reduced real income and employment among working-class and some white-collar sectors.

The grievances caused by increasing inequalities, declining real income, economic and natural catastrophes, and the political dissatisfactions of would-be competing elites led in the mid- and late 1970s to burgeoning agrarian, labor, neighborhood, and community self-help, opposition party mobilization, and to reformist demands upon the state and protests about public policy. Regime coalitions experienced some defections, and the economic resources of all five regimes eroded (Booth 1991).

Regime Responses to Crisis

In both the short and long terms, Central American regimes responded quite differently to unrest, mobilization, and demands for change. In the short run the divergences were most striking. Where regimes responded to reform demands with ameliorative policies to ease poverty and permit the recovery of real wages, with political reform, and with low or modest levels of force or repression, protests failed to escalate or subsided (Booth 1991). Costa Rica's broadly based, capable, and flexible regime managed its challenges and survived intact. Honduras' military authoritarian regime voluntarily enacted ameliorative economic policies and returned power to civilians. In contrast, where regimes responded in the short run by rejecting ameliorative policies and sharply escalating repression, protests and opposition organization and resource mobilization increased, national revolts occurred, and regime crises ensued (Nicaragua, El Salvador, and Guatemala).

In the longer run, the regimes that responded with violent repression and refusal to ameliorate the effects of economic crisis found themselves facing violent, broadly based insurrections. They struggled to mobilize the economic and political resources to resist the revolts, including external assistance derived mainly from the United States. They also eventually undertook fundamental regime change itself (liberalizing and democratizing their rules and broadening their coalitions) and various other policy reforms in the struggle to manage, repress, divide, and isolate their violent challengers.

Outcomes

The outcomes of Central America's regime crises depended upon the relative success of each regime versus its opponents in mobilizing and maintaining domestic and economic and material support and organization. Failure to stabilize the situation (to placate or repress enough outside-the-regime actors) led to regime shifts.

Nicaragua. Dictator Anastasio Somoza Debayle lost U.S. and regional support and vital economic resources, permitting the Sandinistas to oust him and establish the revolutionary regime with a center-left coalition and revolutionary rules. The excluded Somocista Liberals, ex-National Guard elements, and an increasing number of disaffected other economic and political forces formed various outside-the-regime forces, including the U.S.-backed contra rebels. The revolutionary regime's response to its own regime crisis and the counterrevolutionary war included nearly continuous economic and political reform, including the adoption of electoral democratic rules in 1984 and a new constitution in 1987. Soviet economic and political support waned after 1987, as did U.S. support for the contras. The 1987 Central American (Esquipulas) Peace Accord negotiated by Central America's presidents eventually facilitated a cease-fire in Nicaragua and then a negotiated end to the war. In the 1990 election Nicaraguan voters replaced the FSLN government and ended the revolution. This ushered in a new nonrevolutionary civilian regime, with both the left and elements of the right participating. In 1996 Liberal Nationalists returned to the arena and won the election, possibly consolidating a postrevolutionary regime.

Honduras. Faced with domestic turmoil and the Nicaraguan revolution next door, the Honduran military regime made a quick, preemptive transition to civilian democracy. The traditional Liberal and National parties dominate the fairly inclusive regime. The armed forces, flush with massive political, economic and military resources earned by cooperating with U.S. efforts to defeat the revolutionary left in Nicaragua and El Salvador, loomed large in the regime until the mid-1990s. In 1996 the government of Carlos Roberto Peina restructured and demilitarized the police, cut military spending, and implemented other key military reforms (Ruhl 1998, 17-20), ushering in civilian democratic rule.

El Salvador and Guatemala.[9] Coups instituted reformist military regimes that repressed outside-the-regime centrists but failed to defeat leftist rebel coalitions. The failure of this strategy, plus pressure from the United States (a major resource supplier to the Salvadoran regime), led both nations' military regimes to institute civilian transitional governments with broader coalitions and liberalized rules. This strategy won over some of the political center in each country, depriving the rebel coalitions of important allies and resources and contributing to the stagnation of the civil wars. The Central American Peace Accord of 1987 provided a mechanism for eventual negotiations between parties to the stalemated civil conflicts. New elite economic groups linked to transnational capital emerged as powerful contenders for influence within each nation, rising to dominate such key political parties as El Salvador's National Republican Alliance (ARENA) and Guatemala's new National Action Party (PAN). Assisted by international economic reformers, these elites sought to negotiate an end to the wars debilitating their economies and to promote formally democratic regimes that would facilitate their access to the international economy (Robinson 1996). Military exhaustion, U.S. exasperation with the Central American quagmires, and the end of the Cold War also contributed to shifts in all actors' positions, especially recalcitrant oligarchic forces. The United States, other outside actors, national militaries, the civilian reformist regimes, and the rebels all eventually embraced more inclusive civilian democracy and some economic reforms—position changes that helped end both wars.

Table 3.2. Gross Domestic Product Per Capita (in 1990 U.S. $), Central America, Selected Years 1987-1996

	1987	1989	1991	1994	1996	Mean annual growth (90-96)
Costa Rica	1,860	1,909	1,915	2,114	2,054	1.1%
El Salvador	1,015	1,006	1,049	1,202	1,257	3.3%
Guatemala	839	856	863	897	916	1.1%
Honduras	638	654	632	644	648	0.4%
Nicaragua	599	495	464	460	481	0.0%
Latin America	2,706	2,620	2,607	2,781	2,801	1.5%

Source: Inter-American Development Bank (IADB), *Latin America after a Decade of Reforms: Economic and Social Progress in Latin America, 1997 Report* (Baltimore: Johns Hopkins University Press, 1997), p. 221.

Reflections on Guatemala's Democratic Prospects

This broad theory about Central America regime change suggests many possible avenues for the investigation of the prospects for Guatemala's new civilian democratic regime. To a real extent Guatemala's regime crises and shifts have been shaped by global political and economic forces. These forces have also wrought similar effects upon other Central American nations and their regimes. Thus such forces seem likely to continue significantly shaping Guatemala's chances for democratic consolidation. The following focuses mainly upon recent data and developments that give us insights into the political economy, Guatemalans' attitudes and behaviors, and the geopolitical context.

The Political Economy

Turning first to the political economy of the Guatemalan regime, table 3.2 permits a comparison of Guatemala's overall recent economic performance to that of the other Central American nations. The fundamental and obvious lesson in the data is that Guatemala is a poor nation, with 1996 GDP per capita of only $916 and having made only modest progress in earnings per head over the prior decade. During the ten years preceding the year of final settlement in the Guatemalan civil war, Guatemala's relative economic performance remained stable when compared to the trends of Latin America overall and some of its neighbors. Guatemala's GDP per capita (in constant 1990 dollars) was roughly 32 percent of Latin America as a whole in both 1987 and 1996. Similarly, Guatemalan GDP per capita was roughly 45 percent of Costa Rica's in both 1987 and in 1996. Guatemala's growth rate of GDP per capita from 1990 to 1996 was 1.1 percent per annum, equal to Costa Rica's but only a third of El Salvador's. El Salvador's growth rate accelerated after 1992 when that country's civil war ended, fueled partly by a "peace dividend" of new investment and economic recovery and partly by large quantities of international aid. Guatemala may expect to reap something of a peace dividend, but may have considerably less foreign assistance to boost its economic performance.

Table 3.3 provides data on important trends in the Guatemalan economy from 1987 through 1996. GDP growth remained relatively healthy throughout the decade but was attenuated by a population growth rate that ate up much of the new activity. The government ran modest deficits during most of this decade and was able to steadily reduce the burden of its external interest payments. Guatemala's terms of trade improved substantially from 1987 through 1996, contributing to a relatively positive economic performance for a nation plagued by so much political turmoil. The worst aspects of the decade's economic performance came in inflation. Driven by a sharp drop in the value of the quetzal in 1990 and 1991, consumer prices increased 41.2 and 33.2 percent in each of those years. This price jump prompted a sharp drop in real wages that had not yet been made up by 1996 even though inflation was back under control.

High levels of societal prosperity and economic growth are not requisite for successful democratization or democratic survival, but at least some economic resources and economic expansion make democratic consolidation easier (Diamond and Linz 1989, 42-47). The more resources a state may deploy in the public policy arena, to some extent a function of general national economic health, the better the chances for democracy's successful founding and survival. Given these conditions, the data in tables 3.2 and 3.3 suggest that Guatemala has at least a reasonable chance for democratic survival and consolidation. The economy is relatively poor, but considerably stronger than those of two other newly democratic regimes in the area, Honduras and Nicaragua. Recent economic trends (terms of trade, GDP and GDP per capita, foreign debt burden, and deficits) suggest a reasonably favorable economic trajectory for democratic politics.

The more worrisome political economic trends for Guatemala are those for inflation and real wages. The erosion of these factors that so affect the lives of ordinary citizens, at least temporarily curtailed in the mid-1980s (table 3.3), has the potential to generate mass protest and popular sector and labor mobilization. Guatemalan security forces have historically been intolerant of such turmoil, so its occurrence early in the consolidation phase of civilian democracy could imply some risk for institutions.

Table 3.3. Selected Economic Data on Guatemala, 1987-1996

Year	% change in GDP	Central govt. deficit or surplus (-)	% change in consumer prices	% change in real wages	Terms of trade (1990=100)	Interest payments as % of goods
1987	3.5	-1.3	12.3	6.7	99.7	13.6
1988	3.9	-1.7	10.8	5.2	98.8	13.9
1989	3.9	-2.9	11.4	6.5	97.6	11.3
1990	3.1	-1.8	41.2	-14.8	100.0	11.2
1991	3.7	0.0	33.2	-6.3	107.2	7.1
1992	4.8	0.5	10.0	16.2	106.7	8.8
1993	3.9	-1.3	11.9	10.8	103.0	6.2
1994	4.0	-1.4	10.9	7.2	110.5	5.5
1995	4.9	-0.6	8.4	12.0	118.1	4.8
1996	3.1	0.0	11.1	-0.9	112.0	5.0

Source: Inter-American Development Bank (IADB), *Latin America after a Decade of Reforms: Economic and Social Progress in Latin America, 1997 Report* (Baltimore: Johns Hopkins University Press, 1997) p. 280.

Political Culture, Attitudes, and Participation

Another question about Guatemala's democratic prospect is the extent to which the attitudes and behaviors of its citizens may support the civilian democratic regime. While mass culture cannot assure democracy, to the extent that a nation's citizenry embraces democratic norms, eschews authoritarian values, and participates peaceably in politics, the prospects for democratic consolidation are enhanced (Diamond and Linz 1989, 42-47; Diamond 1993, 7-15).

Table 3.4 compares Guatemala to four other Central American nations based upon public opinion surveys conducted in the early 1990s. Nearly identical questions on numerous attitudinal and participation items were asked of the urban residents of each nation.[10] The Guatemalan survey was conducted in 1992 during the second period of the transitional civilian regime that had begun in 1985, but four years prior to the negotiated settlement of the civil conflict that had afflicted the country since the 1960s. It thus serves as something of a benchmark survey of urban

Guatemalans partway through the series of regime changes that led to civilian democracy in 1996.

Table 3.4 first presents data on the level of commitment to democratic norms of Guatemalans and other Central Americans. Each of the four indexes in the "Democratic Norms" portion of the table is a ten-point scale ranging from very low commitment to democratic norms (1.0) to very high commitment (10.0). (A score above 5.0 represents a prodemocratic response. The cell values in table 3.4 are country means on each index.) The data in table 3.4 reveal that each of the five countries' urban citizens averaged in the prodemocracy end of the scale on all but one of the measures. Guatemalans, however, had the lowest commitment to democracy (virtually tied with El Salvador) in the region. Guatemalans also had the region's lowest levels of support for general participation rights and for rights for regime critics. Indeed, on the latter Guatemalans scored in slightly the antidemocratic end of the scale.

Thus, well before Guatemala had completed its transition to civilian democracy, its urban citizens demonstrated what one might describe as cautious support for democratic norms. They did so despite the high levels of political repression the country had experienced, repression to a real extent still present in Guatemala when the survey was conducted. Repression at the level of the political system in Central America has been demonstrated powerfully to depress support for democratic norms (Booth and Richard 1996). One should, therefore, probably emphasize not Guatemala's lower democracy norms scores within the region, but rather that Guatemalans' prodemocracy sentiments in 1992 were remarkably high despite existing within a hostile environment.

The second part of table 3.4 examines urban Guatemalans' opinions on four other indexes, some of which may be labeled authoritarian or undemocratic norms. Anticommunism has been encouraged by and has served as a powerful justification for political repression for Guatemalan regimes. Despite this, Guatemalans expressed only average levels of anticommunist opinions within the regional context. On an index composed of items tapping attitudes supporting or approving the armed forces, Guatemalans also scored in the middle of the Central American distribution (1.27 on a scale of 1.0 to 2.0), well below the midpoint of the index. When asked whether certain circumstances (e.g., economic hardship, student unrest) would justify a military coup, Guatemalans also averaged only 1.20 (index range 1.0 to 2.0), well on the disapproving end of the scale. A strong majority of Guatemalans, like other Central Americans in the early 1990s, thus manifested a healthy skepticism toward the armed forces as a political actor. The final indicator in this group is an index measuring respondents' tolerance of the participation tactics, including protest, confrontation, and even political violence. Most Central Americans disapproved of such tactics, with Guatemalans manifesting the second highest disapproval rate.

Table 3.4. Attitudes, Values, and Political Participation, Urban Central Americans, early 1990s

	Guatemala	Costa Rica	El Salvador	Honduras	Nicaragua
Survey Year	*1992*	*1995*	*1991*	*1991*	*1991*
Democratic Norms					
Support for general participation rights (1 = low, 10 = high)[b]	7.06	8.22	7.47	8.07	8.32
Support for regime critics' rights (1 = low, 10 = high)[c]	4.8	6.12	5.21	6.99	5.69
Opposition to suppression of civil liberties (1 = low, 10 = high)[d]	6.25	7.04	5.25	5.82	6.45
Overall support for democratic liberties (1 = low, 10 = high)[e]	5.97	7.13	5.98	6.96	6.82
Authoritarian Norms					
Anticommunist opinions (1 = weak, 6 = strong)[f]	3.78	4.31	3.59	4.23	2.91
Pro-military attitudes (1 = disagree, 2 = agree)[g]	1.27	---	1.34	1.27	1.23
Justification of military coup (1 = disagree, 2 = agree)[h]	1.20	---	1.26	1.09	1.11
Support civil disobedience (1 = low, 10 = high)[i]	2.01	1.93	2.12	3.41	2.42
Attitudes toward Government					
Diffuse support for the system (1 = low, 7 = high)[j]	4.14	5.06	3.97	3.53	4.51
Evaluation of treatment by gov. offices (1 = poor, 8 = good)[k]	3.53	3.89	4.49	3.83	5.47

Table 3.4—Continued. Attitudes, Values, and Political Participation

Political Participation					
Voting[l]	1.51	1.91	1.39	1.86	1.62
Campaigning[m]	.25	.87	.18	1.08	.47
Contacting public officials[n]	.41	.56	.32	.77	.17
Membership in formal groups[o]	.66	.47	.33	1.05	.46
Activity in community groups[p]	2.10	2.57	2.04	1.68	2.52
Overall political participation[q]	5.02	6.40	4.33	6.44	5.28

Source: All items are drawn from surveys conducted by the author, Mitchell A. Seligson, and other collaborators in urban Central America between mid-1991 and mid-1992, except Costa Rica survey, conducted in 1995. National sample Ns vary between 500 and 900, but all national samples are artificially weighted at 700 respondents to avoid distortions due to population size of country or particular sample.

[a]Regional mean is the unweighted country average (mean of previous column entries).
[b]Index measuring support for general participation rights (range 1-10).
[c]Index measuring tolerance for political rights for regime critics (range 1-10).
[d]Index measuring opposition to governmental suppression of civil liberties (range 1-10).
[e]Index of overall support for democracy (mean of three previous indexes).
[f]Index of disapproval of communism based on three items (range 1-6).
[g]Index of attitudes approving of armed forces in society based on 12 items (range 1-2).
[h]Index of attitiudes justifying military coup under certain circumstances, based on 10 items (range 1-2).
[i]Index of support for civil disobedience and violent political participation (range 1-10).
[j]Index of diffuse support (positive orientations) for the political system (range 1-7).
[k]Index of evaluation of treatment by government offices (range 1-8).
[l]Index of having voted and being registered to vote (range 0-2).
[m]Index of campaign-related behavior and electioneering (range 0-2).
[n]Index of having contacted public officials (mayor, legislative deputy, etc.), (range 0-3).
[o]Index of participation in formal organizations (union, professional and service associations), (range 0-4).
[p]Index of participation in communal-level activism (groups and self-help projects), (range 0-3).
[q]Index of overall political participation (includes all previous participation items), (range 1-14).

These results suggest that urban Guatemalans generally disapproved of these authoritarian, militaristic, or confrontational political norms in the early 1990s. This absence of authoritarian and militaristic values among Guatemalans corresponds with their general sympathy for democratic norms. Such political values constitute a positive sign for Guatemala's democratic prospect.[11]

Table 3.4 also reports on two other political attitudes, each an orientation toward government. One may argue that positive orientations toward the state constitute a resource for government. One such orientation is diffuse support for the system, a sense of pride in various national political institutions that may be loosely interpreted as a measure of legitimacy or patriotism. Guatemalans fell in the midrange among Central Americans on an index of diffuse support for the system, below Costa Ricans and Nicaraguans, but above Salvadorans and Hondurans. In contrast, on an index measuring how well they believed they had been treated by various government agencies, Guatemalans had the lowest scores in the region. Taken together these measures suggest that although Guatemalans may feel some pride in their country and its political system, overcoming the legacy of negative feelings about government treatment may constitute a significant problem for the civilian democratic regime. These data suggest that in 1992 Guatemala's civilian transitional government had only a small reservoir of goodwill from its citizens. Future democratic governments clearly will need to increase popular goodwill in order to build the legitimacy of the civilian democratic system.

Finally, political participation constitutes a key element of democracy. Democracy in its essence consists of citizen participation in rule, so that a country's democratic prospect is to some extent a function of its levels of popular political activity. Participation may be sharply curtailed by repression (Booth and Richard 1996). Guatemala has had a poor human rights record for several decades, and has been widely considered as one of the region's most repressive regimes prior to the 1996 peace accord.

The last group of variables in table 3.4 are measures of citizen participation—voting, campaigning, contacting officials, membership in groups, and communal activism. Urban Guatemalans reported the second lowest levels of voting and campaigning in the region in the early 1990s, a finding that squares with the low levels of voter turnout observed there. Guatemalans were close to the regional mean on three other types of participation: contacting public officials, group membership, and community activism. Overall, however, Guatemalans ranked second lowest in the region in political participation, a finding consistent with expectations given the levels of repression prior to and during the time of the survey. For citizen participation to flourish in Guatemala, as for democratic norms, political repression will have to diminish and remain below its recent high levels.

The External Context

Students of democratization and democratic consolidation have argued that the international context may constrain or shape the likelihood of democratization and democratic consolidation in a particular country (Diamond and Linz 1989; Huntington 1993, 273-74). Pressure to adopt or maintain democracy from a hegemonic power may lead elites involved in forming new regimes to adopt democratic rules of the game. Pressure to democratize or keep democratic rules from key international lenders or trading partners will tend to shape the preferences of local elites in favor of democratic rules. International organizations such as the United Nations or Organization of American States (OAS) may also exercise similar pressures. Pressure from regional neighbors for democracy, and the examples of and interaction with mainly democratic neighboring regimes, can also contribute to a demonstration effect favorable toward establishing and keeping a democratic regime.

Guatemala has clearly been subject to such pressures during its period of transition. U.S. pressure to improve human rights performance began to grow in the late 1970s, followed by a gradual escalation of pressure for elections and further democratization during the 1980s and 1990s. Guatemala's Central American neighbors, Latin American nations, international lenders, and international organizations all gradually escalated diplomatic pressures upon Guatemala to adopt civilian democracy from the mid-1980s on by mechanisms that have been widely discussed elsewhere. Even neighboring Mexico, long a civilian-led authoritarian regime, is undergoing tremendous pressure for democratization and some incipient steps in that direction.

There thus remains in Guatemala's international environment considerable pressure to retain the civilian democratic regime, a factor that should help impede authoritarian reversion in some future regime crisis. Perhaps the best indication of the effectiveness of such pressures came from the coup attempted by Guatemalan president Jorge Serrano Elías on May 24, 1993. Acting with the acquiescence of some parts of the armed forces, Serrano dismissed the Congress and Supreme Court, established press censorship, and announced his intention to rule by decree. In addition to protests by Guatemalan citizens and interest groups, the United States and OAS made clear to Guatemalan political actors, including the armed forces, that these powerful foreign actors and the international financial institutions they heavily influenced would look with great disfavor on a deviation from constitutional practice (Jonas 1995, 35-36; Booth 1995, 1). The resolute and courageous resistance to the coup by domestic actors and institutions, occurring as it did within an international context supportive of institutional democracy, helped save the civilian transitional regime.

Conclusion

Many common forces have battered Central America since the 1970s and in the process have shaped much of the sociopolitical change there. Both internal and external influences shape the internal process of regime change, the reconfiguration of a nation's dominant coalition of political actors, and the prevailing rules of the political game. While specific interactions among local actors and conditions determine much of the detail of what happens in any particular case of regime change, socioeconomic and geopolitical forces operating at and beyond the level of the nation-state may heavily shape the resources and behaviors of local actors.

The work of many scholars has revealed how similar forces drove the widespread social mobilization in five Central American nations in the 1970s and the national revolts that occurred in three of them, including Guatemala. Regime change may be caused and shaped by forces within the global context that are similar to those shaping national revolts and democratization. The flurry of regime changes toward civilian democracy in Central America since the late 1970s, of which Guatemala is a key example, has arisen and taken much of its form and outcome from global forces that include economic strains and geopolitics. One may reasonably assume that this regional move toward democracy did not occur because the dominant elites or their challengers in several countries somehow conspired with each other to this end. Few details have been examined, especially the domestic ones, of Guatemala's regime shifts. While much of what has transpired has arisen because of the decisions and actions of domestic actors, they have not operated in a vacuum.

From the arguments and data presented here, Guatemala's democratic prospect appears better in 1998 than at any time since 1954. Most urban citizens manifest commitment to democratic norms, skepticism about military intervention, and disapproval of antidemocratic methods. While political participation is low for the region, the high repression that kept citizens from engaging in politics has declined. The geopolitical context favors a civilian democratic regime. Economic conditions for the country were reasonably healthy during the 1990s, attenuating the prospects for protest and unrest.

Such positive factors notwithstanding, one must still view Guatemala's prospects with a considerable caution because of the historical role of the security forces and their unwillingness to remain on the sidelines of national politics. The most important question about the consolidation of civilian democracy in Guatemala, I believe, is the extent to which the domestic and global contextual forces can constrain the military until it can institutionalize a new relationship of subordination to civilian rulers and constitutional restraint.

Notes

This is a revised version of a paper presented at the Seminar on Guatemalan Development and Democratization: Proactive Responses to Globalization, Universidad del Valle de Guatemala, Guatemala City, March 26-28, 1998. The theoretical section and illustrations for the region draw heavily upon Booth and Walker (1999). My thanks to Tom Walker for his very significant contributions to these ideas and arguments.

1. This concept of political regimes draws from those of Anderson (1967, 1992) and Higley and Burton (1989), and from Wynia's (1990, 24-45) term "political game." Peeler (1998, xii) employs a formulation that captures the same ideas: "Any political system has a broad range of structures—called the regime—that determine which actors actually have governmental authority; how political conflict and cooperation take place; which actors receive or lose resources; and what role, if any, . . . nonpowerful actors play . . ." See also Casper and Taylor (1996, 16-37).

2. These categories by no means exhaust the range of possible types of regimes. They are proposed as a set that accounts for Central American cases during the period under scrutiny.

3. Experts on particular countries might wish to refine these types further as applied to individual cases, or subdivide particular regimes into subregimes based on changes in either coalition makeup or rules, but not simultaneous to both.

4. Peeler (1998, 192-93) argues that nonelite actors in Latin America play a greater role in provoking regime change toward liberal democracy than they do in the subsequent operation of liberal democracies.

5. Recent work on what focuses citizen's antagonism on the state has emphasized the formation of "cultures of opposition" (Foran 1997a, 1997b).

6. This argument has been applied to Central America by Brockett (1988), Wickham-Crowley (1992), Williams (1986), Booth (1991), and Torres Rivas (1981).

7. The political status of "democracy" at the nation-state level, the transition to which "democratization" refers, is the source of considerable conceptual confusion even among political scientists (Booth 1995). Classical democratic theorists essentially define democracy as citizen participation in rule and, therefore, variable according to the amount and quality of popular participation in all aspects of governance. Another approach—more typical of modern political science—has been to define democracy, especially for operational purposes in comparative research, in minimalist procedural terms as constitutional, representative government with free, competitive elections. This approach has many critics, among them Peeler (1985) and Robinson (1996, 2001). Robinson, for instance, distinguishes the minimalist procedural model (which he calls "polyarchy") from truer forms of democracy with greater and more influential citizen participation grounded in social justice. There is real merit to the criticism that minimalist electoral democratic regimes (polyarchies) are limited in their benefits and degree of democracy. It is also true that these regimes have virtues critics often overlook. In particular, polyarchies have much better human rights records and are less repressive than authoritarian, military-dominated regimes. Thus even without equity-based empowerment of poorer citizens, they permit—even facilitate—much more citizen participation, more intense civil society, and citizen attitudes and norms more supportive of democracy (Booth and Richard, 1998a, 1998b) than do repressive regimes. The difference between polyarchies and authoritarian regimes, therefore, is far from trivial.

8. This combination of alterations—change in the coalition membership plus an adjustment of the rules—constitutes the minimum necessary to be classified as a regime change.

9. For details on El Salvador and Guatemala see especially Montgomery (1995), Baloyra-Herp (1995), and Jonas (1991, 1995).

10. It is an important limitation of this data set that it does not include rural samples. However, the urban populations of each of the Central American countries are those that are closest to the seats of government and the most easily mobilized into political participation that can effect national politics.

11. Of course, one cannot determine whether rural Guatemalans, critically important to national stability, also support democracy and harbor reservations about the military and confrontational political tactics. However, one may reasonably surmise that, because repression was more intense in many rural areas than in the cities, rural dwellers may be somewhat more authoritarian and less democratic than urbanites.

Works Cited

Anderson, Charles W. 1967. The Latin American Political System. In *Politics and Economic Change in Latin America: The Governing of Restless Nations*, edited by Charles W. Anderson. New York: Van Nostrand Reinhold.

———. 1992. Toward a Theory of Latin American Politics. In *Politics and Social Change in Latin America: Still a Distinct Tradition?*, edited by Howard J. Wiarda. Boulder, Colo.: Westview, 239-54.

Aya, Rod. 1979. Theories of Revolution Reconsidered: Contrasting Models of Collective Violence. *Theory and Society* 8 (June-December): 39-100.

Baloyra-Herp, Enrique A. 1995. Elections, Civil War, and Transition in El Salvador. In *Elections and Democracy in Central America, Revisited*, edited by Mitchell A. Seligson and John A. Booth. Chapel Hill: University of North Carolina Press.

Booth, John A. 1991. Socioeconomic and Political Roots of National Revolts in Central America. *Latin American Research Review* 26, no. 1:33-73.

———. 1995. Elections and Democracy in Central America: A Framework for Analysis. In *Elections and Democracy in Central America, Revisited*, edited by Mitchell A. Seligson and John A. Booth. Chapel Hill: University of North Carolina Press.

———. 1998. *Costa Rica: Quest for Democracy*. Boulder, Colo.: Westview.

Booth, John A., and Thomas W. Walker. 1993. *Understanding Central America*. Boulder, Colo.: Westview.

Booth, John A., and Patricia Bayer Richard. 1996. Repression, Participation, and Democratic Norms in Urban Central America. *American Journal of Political Science* 40:1205-232.

———. 1998a. Civil Society and Political Context in Central America. *American Behavioral Scientist* 42:33-46.

———. 1998b. Civil Society, Political Capital, and Democratization in Central America. *Journal of Politics* 60:780-800.

Booth, John A., and Thomas W. Walker. 1993. *Understanding Central America*. Boulder, Colo.: Westview.

———. 1999. *Understanding Central America*. Boulder, Colo.: Westview Press.

Brockett, Charles. 1988. *Land, Power, and Poverty: Agrarian Transformation and Political Conflict in Central America*. Boston: Unwin Hyman.

Carothers, Thomas. 1991. *In the Name of Democracy: U.S. Policy toward Latin America in the Reagan Years*. Berkeley and Los Angeles: University of California Press.

Casper, Gretchen, and Michelle M. Taylor. 1996. *Negotiating Democracy: Transitions from Authoritarianism*. Pittsburgh: University of Pittsburgh Press.

Chase-Dunn, Christopher. 1989. *Global Formation: Structures of the World-Economy*. Cambridge, Mass.: Blackwell.

———. 1998. Globalization from Below in Guatemala. A paper presented at the Conference on Guatemalan Development and Democracy: Proactive Responses to Globalization, Guatemala City, 26-28 March 1998.

DeFronzo, James. 1991. *Revolutions and Revolutionary Movements*. Boulder, Colo.: Westview.

Diamond, Larry. 1993. Introduction: Political Culture and Democracy. In *Political Culture and Democracy in Developing Countries*, edited by Larry Diamond. Boulder, Colo.: Lynne Rienner.

———. 1994a. Causes and Effects. In *Political Culture and Democracy in Developing Countries*, edited by Larry Diamond. Boulder, Colo.: Lynne Rienner.

———. 1994b. Introduction: Political Culture and Democracy. In *Political Culture and Democracy in Developing Countries*, edited by Larry Diamond. Boulder, Colo.: Lynne Rienner.

Diamond, Larry, and Juan J. Linz. 1989. Introduction: Politics, Society, and Democracy in Latin America. In *Democracy in Developing Countries, Volume 4: Latin America*, edited by Larry Diamond, Juan Linz, and Seymour Martin Lipset. Boulder, Colo.: Lynne Rienner.

Foran, John. 1997a. The Comparative-Historical Sociology of Third World Social Revolutions: Why a Few Succeed, Why Most Fail. In *Theorizing Revolutions*, edited by John Foran. London: Routledge.

———. 1997b. Discourses and Social Forces: The Role of Culture and Cultural Studies in Understanding Revolutions. In *Theorizing Revolutions*, edited by John Foran. London: Routledge.

Gasiorowski, Mark J. 1995. Economic Crisis and Regime Change: An Event History Analysis. *American Political Science Review* 89, no. 1:882-97.

———. 1996. An Overview of the Political Regime Dataset. *Comparative Political Studies* 21:469-83.

Goldstone, Jack A. 1991. An Analytical Framework. In *Revolutions of the Late Twentieth Century*, edited by Jack A. Goldstone, Ted Robert Gurr, and Farrokh Moshiri. Boulder, Colo.: Westview.

Gurr, Ted Robert. 1970. *Why Men Rebel*. Princeton: Princeton University Press.

Higley, John, and Michael Burton. 1989. The Elite Variable in Democratic Transitions and Breakdowns. *American Sociological Review* 54, no. 1:17-32.

Higley, John, and Richard Gunther, eds. 1992. *Elites and Democratic Consolidation in Latin America and Southern Europe*. Cambridge: Cambridge University Press.

Huntington, Samuel P. 1993. *The Third Wave: Democratization in the Late Twentieth Century*. Norman: University of Oklahoma Press.

Inglehart, Ronald. 1988. The Renaissance of Political Culture. *American Political Science Review* 82 (November):1203-230.

Inter-American Development Bank. 1997. *Latin America after a Decade of Reforms: Economic and Social Progress in Latin America, 1997 Report*. Baltimore: Johns Hopkins University Press.

———. 1998. Country Profiles. <www.iadb.org/int.sta/english/profile/cty_statprofile_frame.htm>, [accessed 1 December].

Jonas, Susanne. 1991. *The Battle for Guatemala*, Boulder, Colo.: Westview Press.

———. 1995. Electoral Problems and the Democratic Prospect in Guatemala. In *Elections and Democracy in Central America: Revisited*, edited by Mitchell A. Seligson and John A. Booth. Chapel Hill: University of North Carolina Press.

Kriesberg, Louis. 1982. *Social Conflicts*. Englewood Cliffs, N.J.: Prentice-Hall.

Linz, Juan J., and Alfred Stepan, eds. 1978. *The Breakdown of Democratic Regimes*. Baltimore: Johns Hopkins University Press.

Lipset, Seymour Martin. 1959. Social Requisites of Democracy: Economic Development and Political Legitimacy. *American Political Science Review* 53 (March):69-105.

Lowenthal, Abraham F., ed. 1991. *Exporting Democracy: The United States and Latin America*. Baltimore: Johns Hopkins University Press.

Montgomery, Tommie Sue. 1995. *Revolution in El Salvador*. Boulder, Colo.: Westview.

Moore, Barrington. 1966. *Social Origins of Dictatorship and Democracy*. Boston: Beacon.

Moreno, Dario. 1995. Respectable Intervention: The United States and Central American Elections. In *Elections and Democracy in Central America, Revisited*, edited by Mitchell A. Seligson and John A. Booth. Chapel Hill: University of North Carolina Press.

Muller, Edward N., and Mitchell A. Seligson. 1994. Civic Culture and Democracy: The Question of Causal Relationships. *American Political Science Review* 88 (September):645-52.

O'Donnell, Guillermo. 1973. *Modernization and Bureaucratic-Authoritarianism: Studies in South American Politics*. Berkeley and Los Angeles: University of California Press.

O'Donnell, Guillermo, Philippe C. Schmitter, and Lawrence Whitehead, eds. 1986. *Transitions from Authoritarian Rule*. Baltimore: Johns Hopkins University Press.

Olson, Mancur. 1963. Rapid Growth as a Destabilizing Force. *Journal of Economic History* 23, no. 4: 529-52.

Paige, Jeffrey M. 1975. *Agrarian Revolution: Social Movements and Export Agriculture in the Underdeveloped World*. New York: Free Press.

Peeler, John. 1985. *Latin American Democracies: Colombia, Costa Rica, Venezuela*. Chapel Hill: University of North Carolina Press.

———. 1998. *Building Democracy in Latin America*. Boulder, Colo.: Lynne Rienner.

Prevost, Gary, and Harry E. Vanden, eds. 1997. *The Undermining of the Sandinista Revolution*. New York: St. Martin's.

Przeworski, Adam. 1986. Some Problems in the Study of the Transition to Democracy. In *Transitions from Authoritarian Rule*, edited by Guillermo O'Donnell, Philippe Schmitter and Lawrence E. Whitehead. Baltimore: Johns Hopkins University Press.

Putnam, Robert D. 1993. *Making Democracy Work: Civic Traditions in Modern Italy*. Princeton: Princeton University Press.

———. 1996. Bowling Alone: America's Declining Social Capital. *Journal of Democracy* 7 (Summer):38-52.

Robinson, William I. 1996. *Promoting Polyarchy: Globalization, U.S. Intervention and Hegemony*. Cambridge: Cambridge University Press.

———. 2001. Neoliberalism, the Global Elite, and the Guatemalan Transition: A Critical Macrosocial Analysis. In *Globalization on the Ground*, edited by Christopher Chase-Dunn, Susanne Jonas, and Nelson Amaro. Boulder, Colo.: Rowman & Littlefield.

Rueschemeyer, Dietrich, Evelyne Huber Stephens, and John D. Stephens. 1992. *Capitalist Development and Democracy*. Chicago: University of Chicago Press.

Ruhl, Mark. 1998. Militarism and Democratization in Troubled Waters. Paper presented at the 1998 meeting of the Latin American Studies Association, Chicago, Ill., 24-27 September.

Rustow, Dankwart. 1970. Transitions to Democracy: Toward a Dynamic Model. *Comparative Politics* 2 (April):337-63.

Selbin, Eric. 1993. *Modern Latin American Revolutions*. Boulder, Colo.: Westview Press.

Seligson, Mitchell A., and John A. Booth. 1993. Political Culture and Regime Type: Evidence from Nicaragua and Costa Rica. *Journal of Politics* 55 (August):777-92.

———, eds. 1995. *Elections and Democracy in Central America, Revisited*. Chapel Hill: University of North Carolina Press.

Skocpol, Theda. 1979. *States and Social Revolution*. Cambridge: Cambridge University Press.

Tilly, Charles. 1978. *From Mobilization to Revolution*, Reading, Mass.: Addison-Wesley.

Torres Rivas, Edelberto. 1981. *Crisis del Poder in Centroamérica*. San José, Costa Rica: Editorial Universitaria Centroamericana.

Vanhanen, Tatu. 1992. *The Process of Democratization*. New York: Crane Russak.

Walker, Thomas W. 1997. Introduction: Historical Setting and Important Issues. In *Nicaragua without Illusions: Regime Transition and Structural Adjustment in the 1990s*, edited by Thomas W. Walker. Wilmington, Del.: Scholarly Resources.

Walton, John. 1984. *Reluctant Rebels: Comparative Studies in Revolution and Underdevelopment*. New York: Columbia University Press.

Whitehead, Lawrence. 1991. The Imposition of Democracy. In *Exporting Democracy: The United States and Latin America*, edited by Abraham F. Lowenthal. Baltimore: Johns Hopkins University Press.

Wickham-Crowley, Timothy. 1992. *Guerrillas and Revolution in Latin America: A Comparative Study of Insurgents and Regimes since 1956*. Princeton: Princeton University Press.

Williams, Robert. 1986. *Export Agriculture and the Crisis in Central America*. Chapel Hill: University of North Carolina Press.

Wilson, Bruce M. 1998. *Costa Rica: Politics, Economics, and Democracy*. Boulder, Colo.: Lynne Rienner.

Wynia, Gary. 1990. *Politics of Latin American Development*. Cambridge: Cambridge University Press.

Yashar, Deborah J. 1997. *Demanding Democracy: Reform and Reaction in Costa Rica and Guatemala, 1870s-1950s*. Stanford, Calif.: Stanford University Press.

4

Democratization through Peace

Susanne Jonas

The Guatemalan peace process—the negotiation and initial implementation of far-reaching peace accords ending the country's thirty-six-year civil war—provides an excellent opportunity to revisit a number of ongoing discussions about political democratization and social justice in Latin America. The first part of this article summarizes how, beyond ending the war, this peace process contributed significantly to the democratization of Guatemala; it highlights both how the process opened up political space and what gains have (and have not) been achieved in the content of the accords signed. The rest of this article analyzes the Guatemalan experience from the early 1980s to the present and uses that experience to address some broad theoretical debates about democratization and social justice in Latin America.[1]

In engaging the conceptual debates about political democracy, I make no pretense of "settling" these debates; rather, my goal is to interpret (and draw lessons from) Guatemala's political evolution during recent decades. In such an interpretation there should be no disjuncture between the analytical use of terminology about democracy and public discourse about actually lived experience. Hence, we should not assign the label of "democracy" or "democratic transition" to situations and time periods that were not experienced as such by large numbers of Guatemalans. When and how did a genuine democratic transition begin in Guatemala? Can we characterize as a "democratic" transition the period (early 1980s through early 1990s) when the political and electoral transition had begun but prior to the peace process? The answers to these questions rest on an analysis of the interaction between elections and the peace process in opening up Guatemala's exclusionary political system.

From this follows my broader question: What does the Guatemalan experience add to the ongoing debates among different paradigms or schools of analysis about political democracy in Latin America? The most commonly accepted definition in the contemporary political science literature is one or another version of the "procedural minimum." I shall argue here that experiences such as the Guatemalan, involving societal ruptures and decades-long civil wars, cannot be fully understood simply within the context of one (useful but limited) body of literature about democratic transitions. That perspective, which was developed mainly to deal with transitions from authoritarian to democratic rule in southern Europe and the Southern Cone of Latin America, provides partial insights. Nevertheless, for the cases of the Central American countries that underwent revolutionary turmoil during the 1980s, it must be complemented by other bodies of literature that highlight the participatory dimensions of democratization. In particular, key elements of the Guatemalan experience are best captured through the lens of the classical tradition that emphasizes participatory as well as procedural elements of democracy.

In addition, because 60 percent of its population is indigenous, the quality of political democracy in Guatemala will be profoundly affected by issues of cultural diversity ("pluriculturalidad"). Finally, beyond the debates about the nature of political democracy lies the highly contested and still unresolved issue of its relation to social-economic equity or justice—especially in this era of neoliberal economic policies. This issue as well can be reexamined in the light of the Guatemalan peace process experience. This chapter's purpose is to theorize the experience of Guatemala from the early 1980s to the present and hopefully to enrich the broader debates.

Part I: "De-Centaurization" and Other Democratic Gains

The Process of Peace Negotiations

In Guatemala as elsewhere, a peace negotiation is, in the end, a political settlement, and much of what it is able to deliver in the short range concerns postwar political arrangements. Particularly striking in the Guatemalan case are the democratizing elements of both the negotiation process, with its provisions for broad input and participation, and the content of the accords as signed.

It is important to keep in mind that as recently as 1992 to 1993, hardline forces in Guatemala's military and civilian elites were determined not to negotiate a settlement permitting a legal presence or political participation by the insurgent left or its allies; and they regarded virtually all of the organizations of civil society as the guerrillas' allies or "facades." Particularly after the signing of a negotiated peace in neighboring El Salvador in January 1992, the elites vowed "never" to tolerate such an outcome in Guatemala. The extraordinary story of how and why, from 1994 to 1996, the Guatemalan army and government found themselves involved in very much the same kind of process as the Salvadoran, with the United Nations as moderator and verifier of the process, is summarized below (see also Jonas 2000, 1999).

Guatemala's thirty-six-year civil war began in 1960, just a few years after the Central Intelligence Agency (CIA)-orchestrated overthrow of the democratic nationalist government of Jacobo Arbenz in 1954. During the next three and a half decades, there were several phases of the war that pitted leftist insurgent organizations (which united in 1982 as the Unidad Revolucionaria Nacional Guatemalteca, Guatemalan National Revolutionary Unity, URNG) against U.S.-trained and -supported counterinsurgency forces of the Guatemalan army. The first phase of the war, during the middle and late 1960s, was centered in the eastern, primarily ladino (nonindigenous) part of the country. After the devastating army counteroffensive of 1966 to 1968, the guerrillas retreated, regrouped, and reentered the country in the early 1970s.

The subsequent phases of the war took place mainly in Guatemala's "altiplano," or Western Highlands, with many indigenous communities as the major protagonist and support base for the guerrillas. The army responded in the early 1980s with a brutal "scorched-earth" campaign that left 100,000 to 150,000 dead or "disappeared" between 1981 and 1983 alone, and has been widely regarded as genocidal. (See Falla 1978, 1994; Le Bot 1995; Jonas 1991; on U.S. relation to the army, Jonas 1996.) But even as the civil war continued in a lower intensity phase, the late 1980s saw the beginnings of a move toward peace. After the crushing counterinsurgency war of the early 1980s, the URNG recognized that a strategy based on military victory or "taking state power" was unthinkable: the cost of pursuing such a strategy made it totally unacceptable to the noncombatant population. Hence, shortly after the return to elected civilian government in 1986, the URNG began to propose dialogue and negotiations for a political settlement to the war.

For several years, the army and the government (headed by Christian Democrat Vinicio Cerezo, 1986 to 1990) stubbornly refused to negotiate, insisting that the insurgents had been "defeated" and therefore must disarm unilaterally without negotiating any substantive issues. They maintained this stance even in the face of the 1987 Central American Peace Accords negotiated (in Guatemala City) primarily to end the Contra war against the Sandinista government in Nicaragua. By 1990, however, even army and government spokesmen had to acknowledge that Guatemala's war was continuing. The implicit admission that the war could not be "won" militarily by either side created the conditions, for the first time beginning in the spring of 1990, for the negation of the war, that is, serious discussions about ending it.

By this time, considerable political pressure for peace had built up within Guatemala as well as internationally. During 1989, the National Reconciliation Commission (established by the 1987 Central American Peace Accords) sponsored a National Dialogue. Although boycotted by the army, the government, and the private sector, this dialogue expressed a clear national consensus among all other sectors in favor of a substantive political settlement to the war. The dialogue process projected a series of URNG meetings with the political parties and "social sectors" (private enterprise, popular and religious movements) and finally with the government and army. The 1990 sessions included a September meeting between the URNG and the umbrella organization of big business, CACIF (Chamber of Agricultural, Commercial, Industrial and Financial Associations)—an unthinkable event during the previous thirty years. Beyond the formal meetings, the dialogue process opened up spaces within a repressive context for public discussion of issues that had been undiscussable for decades; in this sense, it became an important avenue for beginning to democratize Guatemala.

In early 1991 the newly elected government of Jorge Serrano opened direct negotiations with the URNG. For the first time, top army officials agreed to participate in meetings to set the agenda and procedures for peace talks without demanding that the URNG first disarm—although they still hoped to win URNG demobilization in exchange for minimal, pro forma concessions. During the next year, there were agreements in principle on democratization and partial agreements on human rights. The precariousness of the process became evident when it stagnated in mid-1992 and moved toward total breakdown during the last months of Serrano's crisis-ridden government. The Serrano government turned out to be more interested in imposing a cease-fire deadline than in resolving the substantive issues on the eleven-point agenda (ranging from human rights and demilitarization to indigenous rights and social-economic issues); this stance by the government was unacceptable to the URNG.

The entire peace process was derailed by the May 1993 "Serranazo," or attempted "auto-golpe." Serrano's attempt to seize absolute control (initially but briefly supported by some factions of the army) unleashed a major political and constitutional crisis. After being repudiated by virtually all sectors of civil society and the international community, the Serranazo was resolved through the (most unexpected) ascendance of human rights ombudsman Ramiro de León Carpio to the presidency (see Jonas 1994; McCleary 1997). But the peace process remained at a standstill during the rest of 1993. The new government was closely allied with the dominant wing of the army high command, which supported the idea of civilian presidents but with full autonomy and wide-ranging veto powers for the military. The new government presented unrealistic negotiation proposals that would have discarded previously signed agreements and, in essence, would have required the URNG to disarm without any substantive settlements. Perhaps the army had hoped to use de León Carpio's legitimacy to achieve unilateral surrender by the URNG. These proposals were rejected almost unanimously throughout Guatemalan society (except by the army and private sector) and were viewed as completely nonviable by the international community.

In January 1994, with these tactics having run their course, the negotiations were resumed, but this time on a significantly different basis. During the 1991 to 1993 rounds, Guatemala's peace talks had been moderated by Msgr. Rodolfo Quezada Toruño of the Catholic Bishops' Conference, with the United Nations (UN) in an "observer" role. As of January 1994, both sides agreed that the UN should become the moderator; this paved the way for significantly increased involvement by the international community, raising the stakes in the negotiations and giving the entire process a less reversible dynamic. (See Jonas 2000; Baranyi 1995; Padilla 1995, 1997; Aguilera in Torres Rivas and Aguilera 1998.)

Furthermore, the January 1994 "Framework Accord" established a clear agenda and timetable. (The agenda was maintained, but the deadlines became totally unrealizable in practice.) This accord also formalized a role for a broad-based multisector Assembly of Civil Society (ASC), which included virtually all organized sectors of civil society (even, for the first time, women's organizations) as well as the major political parties. Only the big business sectors represented in CACIF decided not to participate. Having gained new experience during the Serranazo, these grassroots organizations had become increasingly vocal in demanding participation in the peace process. The ASC was also notable for the diversity or plurality of political and ideological positions represented within its ranks; unlike El Salvador's popular organizations in relation to the Farabundo Martí National Liberation Front (FMLN), the ASC was by no means a simple instrument of the URNG. As the main agreements were being hammered out, the ASC—after itself engaging in a fascinating process of consensus building among widely divergent positions—offered proposals to the negotiating parties on each issue. While not binding, the proposals had to be taken into account by the two parties, and the URNG adopted many of the ASC proposals as its own negotiating positions.

The formation of the ASC also gave Guatemala's organized popular sectors their first sustained experience (following upon their initial efforts during the Serranazo) of participating in and considering themselves part of the political process. This was particularly important for sectors that had always rejected electoral participation and prided themselves on their antisystem political culture of *denuncia* (accusations) as a manifestation of political resistance. In the particular unfolding of Guatemalan history, the ASC experience was the precursor to the eventual participation by many of those sectors in the 1995 election.

A breakthrough Human Rights Accord was signed in late March 1994, calling for the immediate establishment of international verification mechanisms to monitor human rights. But for months, the government took no steps to comply with its obligations under the accord, and the mandated UN Verification Mission (MINUGUA) did not arrive until November 1994. At the table, two new accords were signed in June 1994 on the Resettling of Displaced Populations and a watered down Truth Commission (empowered to *esclarecer* or shed light on past human rights crimes, but without naming the individuals responsible)—the latter accord sparking fierce criticism from popular and human rights organizations. On the ground, meanwhile, human rights violations worsened, leaving the definite impression that the government was going through the motions of a peace process without intending to change anything.

For the above reasons as well as the complexity of the issue itself, no agreement was reached on the next theme, Identity and the Rights of Indigenous Peoples, until March 1995. The signing of this accord was a landmark achievement for a country whose population is 60 percent indigenous. It mandated a constitutional redefinition of Guatemala as multiethnic, multicultural, and multilingual, and implied massive changes in the country's institutions (as detailed below). The actual signing, however, was overshadowed by the eruption on March 23 of the scandal in Washington concerning the involvement of a CIA-paid army officer in the murders of an American citizen and an indigenous guerrilla commander married to American lawyer Jennifer Harbury. This scandal remained front-page news for several weeks and left the Guatemalan army (as well as the CIA) even further discredited. Negotiations on the following theme, social-economic issues, directly affecting the interests of Guatemala's economic elites, continued throughout 1995, making some progress but without a final resolution during the lame-duck de León Carpio government.

Inside Guatemala, meanwhile, the dynamics of the November 1995 general election directly impacted the peace process, and vice-versa. (These interactions are explored in detail in Part II.) The most important novelties of this electoral process were as follows: first, the URNG's early 1995 call, urging participation in the vote; second, the formation of a left-of-center electoral front of popular and indigenous organizations (the "left flank" of the ASC), the New Guatemala Democratic Front (FDNG); and third, an August agreement at which the URNG promised not to disrupt the elections in exchange for a commitment by the major political parties to continue the peace negotiations under a new government and to honor the accords already signed.

In the November 1995 general elections, no presidential candidate received an absolute majority. The major surprise of the election was the stronger-than-expected showing of the newly formed FDNG, which won six seats in Congress; additionally, alliances between the FDNG and locally based indigenous "civic committees" won several important mayoralties, including Quetzaltenango. A January 1996 runoff for president pitted modernizing conservative Alvaro Arzú against a stand-in for former dictator Efraín Ríos Montt, who opposed the peace process. Arzú won by a scant 2 percent margin.

Even before taking office, Arzú had already held several direct, secret meetings with the URNG in different venues. Shortly after taking office, Arzú immediately signaled his intention to bring the ongoing peace talks to a successful conclusion. In addition to appointing a "peace cabinet," the new president underscored his intention to establish civilian control over the army by undertaking a series of shake-ups in the army high command and the army-controlled police. These and other actions created a new political climate of confidence and paved the way for an indefinite cease-fire betweeen the rebels and the army in March 1996.

Once the formal peace negotiations were reinitiated, and following intensive consultations with the private sector, the Accord on Socio-Economic and Agrarian Issues was signed in May 1996—this time, finally, with CACIF support. Because of the compromises involved, the accord generated considerable controversy among popular organizations before the ASC eventually endorsed it. The crowning achievement of the peace process came in September 1996, with the signing of the Accord on the Strengthening of Civilian Power and Role of the Armed Forces in a Democratic Society: this accord mandated constitutional reforms subordinating the army to civilian control and restricting the army's role to external defense, while creating a new civilian police force to handle all internal security matters.

A serious crisis, with some lasting effects, nearly derailed the entire process in October 1996, when a high-level cadre of the Organización del Pueblo en Armas (ORPA)—previously regarded as the most pro-negotiation of the URNG organizations—was discovered to be the author of a high-level kidnapping of octagenarian Olga de Novella, from one of Guatemala's richest families and a personal friend of the president. The government suspended the peace talks until ORPA's top leader, Gaspar Ilom, resigned from the negotiating table in November. Once the process was resumed, this time with a deadline set for the end of 1996, the operational accords were signed in December. These dealt with a definitive cease-fire, constitutional and electoral reforms, the legal reintegration of the URNG (entailing a partial amnesty for both the URNG and the army), and a timetable for fulfillment of all of the accords. Following the dramatic return of the URNG leadership to Guatemala on December 28, the historic Final Peace Accord was signed in Guatemala's National Palace on December 29, 1996, amid considerable national celebration and international attention. Thus ended the first phase of the peace process that the Guatemalan elites had vowed "never" to permit in Guatemala.

How did this "never" turn into acceptance? The UN played a role that no other mediating force could have played in facilitating agreements between the government and the URNG. In addition, six governments played an important supportive role as the "Group of Friends" of the peace process.[2] Within Guatemala, slowly but surely, despite fierce resistances and significant delays, the peace process acquired credibility. To be sure, at many times, its volatility and fragility evoked images of the Middle-East negotiations between Israel and the Palestine Liberation Organization (PLO). But with all its difficulties, the logic of the peace process, broadly understood, came to offer Guatemala its best opportunity to democratize a thoroughly exclusionary system and to make important changes that would have been highly unlikely or impossible under any other circumstances.

Even within the recalcitrant CACIF, "modernizing," more pragmatic fractions became invested in the peace process; the CACIF recognized that it was the only way to avoid being isolated and left behind in the world of the twenty-first century. For its part, the seemingly all-powerful army, despite all appearances to the contrary, was increasingly on the defensive and had decreasing legitimacy and authority within Guatemala, especially after the failed Serranazo and the 1995 CIA scandal. Internationally, given the changes in the world and in Guatemala since 1990, open peace resisters in the Guatemalan army could no longer count on U.S. support (Jonas 1996). In short, none of the major Guatemalan players had anywhere to move but forward.

Seen in its totality, the negotiation process was a great step forward for Guatemalan democracy. The accords constituted a truly negotiated settlement, much like El Salvador's of 1992. Rather than being imposed by victors upon the vanquished, they represented a splitting of differences between radically opposed forces, with major concessions from both sides. This exercise in the culture of compromise was a real novelty in Guatemala.

Additional process-related gains for democracy have accumulated since the signing of the peace accords. Most of the accords contain important provisions for participation in decision making—including *comisiones paritarias* (with equal representation from the government and indigenous organizations) and a host of other multisectoral commissions. In addition, the implementation of the accords has given rise to a far-reaching culture and practice of "consultas," involving some (not all) policymakers in direct interchanges with citizens and social organizations —some of them outside the capital city (also a novelty). Finally, the accords provide innovative mechanisms (such as the *Foro de Mujeres*, Women's Forum) for training and "capacity building" among those who have never had such opportunities.

If fully implemented, the accords could open up an opportunity for significant transformations of Guatemalan society—the only such opportunity in half a century (since the CIA-orchestrated overthrow of the democratic reformist Arbenz government in 1954), and likely the only such opportunity that Guatemala will have in another half century. But even after the signing and initial implementation of some accords, the road has remained full of minefields, and the efforts to fully implement the accords have encountered very serious resistances from those who have held power in the old system (see epilogue).

Content of the Accords: Democracy without Social Justice

Taken as a whole, the accords ended forty-two years of painful Cold War history and provided a framework for institutionalizing full political democracy in a country that has not enjoyed such democracy since 1954. Taken one by one, the accords are a mix of genuine achievements and serious limitations; they represent a series of compromises between radically opposing viewpoints. The obligations they impose on the Guatemalan government are written down in black and white and are subject to international (UN) verification.

The first breakthrough achievement was the Human Rights Accord, signed in March 1994. It was important not so much for any new concept of human rights (since these were already guaranteed on paper in the 1985 Constitution) as for the new mechanism it created for ending the systematic violation of those rights in practice: a UN Verification Mission (MINUGUA). The on-the-ground, in-country UN presence signified the international community's intention to monitor respect for human rights, and this definitively altered the political context (see Jonas 1999).

Second, at the heart of the entire arrangement, is the September 1996 demilitarization accord. It requires far-reaching constitutional reforms to limit the functions of the army—which since the 1960s has considered itself the "spinal column" of the Guatemalan state and has involved itself in everything from counterinsurgency and internal security to civic action and vaccinating babies. Henceforth, the accord stipulates, the army will have one single function: defense of the borders and of Guatemala's territorial integrity. The accord also eliminates the dreaded paramilitary Civilian Self-Defense Patrols (PACs) and other counterinsurgency security units, reduces the size and budget of the army by a third, and creates a new civilian police force to guarantee citizen security. Finally, it mandates necessary reforms of the judicial system, to eliminate the pervasive impunity.

Some years ago, Guatemalan writer Carlos Figueroa (1986) gave us the unforgettable image of the "centaurization" of the Guatemalan state, that is, its conversion into a counterinsurgency apparatus that was half-beast, half-human—a mix of civilian and military power, with the military component predominating. The demilitarization accord mandates the "de-centaurization" of the state, as the precondition for strengthening civilian power and genuine democratization. It is also the precondition for Guatemala's governability and viability in the twenty-first century. As we began to see with the failure of the 1993 Serranazo, the state-as-centaur is no longer viable.

If the battle for full implementation is won—which cannot be taken for granted in Guatemala—this accord will stand out as marking profound changes in the rules and principal players of Guatemalan politics—what Booth (1998, 2) denominates a "regime change." For those who have lived under Guatemala's militarized and thoroughly exclusionary political system all these years, ideological pluralism is a significant achievement. The fear of repression, often described as a "culture of terror," has widely permeated human and social interactions during most of Guatemala's recent history. Strange as it sounds, people can celebrate the fact that Guatemala is becoming a "normal" country because they have been living in a virtual state of exception for decades.

The other significant gain is the 1995 Accord on Identity and the Rights of Indigenous Peoples. This accord goes far beyond antidiscrimination protections for Guatemala's indigenous majority—60 percent of the population—to mandate a constitutional reform redefining Guatemala as a multiethnic, multicultural, and multilingual nation. If fully implemented, this agreement will require profound reforms in the country's educational, judicial, and political systems. It lays the formal basis for a new entitlement of Guatemala's indigenous majority and establishes their right to make claims upon the state. As detailed below, democracy and genuine pluralism cannot be divorced from recognition of the diversity that is Guatemala and the strong indigenous component of Guatemala's national identity. This accord, together with independent initiatives by a variety of indigenous organizations, also creates a new context for social and political interactions and for a more democratic political culture.

Of course, there are very serious limitations, flaws, and omissions in some of the accords. Most immediately visible was the weakness on issues of justice to victims of the war. To begin with, Guatemala's Truth Commission was empowered neither to take judicial action nor even to name individually those responsible for unspeakable human rights crimes. This accord, which generated howls of protest in Guatemala when it was first signed in 1994, was compounded by the partial amnesty negotiated in December 1996 for some crimes committed by the army as well as the URNG. The amnesty covers war-related crimes—excluding genocide, torture, and forced disappearances, but not extrajudicial killings.[3] Essentially, the accord kicks the ball back to the courts. But the judicial system, due to be reformed through the Accord on the Strengthening of Civilian Power, still operates within a generalized framework of impunity and threats. The level of impunity still prevailing two years after the peace accords were signed is evident in the failure to resolve the April 1998 Gerardi assassination, the highest level political murder of recent years (see note 2).

Also serious are the shortcomings in the Accord on Socio-Economic and Agrarian Issues. The accord recognizes poverty as a problem—for Guatemala, a step forward—and it accepts, in principle, governmental responsibility for the well-being of the population. It commits the government to increase the ratio of taxes to GDP from under 8 percent (the lowest in the hemisphere) to 12 percent by 2000. (The battle to actually institute the tax reforms has been one of the fiercest of the postwar period—see Jonas 2000.) However, the accord sidesteps the issue of land reform, and it contains no measures to create jobs or address the alarming rate of unemployment and underemployment, now 66 percent.

The compromises and omissions on these issues are not surprising, given the need to get the private sector on board, the government's conservative economic agenda, and the generally neoliberal policies coming from the international financial institutions. The daily lives of most Guatemalans will not improve directly as a result of the accords. As everywhere else in Latin America, socioeconomic policies will be the result of political struggle once all political forces are legalized. The steady deterioration of social conditions in neighboring El Salvador since the signing of peace in 1992 has been an ominous precedent. The Guatemalan accord incorporated measures to prevent a repeat of the Salvadoran experience (i.e., clear contradictions between the negotiated peace agenda and the government's neoliberal agenda). Nevertheless, it remains to be seen whether the resistances to tax reform and social-economic redistribution will become the Achilles' heel of the peace accords, eventually undermining democratic gains. For example, ongoing and worsening poverty is one of the major factors contributing to an increase in social violence and common crime; this, in turn, has sparked calls for maintaining army involvement in internal security—a definite threat to democratic gains.

More generally, Guatemala's democratic reforms are by no means automatically in place, but have required additional battles. Specifically, the most important elements of the peace accords in democratizing Guatemala require changes in the 1985 Constitution. While containing a Bill of Rights on paper, it simultaneously legalized functions and powers for the army that made political democratization almost impossible to achieve in practice. Furthermore, the 1985 Constitution did very little to address indigenous peoples' rights. Hence, the major democratic gains from the peace process cannot be consolidated until the constitutional reforms are in place (see epilogue).

The peace process and the accords have changed many rules of the political game and created a new political scenario. If the forces of the Left are coherent and intelligent enough to use it well, they now have the space to fight for many of the goals not achieved in the accords themselves. Nevertheless, with the signing of the accords, Guatemala's "peace resisters" and defenders of the old order immediately began sharpening their knives. Until the fundamental battles of the second (implementation) phase of the peace process are won, Guatemalan democracy will remain fragile and unconsolidated. Given the level of resistance within Guatemala, concerted international support—and, above all, a conditioning of international aid on compliance with the accords—remains a necessary complement to internal efforts to overcome these resistances.

Part II: Democracy without Adjectives

Fulfillment of the peace accords, particularly on demilitarization, is the necessary precondition for full development of political democracy. The quality of that democracy will also be affected by the degree of citizen participation (both individual and collective) in using democratic institutions to improve their lives. Below, I develop a series of arguments about the Guatemalan experience and implications for the broader debates in Latin America. First, I argue that the transition literature, developed primarily to explain events in the Southern Cone, does not by itself capture the essentials of the democratization process as it actually occurred in Guatemala. In order to fully comprehend experiences such as the Guatemalan (and others in Central America), we must also draw on other paradigms or schools of analysis of democracy. The Schumpeterian/representational tradition, which emphasizes only procedural/institutional democracy, is not "wrong"; but for situations such as the Guatemalan, it includes too much and at the same time describes too little. If that procedural definition is complemented by other theoretical frameworks that make political participation more central, we can gain a better perspective on how much political democratization can mean when it fully develops after a long antidemocratic period. Finally, I address the recurrent issue of socioeconomic equity and its relation to political democracy. I make no pretense of resolving this monumental issue, but its ongoing relevance should be highlighted.

How Democratic Was Guatemala's "Pacted Transition"?

As seen above, the peace process has been a broadly democratizing experience for Guatemala. But how does its contribution compare to that of the electoral democracy restored during the mid-1980s through an interelite pact? This question presupposes another: How shall we characterize the "pacted transition" period from the early 1980s through the early 1990s, before the peace process was fully under way (although it had begun)? By what criteria shall we judge the quality of democracy during that previous period? It was certainly a political transition, but can it be considered a "democratic transition"? And if not, how and when did the transition become more democratic?

During the period from the early 1980s through the early 1990s, Guatemala did experience a transition pacted between civilian and military elites, and did hold elections that were considered "free and fair" (nonfraudulent) as well as competitive. However, those elections were restricted, that is, not representative of all political tendencies (see below). Furthermore, as described more empirically elsewhere (Jonas 1991), at the same time a repressive and coercive counterinsurgency apparatus was effectively stifling basic freedoms (of expression, assembly, and so on) and imposing military control on entire sectors of the rural population. Only the Reagan State Department cheerfully proclaimed Guatemala a "consolidated" and "post-transitional" democracy after nothing more than the 1985 election (Jonas 1989). More sober and rigorous academic analysts implicitly acknowledged the problem when they had to invent new categories of democracy (restricted, pseudo-, "tutelada," "facade," "democradura," and so on) in order to include Guatemala in the "democratic family." When it becomes necessary to add all those qualifiers or adjectives, the definition of democracy is being stretched beyond acceptable limits.

Within Guatemala itself, the debates about the "democratic transition" have been very sharp and contested. Officers of the Guatemalan army and some of their civilian allies generally claim that the army guided Guatemala to democracy, beginning with the 1982 coup, continuing through the Constituent Assembly (1984), the new Constitution (1985), and the 1985 elections that restored civilian government in 1986. Hence, according to this interpretation, farsighted army officials and their civilian allies should go down in history as the fathers of contemporary Guatemalan democracy. Some civilian social scientists concur that the democratic transition began in the early 1980s, although most of them do not credit the army with having "graciously" conceded real power to civilians (e.g., Padilla 1996b, 33; Rosada in ASIES 1998, 32).

A second debate focuses on the period of elected, formally civilian rule beginning in 1986 (the governments of Cerezo, Serrano, and de León Carpio), which a number of Guatemalan analysts take as the starting-point for contemporary Guatemalan democracy (e.g., Aguilera 1996a, 1997; Arévalo 1998; Azpuru 1999). Generally, their argument is not the simplistic one based only on having civilian presidents; in addition, they maintain, despite the large quota of power held by the army, these governments saw the gradual undermining of military power, finally even the subordination of military to civilian power. While it is true that the army lost absolute power and/or saw its power undermined, I agree with those who have challenged the idea of calling this period "democratic" without any further qualification. Edelberto Torres Rivas (1989, 1996), for example, has described it as an "authoritarian transition to democracy." Of course, there were changes (a "transition") beginning in 1982; one could even say in hindsight that it eventually became a "transition toward democracy." But this is quite different from characterizing it as a "democratic transition" per se, particularly the period of 1982 to 1985.

Elsewhere (Jonas 1991, 1995), I have argued in detail that because power was not effectively transferred from the army to civilians, the transition from overt military rule to elected civilian government in Guatemala during the mid-1980s was not so much a "democratic transition" as the top-down liberalization of an authoritarian regime—a process that is generally agreed to be quite different from genuine democratization. In the Guatemalan case, the regimes of the late 1980s and early 1990s made no serious attempt to impose civilian authority over the military (with the brief exception of Serrano, at the very beginning of his government). Liberalizations can be controlled: openings can be shut at will—as was attempted in Guatemala as recently as the 1993 Serranazo. The failure of the Serranazo, in fact, was the first real sign that a deeper, truly democratic transition was beginning (see below).

After the necessary "recomposition" of the counterinsurgency state to resolve its internal and external crises of legitimacy (beginning in 1982 to 1983), what existed from 1986 through the early 1990s can be described as a civilian version of the counterinsurgency state, with its own particularities, but leaving the army with a great deal of power—although not absolute power—over civilian authorities. In essence, what did not change was the prevalence of a predominantly coercive state on an ongoing (not exceptional) basis, and of military domination as opposed to hegemony or creation of social consensus. The counterinsurgency state is a project not simply of the army but of the ruling coalition (including economic elites) as a whole. But civilian counterinsurgency states have their own contradictions, particularly in their responses to popular protest.[4] Formally, the post-1986 civilian government reestablished the rule of law, but on the ground, Guatemalans did not feel protected by it or behave as if their rights were protected. On paper, the 1985 Constitution contained basic liberal democratic guarantees, but that same Constitution codified the counterinsurgency institutions (e.g., army-controlled PACs and "model villages") that violated such guarantees in practice, particularly in rural ex-conflict zones. For the most part from 1986 through the mid-1990s, civilian presidents allowed the army to rule from behind the scenes and were afraid to challenge the army's prerogatives. In short, the ruling coalition ceded and the politicians accepted very restricted spaces for autonomous action.

To be sure, the constitutional framework provided some important spaces from which citizens or popular organizations could organize to force open broader spaces. Nevertheless, as documented by virtually all human rights reports covering the period from 1986 through the mid-1990s, the levels of repression directed against those who tested the limits and the pervasive climate of fear marred the liberalization to such a degree that this could not be considered a climate favorable to citizen participation.[5] In addition, the levels of impunity and arbitrariness, especially by military authorities, and the absence of due process in the judicial system were striking. As late as 1995, MINUGUA reports still identified impunity as the major obstacle to real improvements in the human rights climate.

Elections during this period—specifically, the 1985 and 1990 to 1991 elections—were free of fraud, and certainly featured competing political parties (eighteen or nineteen of them). However, these elections could not be called "representative," as many studies have demonstrated (IHRLG/WOLA 1985; Castañeda 1990; NDI 1991; Jonas 1989, 1995; Trudeau 1989). Far from being fully pluralistic, they were ideologically restricted, with virtually all forces to the left of center excluded as well as persecuted until 1995.[6] As a result, many real issues were left undiscussed in the electoral arena. Many citizens were too inhibited by fear to engage in political activity of any kind. Finally, on the dimension of voter participation, these elections were characterized by ever-declining levels of participation: abstention (among registered voters—not even counting more than 30 percent of the potential electorate that was not registered) rose from 31 percent in the first round of the 1985 presidential election to 44 percent in the first round of the 1990 to 1991 presidential election, and reached the absurd extreme of around 80 percent in the 1994 congressional election.[7]

None of the above should be interpreted as dismissing the critical role of elections in any democratizing process. In particular, the 1985 election, the first serious one in two decades, awakened high hopes among the Guatemalan citizenry about the change from military to civilian rule—although these hopes were subsequently dashed. The main virtue of the 1990 to 1991 election was the transfer of power from one elected civilian government to another—an important advance for Guatemala, but still a "fraudulent pluralism," according to one centrist analyst (Cruz Salazar 1991). The U.S.-based National Democratic Institute (1991), which observed that election, concluded that Guatemala was consolidating an "exclusionary democracy," still lacking in basic political guarantees. In short, these elections overall (through 1994) were so exclusionary as to be insufficient grounds by themselves for establishing a claim to "democracy."

Underneath the surface during those years, in addition, there was an intense debate within the right as to whether to tolerate any autonomous political actor (the URNG, once it laid down its arms, or any other left force). The right was obsessed with the problem of the URNG's insertion into civilian political life—and, more fundamentally, of what forces in civil society would become the social and political bases for parties of the left. Their fears were not unfounded: private presidential polls showed that the URNG came to enjoy a 10 percent *simpatía* in the spring of 1992, even while it was illegal. In fact, many observers agreed that any new force untarnished by the crisis of the existing parties had the potential to gain support rapidly, once its participation was permitted. Because the peace process could potentially open up the previously exclusionary system, it became a source of tensions within the army and the private sector. There were constant pressures to end the process, and thus to close the spaces that it began to open. This was the particular logic underlying human rights violations during that period: hardliners in the security forces were striking out against movements that might function autonomously, precisely in order to avoid a truly pluralistic politics.

To the extent that there were real democratic gains during this period, it was not simply a result of elections by themselves. Rather, the beginning of the peace negotiations opened up new spaces outside the electoral arena, and eventually a sui generis interaction developed between elections and negotiations that democratized the political transition.[8] As argued above, the peace process had its own dynamic—an articulation between the formal negotiations and the concurrent empowerment of (especially Maya indigenous) forces in civil society; this dynamic influenced electoral politics as much as the reverse. It was precisely this complex interplay of forces that differentiated Guatemala's transition from one pacted simply between civilian and military elites—and that helped transform the (sub)minimalist democratic procedures of the late 1980s into a more participatory experience.

A further example of this mutual interaction came in 1995, when the peace process was directly impacted by the dynamics of the campaign for the November general election—as well as vice versa. Early in 1995 the URNG issued an unprecedented call urging people to vote, which was interpreted as signaling an implicit shift toward political means of struggle. Meanwhile, for the first time in forty years—in no small measure as a result of the simultaneous peace process—a left-of-center coalition of popular and indigenous organizations, the FDNG (the "left flank" of the ASC), was formed to participate in the elections. Equally significant was the August 1995 agreement signed on the Panamanian island of Contadora (brokered by the Central American Parliament): the URNG agreed to suspend military actions during the last two weeks of the electoral campaign, in exchange for a commitment by the major political parties to continue the peace negotiations under a new government and honor the accords already signed. For the first time, the Guatemalan political class accepted in principle that the accords constituted "accords of state" and hence could not be jettisoned by any future government or Congress.

In the November 1995 elections, marked by a very low level of participation (47 percent of registered voters), no presidential candidate received an absolute majority, requiring a January 1996 runoff (between modernizing conservative Alvaro Arzú and a stand-in for former dictator Efraín Ríos Montt).[9] In the runoff election, with only 37 percent of registered voters participating, Arzú won by a scant 2 percent of the vote, hence assuring the continuity of the peace negotiations; despite the Contadora agreement, Ríos Montt's party had given signals in the opposite direction. The major surprise of the 1995 election was the far stronger-than-expected showing of the newly formed leftist FDNG. Despite operating at great disadvantage, and weakened by the lack of resources and prior political experience, the FDNG won 8 percent of the presidential vote and six congressional seats, making it the third strongest party in Congress. Additionally, alliances between the FDNG and locally based indigenous *comités cívicos* (civic committees) won several important mayoralties, including Xelajú (Quetzaltenango). These victories resulted from the fact that the early 1990s had also seen the spread of indigenous political movements that were autonomous from the traditional political parties.

This more pluralistic election of 1995 was a result of this complex interplay of forces, and would not have grown simply or automatically out of the electoral system itself. Something similar, involving nonelectoral as well as electoral forces (although without the indigenous or ASC components), had taken place in El Salvador; hence, the particularity of what I call the *camino centroamericano*, the Central American path of democratization. The Central American path is characterized by a true negotiation between armed leftist insurgents and civilian and military elites as two semiequal negotiating parties; it is very different from a more limited "pact" simply between civilian and military elites, as in Chile. The Central American negotiation processes involved mutual compromises in internationally verified political agreements, not counterinsurgent "winners" imposing a settlement on insurgent "losers." Rather than simply moving to the right, leftist and popular forces maintained considerable integrity on issues of democracy and (in Guatemala) indigenous rights—even though they implicitly agreed to defer social justice issues; after all, this was a negotiation, not a revolution.

There are other reasons why the Southern Cone model by itself does not "fit" Central America: whereas the former involved "re-democratization," the latter had no such internal point of reference (with the exception of the brief, long-past 1944 to 1954 interlude in Guatemala). One can even argue that, especially in the light of the extremely exclusionary and retrograde nature of Central America's political systems during recent decades, the gains made in El Salvador and Guatemala are of equal or greater import than those made in some of South America's "pacted transitions"—above all, in Chile.[10] It is beyond my purpose here to develop the comparison in more detail; Southern Cone critics of the pacted transition experiences have addressed the shortcomings of those experiences in their own countries, as the basis for alternative concepts of democracy.[11]

In any case, in Central America, even nonrevolutionary demands such as participation in elections had to be won through armed revolutionary insurgencies that confronted counterinsurgency armies and exclusionary civilian elites—followed by negotiated solutions to the civil wars, centered around the dismantling of the counterinsurgency apparatus. There simply were no electoral options for many citizens until the revolutionary left and other left forces created them. In El Salvador, the FMLN invented "new political practices" for consensus building during the course of its negotiations (see Lungo 1994). In Guatemala, it was the ASC, with its plurality of forces—some sympathetic to the URNG, some not, but most of them (except political parties) excluded from the electoral arena—that ultimately created space for the emergence of the FDNG as a left electoral option in 1995, the first such force since 1954.

The above analysis of the period from the early 1980s through the mid-1990s is not meant to suggest that there was one identifiable moment when Guatemala ceased to be a counterinsurgency state and became democratic. The evolution or process of change that I have described here—in which what began as an army-controlled, top-down "authoritarian transition" eventually became a "democratic transition"—was very complex and contradictory. Even the three civilian presidents who subordinated themselves to the army—Cerezo, Serrano, and de León Carpio—were part of a process of liberalization or "political opening" that eventually permitted the formation of important democratic counterinstitutions (e.g., Human Rights Ombudsman). The 1993 Serranazo itself was an important moment in galvanizing all of Guatemalan society for a return to the constitutional order, and it demonstrated the nonviability of military coups or other expressions of the state-as-centaur. If not "the" moment when a more genuinely democratic transition began, this was most certainly a key turning point.

Theoretically, the point is that political and electoral openings or liberalizations of right-wing authoritarian regimes do not automatically or inevitably lead to full democratization, as Jeane Kirkpatrick (1979) argued. There was no way to predict in 1986 (much less in 1982) that a genuine democratization, going beyond a liberalization or political "opening," would occur in Guatemala. This process has begun now, in large measure because the negotiation of internationally verifiable peace accords, as well as MINUGUA's in-country presence, extracted democratic concessions that no election could guarantee—above all, and as the precondition for all else, the demilitarization of state and society. Furthermore, in the Guatemalan case, only the force of such accords has the potential to overcome the exclusionary internal resistances and hopefully ensure the irreversibility of the democratic changes.

Dimensions of the Democratic Project

It has come to be widely accepted among students of democratic transitions that civilian control over the military is a necessary condition for functional democracy. Hence, they have included this criterion in their "expanded procedural minimum" definition of democracy. But is this a sufficient description? Does it fully capture the richness and complexity of the real experience—above all, in a country such as Guatemala, where the indigenous majority makes cultural pluralism a central issue? I argue that the multidimensional democratization that is occurring in Guatemala today requires broader theoretical horizons than are comprehended in the transition literature by itself.

Much of the theoretical literature on democratic transitions has taken as its starting point the Schumpeterian model, refined by Dahl's "polyarchy"—from which are derived various "procedural minimum" conceptions, ranging from very minimalist to more "expanded."[12] However, there are other traditions from which to draw for our discussions of democracy: first, the formulations based on classical conceptions of democracy, as laid out by theorists such as Carole Pateman (1970) and Leonardo Morlino (1985), and applied to Central America, for example, by

John Booth (1989 and 1995) and Manuel Montobbio de Balanzó (1997); and second, a number of contemporary contributions to the democracy literature drawing largely on the experience of social movements (e.g., feminist, indigenous). These traditions, which fall outside the transition literature, provide a context for my broader argument about the potential for Guatemala's democratic project.

Taking the broadest of the procedural definitions, the "expanded procedural minimum" goes beyond Dahl, by adding two further conditions that are essential in the Latin American cases: the polity must be self-governing (sovereign); and there must be civilian control over the military (Karl 1990, 2), or at least the absence of a military veto. But even though this formulation adds civilian control over the military, it explicitly excludes extensive "participation" as a requisite, stipulating that "all citizens may not take an active and equal part in politics, although it must be legally possible for them to do so" (Schmitter and Karl 1991, 83). Without begging the question of whether "all citizens" are active participants, there is a real issue of the relative weight given to the participatory element.

Booth (1995, 5) spells out an alternative approach to what he calls the "pluralist-elitist conception." His alternative is rooted in the classical conception as laid out by Pateman (1970), among others: "participation by the mass of people in a community in its governance (the making and carrying out of decisions)." As Montobbio (1997, 18-21) argues regarding El Salvador, the classical tradition is particularly appropriate in cases (such as the Central American) involving ruptures of the social contract—that is, civil wars—as contrasted with "peaceful transitions." This tradition is based on a broad conception of citizens' rights and goes back to theorists from Aristotle through Mill; beyond not being legally precluded, political participation lies at the heart of democracy. Although the degrees of democracy may vary, this depends on "the amount and quality of public participation in decision-making and rule" (Booth 1995, 6). Hence, according to Booth and others,[13] electoral participation is one important aspect—but only one among others. Referring specifically to Guatemala, René Poitevín (1992, 27) speaks of a concept of citizenship in which the population is more than an "occasional legitimator" of the existing power structure (through elections), and in which all sectors enjoy full freedom to organize and exercise effective power.

Why insist on the participatory element? First, even in regard to elections, it implies going beyond the absence-of-fraud measure, to permit a critique of elections held in an overall context of a system that excludes certain ideological positions and retains many coercive and repressive elements. Second, starting from a broader conception of politics, it permits us to take into account participation outside the electoral arena, as well as formal electoral participation, and the interaction between them. Third, and perhaps most important, it provides a basis for appreciating the dimensions of democracy when it finally does come to exist; these include ideological and cultural diversity, the growing effectiveness of civil society, and an expanded conception of citizenship to include rights beyond those associated with the legal status.

These points can be developed by referring to several relatively "newer" or more contemporary bodies of literature that deal with noninstitutional aspects of democracy; most of these grow out of practical social movement experiences in Latin America and elsewhere. To mention a few examples of the themes emphasized in these newer literatures: citizenship and social citizenship (including cross-border rights), civil society, human rights, local power, feminism and its critiques of earlier conceptions of democracy, indigenous peoples' rights, Liberation Theology, and ecology and environmental justice. Much of the literature growing out of social movements emphasizes group rights as well as strictly individual rights.[14]

All of the above dimensions have great relevance to Guatemala. Many of them were expressed in the organizations that came together to form the ASC in the early 1990s, and others are taking shape in new forms of social organization today. Rather than spelling out what each of them means in Guatemala—a project for a future book—I emphasize here the dimensions most relevant to political democracy in a country that is 60 percent Maya: cultural rights alongside civil and human rights. As seen above, many of these are codified in the Accord on Identity and the Rights of Indigenous Peoples, which mandates a constitutional reform redefining Guatemala's identity as a multiethnic, multicultural, multilingual nation. It is an implicit premise of that accord that political democracy cannot be fully achieved in Guatemala without recognizing and acting on the basis of the country's cultural diversity.

Aside from the indigenous accord, other on-the-ground advances by indigenous movements in recent years include the broader use of alternative forms of political organization. Among the most prominent of these have been *comités cívicos* formed outside the traditional political parties that did not fully represent the interests of indigenous communities (Ochoa et al. 1995; Gálvez et al. 1997; ASIES 1998). In the 1995 election, these comités were able to win the mayoralty of Guatemala's second largest city, Quetzaltenango, creating the previously inconceivable situation of an indigenous mayor in a city that is half indigenous, half ladino. Various other initiatives promise to profoundly enrich the content of Guatemala's democratic project by incorporating indigenous traditions of community democracy and customary law (*derecho consuetudinario*).[15]

Although some of these issues are still very much contested by ladinos as "divisive" or threats to "national unity," they are central to the quality of democracy not only for Guatemala's indigenous peoples, but also for Guatemala as a whole. They raise the issue of building a tolerant, pluralistic political culture among all Guatemalans, in a society that has been as exclusionary as South Africa or the slave South in the United States. Anything less than a new framework of this kind would mean electoral democracy within the context of de facto apartheid. The assertion of cultural rights in this case is not "identity politics" but a new political framework for Maya-ladino social relations; it is now being reformulated in a discourse of intercultural as well as multicultural relations. From a more positive perspective, if advances are made and consolidated in this area, they will not only have an impact internally but also be recognized as an example outside Guatemala.

The above reflections suggest that minimalist or primarily procedural conceptions of democratization, even when "expanded," often sell democracy short, by not emphasizing the full ideological and cultural diversity that is central to the participatory dimensions of political democracy and by not emphasizing—indeed, often entirely missing—some of the most profound transformations in the rules of the political game. In Guatemala, the symbolic "moment" when these democratic transformations came closest to being formally "adopted" as a national project or agenda will be remembered in the signing of the peace accords more clearly than in any other moment since 1954—certainly more than in any of the elections between 1954 and 1996. (This is not to deny that the changes had begun several years before the signing of peace, and that their realization will take many years.) To use a crude indicator, on the evening of the signing, a telephone poll by the conservative daily newspaper *Prensa Libre* elicited a 77 percent "happiness" response; and despite limited expectations, "the prevailing mood [in the Plaza Central] was of being at the ushering in of a new historical era" (Hernández Pico 1997).

Experiences such as these also signify a potential transformation in political/ cultural/ social relations. As Carlos Vilas put it in a recent talk about Central America, even if a revolution fails, nothing in the country is the same as before, and people do not behave in the old ways. To illustrate from our discussion above: the redefinition of the nation as multicultural poses the possiblity of transforming the collective political culture of Guatemalan society as a whole; certainly the indigenous population is engaging in new forms of behavior, and it is to be hoped that this will eventually elicit new responses from ladinos. In Guatemala, furthermore, lifting the blanket of fear that permeated virtually all human interactions since 1954 constitutes, if not a revolution in the old sense, at least a very profound transformation. Subjectively, it opens up space for a "revolution of rising expectations" among many previously excluded sectors, despite the fact that they still live in poverty and face deeply entrenched opposition to change from powerful elites. Guatemalans are beginning to feel entitled to nothing less than what is enjoyed by citizens in the traditional Western democracies.

Some of the above-mentioned general observations have been substantiated by the findings of at least one major empirical survey documenting the expansion of political participation and a democratic political culture in Guatemala in the mid- to late 1990s (Development Associates et al. 1998). Among the survey's most important findings and conclusions were the significant increases (between 1993 and 1997) in the levels of political tolerance and of participation in local government and, even more notably, in organizations of civil society (educational, religious, community development, and so on). By 1997, 78 percent of the 1,200 interviewees participated in at least one such organization. (A significant contrast was the ongoing lack of confidence in the judicial system and in the central government more generally—which could explain the gap between the high level of social participation and the low level of voting.) Overall, the 1997 survey concluded that the signing of the peace accords was crucial in the changes between 1993 and 1997, that there now exist opportunities to consolidate *democracia desde abajo* (democracy from below), and that the stereotype of the unmovably authoritarian Guatemalan political culture is misleading—particularly among the indigenous population.

From a historical perspective, Guatemala stands today on the threshold of possibly completing its long-interrupted national democratic revolution of 1944 to 1954; but this time, having suffered the interlude of a forty-two-year nightmare and thirty years of Cold War counterinsurgency war, people are experiencing democracy in a new way. This time (unlike 1954), it is to be hoped that Guatemalans will fight to defend their gains if those gains are threatened. Today, moreover, the incipient democratic revolution is broader than fifty years ago, as it includes new—or, more precisely, newly recognized—social protagonists, most notably, indigenous peoples and women. It also includes new forms of organization that are mobilizational as well as electoral. Although Guatemalan democracy remains very fragile and unconsolidated, one can begin to catch a glimpse of what "full democracy" might mean in the twenty-first century, in all of its political, ideological, and cultural dimensions.

The Unresolved Question of Social Justice

One of the consistently troublesome and unresolved discussions about political democracy is its relation to social justice. While I cannot fully address the issue here, I discuss some reasons for its relevance to the case at hand. It is widely argued that, without being definitionally part of political democracy, social justice issues have profoundly affected the fate of "new" democracies (and older ones) in practice—or, as some analysts have put it, the "quality of democracy." Others have begun to take this up as an issue of "social citizenship." Adam Przeworski (1996) warned of the dangers of a new "monster": democracy without citizenship, that is, without the minimal conditions necessary for citizens to exercise their rights in practice. Guillermo O'Donnell (1997) has expressed similar concerns. Montobbio (1997, 25) put it in slightly different terms for El Salvador, warning of a *congelación* (freezing-up), in which "authoritarian enclaves" retain considerable power, and the democratic transition is never fully consolidated, stable, or lasting. Consolidation, he continues, implies dealing not only with the elimination of military control but also addressing the country's historical problems, including massive social inequalities.

In recent Latin American experience, formal political democracy has generally been regarded as a precondition for struggles for greater social equality. But beyond that, there are two opinions about whether a fully democratic system can be sustained amidst major social disparities or whether, eventually, the huge socioeconomic gaps will (directly or indirectly) undermine democratic gains. The experiences of the past two decades in Latin America are mixed and open to a variety of interpretations. Some situations in South America suggest the difficulties of consolidating political democracy on a lasting and stable basis while simultaneously institutionalizing neoliberal measures that increase social inequalities (see note 10). Venezuela illustrates the complexities: Since the late 1980s, austerity policies have generated food riots, populist military coup attempts, and in December 1998, electoral victory by the coup leader—all this in a country regarded for the last forty years as a stable, consolidated democracy.

But there are particular dynamics in countries emerging from longstanding civil wars or national liberation struggles inspired by revolutionary visions, such as Central America in recent decades—not unlike South Africa's African National Congress (ANC)-led struggle (see Wallerstein 1996). The traditional socialist revolutionary visions have clearly been modified in the last twenty years; but democratization has brought rising expectations about greater social justice. In the Central American cases, there is much discussion about whether the "structural causes" that gave rise to the revolutionary movements of the 1960s to the 1980s are being addressed by the peace settlements of the 1990s. Clearly these problems have not been resolved thus far; in this sense, peace did not bring social justice. But the widespread expectation or demand remains very much alive. Minimally, this means building an internal market economy, even in this age of world-market export frenzy; this presumes a concern (and state intervention) to raise wages and living standards for the majority of the population, in order to create an internal comsumer market. Social equity is not part of the definition of democracy, but it is unquestionably part of the panorama of issues opened up by democratization. If the rising expectations are frustrated, and significant numbers of citizens perceive that "nothing has changed," democracy itself can be delegitimized, undermined, or destabilized.

Coming out of a thirty-six-year civil war, Guatemala is certainly experiencing this revolution of rising expectations. Yet, as seen above, the socioeconomic accord does not directly resolve the social issues; and Guatemala is surrounded by the chilling realities of social deterioration in El Salvador and, even more, in Nicaragua. El Salvador's peace agenda has been undermined by the government's neoliberal economic agenda (see de Soto and del Castillo 1994; Boyce 1996; Montobbio 1997). Guatemala faces a host of dangers that typically plague post-war societies, as well as some that are particular to Guatemala, which could undermine rather than consolidate democratic gains. One very immediate source of undermining is a rise in common crime (partly driven by poverty and the lack of jobs) and authoritarian responses to that situation—already a serious problem in Guatemala.

Few Guatemalans seriously discuss democracy without addressing these issues, because they believe that, so long as nearly three-fourths of the population lives in extreme poverty, formal democracy will remain forever fragile. (In the Guatemalan case, the socioeconomic structure has been so skewed that even the World Bank recommends more state spending.) As Guatemalan analysts Poitevín (1992, 35-37) and Torres Rivas (1991) argue, social struggles have become the condition for liberal democracy: "a democratic process is not possible without a minimum basis for developing social relations of equality," without a material basis for the exercise of citizen rights. Moreover, liberal democracy has arrived in Guatemala linked to a much broader national project or *imaginario* (vision) contained in the peace accords (Aguilera 1997). Torres Rivas (1995, 46 ff) refers to something similar in the concept of good government, which "seeks a permanent link between political freedom and social justice."[16] Gálvez (1995) and others use the concept of "governability" in a similar manner, that is, beyond formal institutionality, to refer more broadly to the relation between the state and civil society, particularly in meeting popular expectations. Hence, without being substituted for "political democracy," the broader social dimension is linked to it time and again by a wide range of Guatemalans and Latin Americans in general; and the experience of recent years demonstrates the importance of this link in moving toward a society that is viable and stable—"governable"—as well as humane.

At the theoretical level, Immanuel Wallerstein (1991) has written about the ongoing battle since the time of the French Revolution, over the interpretation of its legacy, in particular between the libertarian and social emphases. Theoretically, there is not one correct answer, but rather, an ambivalent legacy (hence the battle for the interpretation). It is one of the great ironies of history since the French Revolution that struggles for "liberty" (liberal democracy) have been led and won by revolutionaries—that is, those who also had a social justice agenda. As Vilas (1994, 99) put it, "At the root of popular acceptance of calls for revolution is an unavoidable democratic demand." But while successful in winning democracy, revolutionaries have generally not won the struggles for social equality. In the cases of Central America during the 1980s and 1990s, we have seen a continuation of this historical tendency. Furthermore, their ability to win social justice is even more constrained in an era dominated internationally by neoliberal policy prescriptions (privatization, dismantling of the social safety net, and so on). The unanswered question for progressive and leftist forces in Guatemala and the rest of Central America today is whether they will be able to use the political space won through the peace accords to make significant social justice gains in the future. The answer to this question—which will have to be revisited many times during the next ten to fifteen years—will be essential to our long-range assessments of the *camino centroamericano*.

Epilogue

As of mid-1999, two and a half years after the signing of the final peace accords, it is evident that the implementation phase of Guatemala's peace process is just as difficult and dangerous as the negotiations. Particularly after the beginning of 1998, the battles for implementation became more intense, as Guatemala's veteran peace resisters challenged the substance and the continuity of the process itself. The Arzú government, which had taken such bold initiatives to finalize the peace negotiations, was much more timid—on many occasions resistant—in regard to compliance with the accords.

The most difficult moment for the entire peace process came in May 1999, in regard to the constitutional reforms required to put into effect the most significant provisions of the accords on indigenous rights and on strengthening civilian power (limiting the functions of the army). It had taken one and a half years to gain congressional approval of those accords (which was finally accomplished in October 1998, largely as a result of international pressures). But in the congressional package of reforms submitted for approval by a public referendum (as required by the Constitution), the reforms stemming from the peace accords were swamped by dozens of others that were unrelated to the accords. And while polls had shown ahead of time that the reforms were likely to be approved, a well-financed last-month blitzkrieg campaign by peace resisters (who urged a "No" vote) succeeded in defeating the reforms—that is, in getting a 55 percent majority for the "No" among the bare 18.5 percent of the electorate that voted. Clearly, the main winner of this vote was abstention, and the main loser was the peace process itself. (For a detailed analysis, see Jonas 2000, chapter 8.)

In the wake of this political disaster, the peace agenda was placed on hold until after the November 1999 election. Two and a half years after the signing of peace, it remains to be seen whether the combination of domestic pro-peace forces and their supporters in the international community can consolidate the incipient gains from the previous decade's peace process.

Notes

1. This article was written in 1998, before the May 1999 referendum on constitutional reforms (see epilogue). Despite the changes that may develop after that referendum, I have not substantially altered this article, since its focus is the democratic project of the peace process, rather than its vicissitudes.

Beyond the literature on democratization and on the Guatemalan and Salvadoran peace processes, this article is based primarily on several hundred author interviews, carried out between 1990 and 1999, with virtually all of the key domestic and international players in the Guatemalan peace process and political arena, from all political perspectives. I am deeply grateful to them for cooperating generously and, in some cases, year after year. I wish to thank the North-South Center of the University of Miami, the Stevenson Program on Global Security at the University of California, Santa Cruz, and FLACSO/Guatemala for supporting the research for this article—and for the larger book, *Of Centaurs and Doves: Guatemala's Peace Process* (Westview 2000).

I am grateful to numerous colleagues, both in Guatemala and the United States, for critical and stimulating feedback on earlier drafts and presentations of the arguments developed here—among them John Booth, Jeff Stark, Ronnie Lipschutz, Christopher Chase-

Dunn, Tom Walker, Larry Diamond, Paul Sigmund, Rachel Sieder, Jenny Pearce, Dinorah Azpuru, René Poitevín, Edelberto Torres Rivas, Bernardo Arévalo, Manuel Montobbio, and Gabriel Aguilera.

2. The leading governments in the "Group of Friends" were Mexico, Spain, Norway, and the United States; Colombia and Venezuela were also nominal members, but less influential.

3. To compensate for the weaknesses of the Truth Commission Accord and the partial amnesty law, several organizations and coalitions of Guatemalan civil society took their own initiatives to hold human rights criminals responsible. The Catholic Church developed a massive nationwide project, "Recovery of Historical Memory," to bring forth testimony from victims. In the most brutal postwar act of political violence, the chief architect of the report, Auxiliary Bishop Msgr. Juan Gerardi, was assassinated two days after the public presentation of the report in late April 1998. (The actual Report of the Truth Commission, issued in February 1999, far exceeded all expectations, despite the limitations in its mandate.)

4. For a fuller argument that Guatemala under civilian rule during the late 1980s remained essentially a counterinsurgency state, see Jonas (1991, 171 ff). I also argue there against exaggerated versions of the counterinsurgency state thesis, which view such a state as permanent, stable, self-perpetuating, or all-controlling.

5. For examples as recent as 1994, see annual reports by Americas Watch, Amnesty International, and even the U.S. State Department's Human Rights reports; also Jonas 1994.

6. The very small social democratic Partido Socialista Democrática (PSD) was permitted to participate, once its politicians had accepted the "rules of the game" (which included rejection of any possible alliance with the URNG) and the unspoken limits on its platform imposed by the military; meanwhile, some of its leaders remained in exile.

7. The figures are more extreme if we take into account two additional considerations. First, well over 30 percent of eligible voters were not even registered; this would bring the effective voter abstention rate to 52 percent in 1985 and 69 percent in 1990. (More recent estimates of nonregistration are as high as 35 to 40 percent.) Second, in both cases, abstention among registered voters increased significantly in the presidential runoff elections (from 31 percent to 35 percent in 1985, and from 44 percent to 55 percent in 1990 to 1991). Third, at least 12 percent of ballots, in some cases higher, were not valid (null or blank votes). (Sources: OAS 1997, Aguilera 1996b, based on official figures from the Supreme Electoral Tribunal.)

8. Other analysts characterize that interaction in a very different way. For example, Padilla (1996a, iii) argues that "democratization [i.e., elected civilian rule] made peace possible, not vice-versa." See also Azpuru (1999).

9. In terms of voter participation and abstention in the 1995 to 1996 elections: In the November 1995 first round, participation was only 47 percent of registered voters (i.e., abstention was 53 percent); these figures worsened to 37 percent participation (63 percent abstention) in the January 1996 runoff. Here again, around 30 percent of eligible voters were not registered to vote, meaning that effective participation rates were substantially lower (33 percent in November, 26 percent in January).

Why did this happen despite the first-time option of a leftist party (FDNG)? Among other explanations, what stands out are the following: First, the FDNG came together very late in the game, and virtually at the same time as the deadline for registration of new voters. Second, political parties in general remained totally discredited by their corruption and inefficacy during the first decade after the return to civilian rule. (For more detailed analyses of the obstacles to voting in the electoral system itself, see OAS 1997, Aguilera 1996b, Jonas 2000, chapter 8.)

A further troubling question arises: The January 1996 presidential runoff, with participation by a bare 26 percent of those eligible to vote, came within a hair's breadth of restoring to (indirect but virtual) power an ex-dictator whose policies would have ended the peace process. If the antipeace Ríos Montt forces had won this low-turnout runoff election, even without fraud, the victory would have been for a "democracy" of the iron fist, another *democradura*, and the peace negotiations might well have been scuttled. Could such an outcome really have been regarded as advancing the cause of democracy in Guatemala?

10. Even in the late 1990s, Chile's General Pinochet retained substantial veto power, and in November 1996, a leading Communist Party politician was jailed for verbally insulting him. According to the constitution written under his dictatorship, the military retains four reserved seats in the Senate, as well as half of the seats on the National Security Council (NYT November 10, 1996). In 1998, Pinochet refused to resign as defense minister unless he was guaranteed a seat as senator-for-life—which he subsequently obtained. Finally, it took international initiatives in the fall of 1998—by European judges and governments—to finally re-raise the issue of holding Pinochet accountable for crimes against humanity; even then, the democratically elected civilian government of Chile opposed those initiatives and sided with Pinochet in resisting them.

11. Various Southern Cone analysts have argued that participatory democracy is essential to representative democracy and have associated participatory democracy with a commitment to reducing socioeconomic inequality; to cite only a few examples, Argentine analysts Nun (1993) and Borón (1993, 1998)—both of whom cite Dahl to bolster their arguments; and Brazilian analyst Weffort (1992).

12. In her pioneering treatment of the subject, Pateman (1970) suggested that the initial antipathy to including participation and mobilization emphases in discussions of democracy in U.S. political science models was in part a function of the Cold War ideological bias against "the other model" (that of Soviet/Third World socialism). Some even suggested that too much participation could be dangerous to democratic stability (see Pateman 1970, 10). Looking at the recent literature regarding Latin America, the most careful constructions of the "expanded procedural minimum" can be found in Karl 1990 and Schmitter and Karl 1991. For a survey of the literature on this topic, see Collier and Levitsky 1997. Recently, several prominent "transitologists" have been moving toward discussing the importance of nonformal criteria and even some social issues as they affect political democracy. This can be seen in recent presentations by O'Donnell, Przeworski, Schmitter, and Karl, among others.

13. In addition, see Fagen's (1986, 258) "working definition" of the "constituent elements" of democracy, which include "effective participation by individuals and groups in the decisions that most affect their lives" along with classical individual rights and equality before the law. Similar emphases are found in writings by González Casanova, Vilas, and others.

14. To give a few examples of these participatory social movements and themes, as described and theorized in recent literature: citizenship and social citizenship—some, but not all of it developed out of feminist critiques of older models, both left and right (e.g., Dagnino 1993, Jelin 1990 and 1995, Falk 1993); civil society and its relation to formal politics (e.g., Fox 1996, Foley 1996, Lungo 1994, Pearce 1998); local power (e.g., Sader 1992, Bittar 1992, NACLA 1995; for Guatemala, Gálvez et al. 1998); Liberation Theology (e.g., Boff 1981, 1986; Richard 1995); ecological and environmental justice movements and other "new social movements" (e.g., articles in Escobar and Alvarez 1992); group rights, as opposed to strictly individual rights (e.g., Falk 1989, Felice 1996). Many of the above themes and tendencies are also illustrated in Jonas and McCaughan 1994, Alvarez et al.

1998, Jelin and Hershberg 1996.

15. See Cojtí 1991, Poitevín 1991 and 1992, Solares 1992, Bastos and Camus 1993, Esquit and Gálvez 1997, Adams 1994 and 1995, Warren 1998; on the contributions of *derecho consuetudinario*, see Rojas Lima 1995, Sieder 1996.

16. To expand on Torres Rivas's (1995) concept: Good government is "a metaphor for the democratic search to put public order in the service of addressing the problems of the majority." The link between democracy and social justice is necessary "to avoid discrediting the electoral system, the democratic premise, civilian governments chosen for their promises and programs, or politics itself."

Works Cited

Adams, Richard N. 1995. Ethnic Conflict, Governance and Globalization in Latin America, with Special Attention to Guatemala. Latin American Program Working Paper Series No. 215, *Ethnic Conflict and Governance in Comparative Perspective*. September, pp. 51-69.

———. 1994. A Report on the Political Status of the Guatemalan Maya. In *Indigenous Peoples and Democracy in Latin America*, edited by Donna Lee Van Cott. New York: St. Martin's.

Aguero, Felipe, and Jeffrey Stark, eds. 1998. *Fault Lines of Democracy in Post-Transition Latin America*. Coral Gables, Fla.: North-South Center Press.

Aguilera, Gabriel. 1997. Negociar lo imposible: El proceso de paz en Guatemala. Manuscript.

———. 1996a. El proceso de paz en Guatemala. *Estudios Internacionales*. (July-December):1-19. Guatemala: Instituto de Relaciones Internacionales y de Investigación para la Paz (IRIPAZ).

———. 1996b. Democracia y elecciones en Guatemala. Manuscript presented at XIX Congreso de LASA (September).

———. 1994. Los temas sustantivos en las propuestas para la paz. Debate No. 24. Guatemala: FLACSO.

———. 1986. Notas sobre elecciones y transición en Guatemala. *Economía* (Guatemala), no. 88 (April-June).

Alvarez, Sonia, Evelina Dagnino, and Arturo Escobar, eds. 1998. *Cultures of Politics, Politics of Cultures: Re-visioning Latin American Social Movements*. Boulder, Colo.: Westview.

Amin, Samir. 1991. El problema de la democracia en el Tercer Mundo contemporaneo. *Nueva Sociedad*, no. 112 (Marzo-Abril).

Arévalo, Bernardo. 1998. *Sobre arenas movedizas: Sociedad, estado y ejército en Guatemala, 1997*. Guatemala: FLACSO.

Asociación de Investigación y Estudios Sociales (ASIES). 1998. XIII Seminario sobre el rol de los partidos políticos (1997): Regimen electoral y organización política: Instrumentos de transformación democr tica en Guatemala. Guatemala: ASIES.

Azpuru, Dinorah. 1999. Peace and Democratization in Guatemala: Two Parallel Processes. In *Comparative Peace Processes in Latin America*, edited by Cynthia Arnson. Stanford, Calif. and Washington D.C.: Stanford University Press and Woodrow Wilson Center Press.

Baranyi, Stephen. 1995. The Challenge in Guatemala: Verifying Human Rights, Strengthening National Institutions and Enhancing an Integrated UN Approach to Peace. London: The Centre for the Study of Global Governance, London School of Economics.

Bastos, Santiago, and Manuela Camus. 1993. *Quebrando el Silencio*. Guatemala: Facultad Latinoamericana de Ciencias Sociales (FLACSO).

Bittar, Jorge, ed. 1992. *O Modo Petista de Governar*. Sao Paolo: Teoria y Debate.

Boff, Leonardo. 1986. *E a Igreja se Fez Povo*. Petrópolis, Brazil: Voces.

———. 1981. *Igreja: Carisma e Poder*. Petrópolis, Brazil: Vozes.

Booth, John A. 1998. Global Forces and Regime Change: Guatemala within the Central American Context. Manuscript for Conference on Guatemalan Development and Democratization. Cited by permission.

———. 1995. Introduction. Elections and Democracy in Central America: A Framework for Analysis. In *Elections and Democracy in Central America*, edited by Mitchell Seligson and John Booth. Chapel Hill: University of North Carolina Press.

———. 1989. Elections and Democracy in Central America: A Framework for Analysis. In *Elections and Democracy in Central America*, edited by Mitchell Seligson and John Booth. Chapel Hill: University of North Carolina Press.

Booth, John, and Mitchell Seligson, eds. 1989. *Elections and Democracy in Central America*. Chapel Hill: University of North Carolina Press.

Borón, Atilio. 1998. Faulty Democracies? In *Fault Lines of Democracy in Post-Transition Latin America*, edited by Felipe Aguero and Jeffrey Stark. Coral Gables, Fla.: North-South Center Press.

———. 1993. Estado, democracia y movimientos sociales en América Latina. *Crisol* (Mexico), no. 5 (Summer).

Boyce, James, ed. 1996. *Economic Policy for Building Peace: The Lessons of El Salvador*. Boulder, Colo.: Lynne Rienner.

Bran, Rosalinda, and Claudinne Ogaldes. 1996. *Los retos de la paz, la democracia y el desarrollo sostenible en Guatemala*. Guatemala: FLACSO.

Castañeda, Jorge. 1990. Is Squeaky Clean Squeaky Fair? *Los Angeles Times* (November 18).

Cavarozzi, Marcelo. 1992. Beyond Transitions to Democracy in Latin America. *Journal of Latin American Studies* 24, part 3 (October):665-84.

Cojtí Cuxil, Demetrio. 1997. Gobernabilidad democrática y derechos indígenas en Guatemala. Manuscript.

———. 1991. *La configuración del pensamiento político del pueblo maya*. Guatemala: Asociación de Escritores Mayances de Guatemala.

Collier, David, and Steven Levitsky. 1997. Democracy with Adjectives: Conceptual Innovation in Comparative Research. *World Politics* 49 (April):430-51.

Comisión de Reforma Electoral. 1997. Comítes cívicos electorales (documento para discusión) (June). Guatemala: Comisión de Reforma Electoral.

Consejo Nacional de Educación Maya (CNEM). 1998. *Analisis del proceso de paz desde la perspectiva indígena*. Guatemala: CNEM.

Cruz Salazar, José Luis. 1991. El Proceso Electoral Guatemalteco, 1990-91. Manuscript. Guatemala: ASIES.

Dagnino, Evelina. 1993. An Alternative World Order and the Meaning of Democracy. In *Global Visions: Beyond the New World Order*, edited by Jeremy Brecher, John Brown Childs, and Jill Cutler. Boston: South End Press.

de Soto, Alvaro, and Graciana del Castillo. 1994. Obstacles to "Peace Building." *Foreign Policy* (Spring):69-83.

Development Associates, Inc., University of Pittsburgh, and ASIES. 1998. La cultura

democrática de los guatemaltecos (Tercer Estudio, 1997) (January). Guatemala.
Diamond, Larry. 1997. Consolidating Democracy in the Americas. *Annals, AAPSS* 550 (March):12-41.
Diamond, Larry, and Marc Plattner, eds. 1996. *Civil-Military Relations and Democracy.* Baltimore: Johns Hopkins University Press.
Domínguez, Jorge, and Marc Lindenberg, eds. 1997. *Democratic Transitions in Central America.* Gainesville: University Press of Florida.
Domínguez, Jorge, and Abraham Lowenthal, eds. 1996. *Constructing Democratic Governance: Mexico, Central America, and the Caribbean in the 1990s.* Baltimore: Johns Hopkins University Press.
Drake, Paul, and Eduardo Silva, eds. 1986. *Elections and Democratization in Latin America, 1980-85.* San Diego: University of California, Center for Iberian and Latin American Studies.
Escobar, Arturo, and Sonia Alvarez, eds. 1992. *The Making of Social Movements in Latin America.* Boulder, Colo.: Westview.
Esquit, Alberto, and Victor Gálvez. 1997. *The Mayan Movement Today: Issues of Indigenous Culture and Development in Guatemala.* Guatemala: FLACSO.
Fagen, Richard. 1986. The politics of transition. In *Transition and Development*, edited by Richard Fagan, Carmen Diana Deere, and José Luis Corragio. New York: Monthly Review.
Falk, Richard. 1993. The Making of Global Citizenship. In *Global Visions: Beyond the New World Order*, edited by Jeremy Brecher, et al. Boston: South End Press.
———. 1989. Group Claims and the Nation-State within the United Nations System. Conference on Ethnic Conflict and the UN Human Rights System. Oxford: St. Ann's College.
Falla, Ricardo. 1998. *The Story of a Great Love.* Washington, D.C.: EPICA.
———.1994. *Massacres of the Jungle.* Boulder, Colo.: Westview.
———. 1978. *Quiché Rebelde.* Guatemala: Editorial Universitaria.
Felice, William. 1996. *Taking Suffering Seriously: The Importance of Collective Human Rights.* Albany, N.Y.: State University of New York Press.
Figueroa Ibarra, Carlos. 1986. *La centaurización estatal en Guatemala.* Polémica. No. 19 (January-April).
Foley, Michael. 1996. Laying the Groundwork: The Struggle for Civil Society in El Salvador. *Journal of Interamerican Studies and World Affairs* (Spring):67-104.
Fox, Jonathan. 1996. How Does Civil Society Thicken? The Political Construction of Social Capital in Rural Mexico. *World Development* 24, no. 6:1089-103.
Gálvez, Victor. 1995. *La gobernabilidad en centroamérica: Sectores populares y gobernabilidad precaria en Guatemala.* Guatemala: FLACSO.
Gálvez, Victor, and Roberto Camposeco Hurtado. 1996. *Guatemala: Políticas de descentralización y capacidades de gestión administrativa y financiera de las municipalidades.* San Salvador: FLACSO.
Gálvez, Victor, Claudia Dary, Edgar Esquit, and Isabel Rodas. 1997. *Qué sociedad queremos?* Guatemala: FLACSO.
Gálvez, Victor, Carlos Hoffman, and Luis Mack. 1998. *Poder local y participación democrática.* Debate No. 40. Guatemala: FLACSO.
Garreton, Manuel Antonio. 1995. Transiciones Ambivalentes. *Memoria 80* (August):39-44. Mexico: CEMOS.
González Casanova, Pablo. 1995. La democracia de los debajo y los movimientos sociales.

Nueva Sociedad (Caracas, Venezuela) (March-April):37-40.

———. 1989. La crisis del Estado y la lucha por la democracia en América Latina. *Nueva Sociedad* (Caracas, Venezuela), no. 104 (November-December): 95-104.

Hernández Pico, Juan. 1997. Peace Accords: Return of the Quetzal. *Envio* (February-March):14-21.

Hinkelammert, Franz. 1994. Our Project for the New Society in Latin America. In *Latin America Faces the Twenty-First Century*, edited by Susanne Jonas and Edward McCaughan. Boulder, Colo.: Westview.

Holiday, David, and Tania Palencia. 1995. Organización ciudadana y estado en Guatemala. Manuscript.

Huntington, Samuel P. 1991. *The Third Wave: Democratization in the Late Twentieth Century*. Norman: University of Oklahoma Press.

Inforpress Centroamericana (IC). Guatemala: weekly

International Human Rights Law Group and Washington Office on Latin America (IHRLG/WOLA). 1985. *The 1985 Guatemalan Elections: Will the Military Relinquish Power?* Washington, D.C.: IHRLG and WOLA.

Jelin, Elizabeth. 1995. Building Citizenship: A Balance between Solidarity and Responsibility. In *The Consolidation of Democracy in Latin America*, edited by Joseph S. Tulchin and Bernice Romero. Boulder, Colo.: Lynne Rienner.

———. 1990. Citizenship and Identity: Final Reflections. In *Women and Social Change in Latin America*, edited by Elizabeth Jelin. London: ZED and UN Research Institute for Social Development.

Jelin, Elizabeth, and Eric Hershberg, eds. 1996. *Constructing Democracy: Human Rights, Citizenship, and Society in Latin America*. Boulder, Colo.: Westview.

Jonas, Susanne. 2000 (forthcoming). *Of Centaurs and Doves: Guatemala's Peace Process*. Boulder, Colo.: Westview.

———. 1999 (forthcoming). Between Two Worlds: The U.N. in Guatemala. In *Peacemaking and Democratization in the Western Hemisphere*, edited by Tommie Sue Montgomery. Coral Gables, Fla.: North-South Center Press.

———. 1997. Guatemala's Peace Accords: An End and a Beginning. *NACLA Report on the Americas*. May-June.

———. 1996. Dangerous Liaisons: The U.S. in Guatemala. *Foreign Policy* (Summer):144-60.

———. 1995. Electoral Problems and the Democratic Project in Guatemala. In *Elections and Democracy in Central America: Revisited*, edited by Mitchell Seligson and John Booth. Chapel Hill: University of North Carolina Press.

———. 1994. Text and Subtext of the Guatemalan Political Drama. *LASA Forum* (Winter). Latin American Studies Association (LASA).

———. 1991. *The Battle for Guatemala: Rebels, Death Squads, and U.S. Power*. Boulder, Colo.: Westview.

———. 1989. Elections and Transitions: The Guatemalan and Nicaraguan Cases. In *Elections and Democracy in Central America: Revisited*, edited by Mitchell Seligson and John Booth. Chapel Hill: University of North Carolina Press.

Jonas, Susanne, and Edward McCaughan, eds. 1994. *Latin America Faces the Twenty-First Century*. Boulder, Colo.: Westview.

Jonas, Susanne, and Nancy Stein, eds. 1990a. *Democracy in Latin America: Visions and Realities*. New York: Greenwood/Bergin and Garvey.

———. 1990b. The Construction of Democracy in Nicaragua. *Latin American Perspectives*

(Summer):10-37.
Karl, Terry. 1995. The Hybrid Regimes of Central America. *Journal of Democracy* (July):72-86.
———. 1992. El Salvador's Negotiated Revolution. *Foreign Affairs* (Spring):147-64.
———. 1990. Dilemmas of Democratization in Latin America. *Comparative Politics* (October).
Kirkpatrick, Jeane. 1979. Dictatorships and Double Standards. In *Commentary* (November).
Lechner, Norbert. 1997. Los condicionantes de la gobernabilidad democr tica en la América Latina de fin de Siglo. *Diálogo* (November). Guatemala: FLACSO.
Le Bot, Yvon. 1995. *La guerra en tierras mayas: Comunidad, violencia y modernidad en Guatemala (1970-1992)*. Mexico, D.F.: Fondo de Cultura Económica.
Lungo, Mario. 1994. Redefining Democracy in El Salvador. In *Latin America Faces the Twenty-First Century*, edited by Susanne Jonas and Edward McCaughan. Boulder, Colo.: Westview.
MacPherson, C.B. 1973. *Democratic Theory: Essays in Retrieval*. Oxford, U.K.: Clarendon Press.
McCleary, Rachel M. 1997. Guatemala's Postwar Prospects. *Journal of Democracy* (April):129-43.
Montgomery, Tommie Sue. 2000. *Peacemaking and Democratization in the Western Hemisphere*. Coral Gables, Fla.: North-South Center Press.
Montobbio de Balanzó, Manuel. 1997. La construcción de la democracia en El Salvador. (February). Madrid: Centro de Estudios Políticos Americanos.
Morlino, Leonardo. 1985. *Como cambian los regimenes políticos*. Madrid: Centro de Estudios Constitucionales.
North American Congress on Latin America (NACLA). 1995. The Left in Local Politics. *NACLA Report on the Americas* (July-August):14-44.
National Democratic Institute for International Affairs (NDI). 1991. *The 1990 National Elections in Guatemala: International Delegation Report*. Washington, D.C.: NDI.
Nun, José. 1993. Democracy and Modernization, Thirty Years Later. *Latin American Perspectives* (Fall):7-27.
Ochoa, Carlos, Rosa Sánchez, and Armando Pacay. 1995. *Los Comités Cívicos: Gestión local de la acción política*. Guatemala: IRIPAZ.
O'Donnell, Guillermo. 1997. Rendición de cuentas horizontal y nuevas poliarquías. *Nueva Sociedad*, no. 152 (November-December):143-67.
O'Donnell, Guillermo, Phillipe Schmitter, and Laurence Whitehead, eds. 1986. *Transitions from Authoritarian Rule*. Baltimore: Johns Hopkins University Press.
Organization of American States (OAS). 1997. *Electoral Observation: Guatemala, 1995-1996*. Washington, D.C.: OAS.
Padilla, Luis Alberto. 1997. Peacemaking and Conflict Transformation in Guatemala. *Estudios Internacionales* (January-July):82-108.
———. 1996a. Presentación. *Estudios Internacionales* (July-December):i-viii. Guatemala: IRIPAZ.
———. 1996b. Las nuevas relaciones cívico-militares en el marco del proceso de paz en Guatemala. *Estudios Internacionales* (July-December):27-41. Guatemala: IRIPAZ.
———. 1995. La negociación bajo el signo de las mediaciones interna y externa. *Estudios Internacionales* (January-July):30-60. Guatemala: IRIPAZ.
Pateman, Carole. 1970. *Participation and Democratic Theory*. Cambridge: Cambridge University Press.

Pearce, Jenny. 1998. Building Civil Society from the Outside: the Problematic Democratisation of Central America. *Global Society* 12, no. 2.
Peeler, John. 1995. Elites and Democracy in Central America. In *Elections and Democracy in Central America, Revisited*, edited by Mitchell Seligson and John Booth. Chapel Hill: University of North Carolina Press.
Poitevín, René. 1992. Los problemas de la democracia. In *Los problemas de la democracia*. Guatemala: FLACSO.
———. 1991. En busca de la identidad. *Cuaderno de FLACSO*, no. 1. Guatemala: FLACSO.
Przeworski, Adam. 1996. Studying Democratization: Twenty Years Later. Manuscript. Cited by permission.
Richard, Pablo. 1995. La fuerza del espíritu: Religión y teología en América Latina. *Nueva Sociedad* (March-April):128-41.
Rojas Lima, Flavio. 1995. *El derecho consuetudiario en el contexto de la etnicidad Guatemalteca*. Guatemala: Procurador de los Derechos Humanos.
Rosada, Héctor. 1997. El desafío de la paz. *Nueva Sociedad* (January-February):18-26.
———. 1996. El impacto de las negociaciones de paz en Guatemala. *Estudios Internacionales* (July-December):20-26. Guatemala: IRIPAZ.
Sader, Emir. 1992. *Governar para todos*. São Paolo: Editora Página Aberta Ltda.
Schmitter, Philippe, and Terry Karl. 1991. What Democracy Is And Is Not. *Journal of Democracy* (Summer).
Seligson, Mitchell, and John Booth, eds. 1995. *Elections and Democracy in Central America, Revisited*. Chapel Hill: University of North Carolina Press.
Sieder, Rachel. 1996. *Derecho consuetudinario y transición democrática en Guatemala*. Guatemala: FLACSO.
Solares, Jorge. 1992. Guatemala: Etnicidad y democracia. In *Los problemas de la democracia*. Guatemala: FLACSO.
Torres Rivas, Edelberto. 1996. Los desafíos del desarrollo democr tico en Centroamérica. *Anuario de Estudios Centroamericanos* 22, no. 1:7-40. Universidad de Costa Rica.
———. 1995. Democracy and the Metaphor of Good Government. In *The Consolidation of Democracy in Latin America*, edited by Joseph S. Tulchin and Bernice Romero. Boulder, Colo.: Lynne Rienner.
———. 1991. La democracia electoral y sus dificultades en América Latina. *Memoria* (January-February). Mexico: CEMOS.
———. 1989. Authoritarian Transition to Democracy in Central America. In *Sociology of Developing Societies: Central America*, edited by Jan Flora and Edelberto Torres Rivas. New York: Monthly Review Press.
Torres Rivas, Edelberto, and Gabriel Aguilera. 1998. *Del autoritarismo a la paz*. Guatemala: FLASCO.
Touraine, Alain. 1991. Lecture for "Tribuna 92." *El Gallo Ilustrado*, Supplement of *El Día* (Mexico) 29 September.
Trudeau, Robert. 1989. The Guatemalan Election of 1985: Prospects for Democracy. In *Elections and Democracy in Central America, Revisited*, edited by Mitchell Seligson and John Booth. Chapel Hill: University of North Carolina Press.
Tulchin, Joseph S., and Bernice Romero, eds. 1995. *The Consolidation of Democracy in Latin America*. Boulder, Colo.: Lynne Rienner.
Vilas, Carlos M. 1997. Inequality and the Dismantling of Citizenship in Latin America. *NACLA Report on the Americas* (July-August):57-63.

———. 1996. Prospects for Democratisation in a Post-Revolutionary Setting: Central America. *Journal of Latin American Studies* (May):461-503.

Vilas, Carlos. 1994. Latin America: Socialist Perspectives in Times of Cholera. In *Latin America Faces the Twenty-First Century*, edited by Susanne Jonas and Edward McCaughan. Boulder, Colo.: Westview.

Wallerstein, Immanuel. 1996. *The ANC and South Africa: The Past and Future of Liberation Movements in the World-System*. Binghamton, N.Y.: Fernand Braudel Center, SUNY.

———. 1995. *After Liberalism*. New York: New Press.

———. 1991. *Unthinking Social Science: The Limits of Nineteenth-Century Paradigms*. Cambridge, U.K.: Polity Press.

Warren, Kay B. 1998. *Indigenous Movements and Their Critics: Pan-Maya Activism in Guatemala*. Princeton, N.J.: Princeton University Press.

Weffort, Francisco. 1992. New Democracies. Which Democracies? Manuscript, prepared for East-South System Transformations Seminar.

5

Decentralization, Local Government, and Citizen Participation: Unsolved Problems in the Guatemalan Democratization Process

Nelson Amaro
(Translated by Patricia Landolt)

The triad of decentralization, local government, and citizen participation is intimately connected to democracy and the development process. Democracy presupposes multiple foci of power and decision making. Decentralization involves the transmission of a set of "rights and responsibilities"—legal norms, authority, functions, and resources—from higher levels of command toward lower, disaggregated levels of command. It is, in effect, the operationalization of a democratic structure of power.

Likewise, the state apparatus and public administration are major determinants of a nation's development strategy and outcomes. Guatemala is a unitary republic with 8 regions, 22 departments, and 330 *municipios*. Government is divided among the executive, unicameral Congress, and the judiciary. Elections are held each four years for the executive, Congress [including the Central American Parliament (PARLACEN)] and the municipalities.[1] Nevertheless, few ministries have taken into account the regional layer.

In addition, those that are deconcentrated at the departmental and municipal level depend hierarchically from the top in Guatemala City. All civil servants depend on the central level, with the exception of some innovative programs that are very limited in scope. Municipal officers lack any legal uniform framework that could enhance their career development with the exception of some limited social benefits.[2] They do not have salary scales, seniority, employment stability, or promotion rules.

Determination of needs, program formulation, and evaluation are also centralized. Although there has been some fiscal decentralization measures still they are disbursed as transfers from the central level. Revenues are overwhelmingly centralized though some forty municipios have been granted autonomy regarding the collection of real estate taxes. Centralization is not new. It may be traced back to colonial times when this same picture emerged from the Spanish Crown that ruled Guatemala for almost three hundred years.

Decentralization can bring greater efficiency and equity in development when policies reflect the needs of the population. In Guatemala, municipio is the political expression of the local government. It should establish the goals that accord with the general interest, and it should have the administrative and financial means to achieve these goals. The notion of citizen participation suggests that neighbors in a municipio have regular access to elected officials and that they can shape and influence the decision making of the elected authorities. Democracy is strengthened and development achieved when decentralization and citizen participation are advanced.

In Guatemala, decentralization has experienced both breakthroughs and breakdowns. In this chapter, I map the different policies that have been intended to implement the decentralization process. Our evaluation of the decentralization process focuses on the quality of service delivery. We are less concerned with the intentions of decentralization programs than with their actual effects. The current situation suggests that decentralization needs to be extended to the regional and local levels if it is to have any effect. Future reforms must address two key issues: (1) the delivery of services has to be more effective and (2) local government policies must reflect the needs of the population.

The National System of Urban and Rural Development Councils: Ideal and Reality

Guatemala's National System of Urban and Rural Development Councils (SINACODUR)[3] was instituted in 1987 on the basis of Decree 52-87 passed the same year. It was built having as an antecedent the 1985 Constitution where national, regional and departmental urban and rural development councils were defined. The latter, however, was not conceived as a system. Decree 52-87 gives this step. Simultaneously, it widens its scope by incorporating the municipal and local level. The purpose of the SINACODUR is to provide channels of citizen participation in the process of determination of priorities, policies, programs and projects formulation, implementation, resources allocation, and evaluation of any public endeavor. In addition, it had the responsibility of territorial planning and the organization and coordination of public administration considering the participation of the population in SINACODUR.

From its inception, the SINACODUR did not achieve the ideal of decentralization it sought to establish. In design and in the mind of those who were its supporters, SINACODUR resembles a dual pyramid structure of authority. Originally, it was conceived as a two-way avenue. But in reality, observers and many actors wrongly regard it as a simple pyramid of authority with the president of the Republic at the top, and the local development councils (CODURs) at the base (See Gálvez Borrell, Mack, and Camposeco Hurtado 1998). Nevertheless, even this idealization does not approximate completely what has actually happened.

Several factors have produced this gap between the ideal and the reality. First, it has been suggested that there were defects in the analysis leading up to the design and installation of the system and that the institutional structure of the system is too complicated and top-heavy. Also, there has been too much emphasis on planning and coordination, and not enough on the actual execution of the system. Underlying these issues has been a more fundamental problem, which is that the central administration has a "deep distrust of those that should have been involved in the planning and design stages of the program" (Gálvez Borrell, Mack, and Camposeco Hurtado 1998).

Since its inception in 1985, legal battles and political controversies have eroded the structure and undermined the functioning of the SINACODUR. Given the political compromises required to pass Decree 52-87, the municipal and local levels never really got off the ground. In 1987, the opposition in Congress argued that the municipal urban and rural development councils actually resulted in diminishing the exercise of local power by elected authorities subtracting from the autonomy enjoyed by the town council in the same Constitution. As a compromise, municipal councils with citizen participation representation, along with elected authorities, were vanished from Decree 52-87. The following year, the same argument was put forward regarding the local urban and rural development councils. The issue was taken to the Constitutional Court, which in 1988 ruled in favor of the opposition. The local urban and rural development councils were held to be a violation of municipal autonomy.

The 1988 legal ruling called for the dismantling of the local development councils. As a result of this decision, local levels of government that were being actively constituted throughout the country were left without a legal basis for their existence. According to reports of the Ministry of Urban and Rural Development, by October 1988 1,582 local development councils had been created or were in the process of being instituted (Amaro 1990). The capacity of the municipality to open itself to citizen participation was already severely curtailed by Decree 52-87. After the adjustments made to the structure following the decision of the Constitutional Court in 1988, SINACODUR resembled a structure "without feet and head".

Given the legal dismantling of local-level councils, in 1988 the SINACODUR basically resembled the structure called for in the 1985 Constitution, which only sought to create councils at the national, regional, and departmental level. In practice, as the administration of President Cerezo (1986 to 1991) was consolidated, the three-tiered system became increasingly less relevant. The national level was not a priority and hardly received any political support. The president only engaged in the council process twice, and this for public functions. Otherwise, activities were delegated to the vice president. Each year the national level had less meetings.

At the regional level, discussions centered on which departmental capital would head each particular region: coordination without resources produced no results. The regional administration structure went into crisis when the national government drastically cut its budget. The never-ending call to hold meetings began to wear on participants, and attendance began to diminish. Finally, since departmental politics had never played an important role in national politics, this level of the SINACODUR system remained essentially ornamental.

When, in 1991, Jorge Serrano assumed the presidency, the council system structure resembled an inverse pyramid with a very narrow and weak base that survived largely because it had a budget and for no other reason. The CODURs were absent from public life. Partisan considerations aside, it was quite clear at this time that SINACODUR was unable to motivate or sustain the voluntary participation of institutions and sectors of civil society. All project and program decisions were made at the central posts. These in turn felt no pressure to initiate or complete projects since they were totally disconnected from the local communities and their needs and concerns.

The political crisis of 1993 brought Guatemala's political process to a standstill. During this period tensions originating in the legislature and judiciary paralyzed the presidential office and the cabinet. Following a failed coup attempt, Serrano was forced to resign, and Ramiro de León Carpio, formerly the human rights ombudsman, was elected by Congress to assume the presidency. Carpio lacked the legitimacy to fully exercise power, so that the political process remained deadlocked. Carpio finally called for a renovation of Congress, since it was felt that during the crisis its members had strayed far from their mandate.

The fallout from this political crisis and institutional shuffling requires another examination of the institutional framework of the SINACODUR and its supporting institutions. Despite the breakdown of the political process, during both the Serrano and Carpio administrations, the approval of moneys earmarked for specific funds accelerated. As a result, there were seventeen schemes, of which thirteen have been fully funded (FUNCEDE 1997). These include the Social Investment Fund, which served as the model for the other sixteen schemes and the Solidarity and Community Development Fund (FSDC), which has the largest budget.[4] The fragmentation of the budgetary process culminated with the elimination of the Ministry of Urban and Rural Development (MINDUR), which was originally charged with the executive direction of the SINACODUR.

The FSDC came under the supervision of the Secretariat of the Presidency (SEP), which, according to the Law of the Executive Organ passed in 1997, is charged with the administration of the CODURs at the national, regional, and departmental level. In its functions, the FSDC is structurally equivalent to the now defunct MINDUR. Substantively, there are major differences between the MINDUR and the FSDC. The FSDC has made little effort to revitalize the SINACODUR's national level structures. There has been no policy to reincorporate civil society at the regional, municipal, or local level. Even at the departmental level, where it has been more visible, the participation of sectors such as cooperatives, the private sector, the unions, non-governmental organizations, and political parties varies across departments and is quite limited in many of them. There is no organic link (namely, rules for representativeness, decision-making procedures, rotation, and so on) between the institutions of civil society and the departmental councils.[5]

The FSDC has also been conceived as a coordinating body. Its role is to serve as an intermediary between the communities and the municipios, and the municipal, regional, and departmental administrations. It is charged with presenting the project proposals of the local population to the different levels of administration. The budget for the portfolio of projects that is approved constitutes the annual budget requested by the FSDC from the Ministry of Finances. Once the budget is approved, the Ministry of Finances makes trimestral disbursements to the FSDC, which in turn distributes the funds to the regional and departmental administrations. Finally, the regional and departmental administrations allocate these funds to municipal and local projects.

The goal of the Secretariat of the Presidency is to strengthen the SINACODUR, focusing in particular on the departmental level. Thus, it is really at the departmental level that local community and municipal projects are evaluated and approved. As a result, the departmental level administration of the SINACODUR has acquired an importance not anticipated in the original proposal. There is a lack of representation of civil society at the municipal level. In addition, although agreed to in the peace accords of 1994, there was still an unwillingness to reestablish the local councils. Finally, as part of a new reform plan for the SINACODUR, the reinstitution of the local councils was again under discussion in Congress in 1998 and 1999. As of March 1999, this legislation had not been approved.

The last episode on the rise and fall of SINACODUR took place on May 16, 1999. The electorate was called to a referendum where significant changes were to be approved. The so-called Consulta Popular put before the population a complex agenda that covered changes in the constitutional charter on issues such as ethnic relations extending the legitimacy of the Indian population in linguistic as well as in cultural terms; army restructuring sponsoring, among other things, a civilian as Secretary (*Ministro*) of Defense; an overhaul of the justice system, strengthening its operations against corruption practices; and the inclusion of local and municipal bodies with citizen participation to share decision making with municipal political authorities. Only 18.5 percent of the electorate attended, and those who deposited their ballot preferred to answer "no" instead of "yes".[6] A sense of perplexity before so many and profound issues; a negative stance against any kind of government; and a polarization of the "ethnic" issue that "may lead Guatemala to a racial war," in addition to the secular indifference of people suffering a "social deficit" in education, health, and quality of life, may account for this result. This presumption was corroborated on December 26, 1999, when the second round of presidential elections gave the triumph to the opposition with an advantage of almost forty points.

The Absence of Institutional Support Structures for the Municipios

Guatemala's fiscal decentralization plan is recognized internationally. It is estimated that approximately 20 percent of the national budget's current revenues is allocated to the municipalities (USAID 1998). As a result of the peace accords, this sum includes both the 10 percent guaranteed by the constitution, and 1 percent of the national revenues from the value-added tax and the tax on gasoline, automobiles, and other consumer items (Calderón González 1995). This compares quite favorably with the situation in the rest of Latin America. In Central America, El Salvador passed a similar fiscal decentralization measure in 1997 that allocates only 6 percent of the national budget's current revenues to the municipalities.

In Costa Rica, a fiscal decentralization bill has been before Congress since the 1960s without approval. In 1990, Honduras passed a similar measure, but again it allots municipalities only 5 percent of the national budget. In South America, Ecuador assigns 8 percent of the budget to the municipalities without any regulation; and Venezuela assigns 20 percent of the federal budget to the states, which in turn allocate 20 percent of their state budgets to the municipalities. The income stemming from the states is almost negligible. Therefore, municipalities reach a little more than the 4 percent given by the federal government.

A program to strengthen the institutional apparatus of the municipios has not accompanied fiscal decentralization, as Eduardo Wiesner explains:

> In the case of decentralization, the externalities of certain policies can be the key to success or failure. The cornerstone of this process should be institutional development at the local level. For this reason, it is always recommended that institutional development accompany the processes of political and fiscal decentralization. In various countries of Latin America, this has included the development of seminars, courses, and pamphlets that emphasize institutional reform as part of the decentralization of resources and management. (Wiesner 1997: 236-37)

The theoretical need to have qualified personnel with technical, administrative, and financial expertise stands in stark contrast to Guatemala's reality. In spite of some notable but isolated efforts, technical and financial assistance, training of those charged with decision making and fund management falls far short of the very minimum required to make the system function effectively. The majority of the municipalities do not have any sort of concrete plans or development projects. Municipal administrators have neither a clearly specified hierarchy, nor clearly defined functions. Procedures are excessively bureaucratic, budgetary accountability is inadequate, and information, follow-up, and evaluations systems are lacking

(INFOM 1992).

The average municipality has only one elected official paid, the mayor. There is also a trustee and a municipal secretary who receive salaries. Sometimes other personnel are hired on a short-term basis. In Mayan municipalities where there still exists a civic-religious hierarchy, the municipal structure includes volunteer positions for these leaders. Larger municipalities commonly also have a treasurer, a person in charge of the municipal registry, and an accountant. An editorial by the newspaper of greatest circulation in the country, regarding the enormous municipal debt that had been public after the former administration left, comments:

> A high percentage of the Mayors used funds for pharaonic works .... Others, used them with the simplistic criterion that the more the expenditure, the greater the sum of illegal pay backs ... while still others ... simply did nothing and put the money into their pockets. ... There was neither ... any priority criteria ... nor any cost-benefit analysis. ... This vice is the reason for many villages having basket ball courts and community saloons while water, sanitary services and health posts are lacking.[7]

In general, the notion of a career in municipal administration is absent. An investigation of a representative sample of municipalities (N = 45) concludes that over 30 percent of municipal personnel have held their post for ten or more years, and 24 percent have held their post for less than three years. While the data suggest a degree of institutional stability, it is the low wages that sabotage the system. Guatemala's monthly minimum wage is set at Q535.50 at the time of the survey. Eighty-nine percent of municipal employees surveyed earn less than two minimum salaries, or the equivalent of U.S.$172 (Gálvez Borrell, Mack, and Camposeco Hurtado 1998). There are no monetary incentives for remaining in a post or doing a job well. Municipal secretaries most closely approximate the career civil servant. During their career, which is usually quite lengthy, they move from one to another municipio, and in cases where the mayor has little education, will basically assume the functions of the maximum local authority. In spite of this track record, municipal secretaries have no job security, and there are no policies in place to encourage the retention of these personnel (USAID 1998).

There are two key institutions that shape the political process at the municipal level: the Municipal Promotion Institute (INFOM) and the National Association of Municipalities (ANAM). Here we examine the legacies, strengths, and weaknesses of these two institutions and suggest key issues that must be addressed to make these institutions effective. We turn first to an examination of INFOM.

INFOM was founded in 1957 when Guatemala was a very different place. In 1997, when INFOM was called on to participate in the decentralization process, it was a weak institution with an anachronistic structure. With the support of the German Cooperation Fund (GTZ), INFOM is being restructured. The main goal is to adapt INFOM to a national context in which the number of actors actively engaged in municipal politics and administration has grown exponentially. Universities, nongovernmental organizations, and even the private sector via social branches of the sugar and coffee growers associations have entered into the municipal arena to offer technical assistance and training.[8]

INFOM is still weighed down by its institutional history. In the early 1990s, INFOM was found by expert evaluators to be an incompetent institution. According to Luis Everardo Estrada et al. (1990), INFOM had focused its attention almost exclusively on financial, technical, and administrative assistance to municipal governments. It had neglected the task of mediating between national and municipal development plans. It had also not engaged in the socioeconomic promotion of municipalities. As an institution, INFOM had favored urban over rural areas, infrastructure projects over the development of a sustainable economic basis for municipios, and the municipal bureaucracy over the social organizations of the municipios.

At this point, the needs of the municipios far exceeded the capacities of INFOM to deliver either projects or financial support. INFOM's highly centralized decision-making process and its inability to consolidate a presence in more remote regions of the country restrict its engagement with the municipalities. By 1999, INFOM was argued to have changed little. According to this criticism it has produced ineffective and erratic results due to its size, the instability of its clientele, and the traditional nature of the activities it undertook, which focused on imposing INFOM services, rather than on responding to the genuine demands of local institutions.

Nevertheless, since 1996, INFOM has undergone a major internal reorganization. In 1997, INFOM stopped receiving funding from the central government and became self-financing with the interest earned on loans it had been allotted earlier. Its lending system has been decentralized and is now under the supervision of regional-level decision makers. Technical assistance has been given to one hundred municipios in the process of elaborating projects to be presented to the Social Investment Fund. INFOM has also been strengthened by the incorporation of new institutions into its structure. In particular, UNEPAR, the National Unit for Rural Water, an entity with expertise in the introduction of potable water systems that was originally housed within the Ministry of Transportation and Public Works, now functions as part of INFOM. Potable water is a key demand of municipalities, so that INFOM's capacity to deliver this service has increased municipality satisfaction with INFOM.

Another major problem of the INFOM structure has to do with resource distribution. INFOM establishes the criteria for how municipal funds are to be distributed and spent according to the legislation that gives municipalities 10 percent of the budget. Given that it is the sole decision maker, it is important that INFOM keep abreast of local issues and developments. Yet INFOM has never established a permanent or visible presence in Guatemala's rural regions. Only 59 of INFOM's 340 personnel were located in rural areas, and 291 of them were located in Guatemala City in 1998.

Finally, in keeping with the mandate of the peace accords, INFOM has constructed a Technical Training Plan for the municipalities that seeks to coordinate collaborative activities across thirty-three institutions (RENICAM 1997). INFOM has traditionally funded technical training for municipios. Yet results for the current program are mixed. Participants have determined that only 40 percent of the municipalities and 20 percent of the target population are actually receiving training when this program was launched. One of the problems of this plan is a shortage of funding. But more troubling is unwillingness on the part of municipal civil servants to dedicate time to the training sessions. A recent evaluative report contends that even when municipal functionaries recognize the importance of training, they do not demand it. Most mayors, as well as the other members of the Municipal Council, resist making any efforts to engage in the training programs because they don't see any immediate personal advantage in it, and also because they do not have the time to do so. Training is, unfortunately, not a priority.

The National Association of Municipalities (ANAM) is the second organization that must play an important role in the modernization and decentralization reforms. In the past, ANAM failed to strengthen the municipalities and has been slow to recognize and respond to the exigencies of its current role. For example, between 1974 and 1987 ANAM did not hold a single meeting of mayors. Part of the problem stems from the fact that the municipality of Guatemala City, from which it gained its autonomy only in 1992, traditionally monopolized ANAM. Before 1992, the mayor of Guatemala City was automatically appointed president of ANAM. Also, its resources have always been limited, in part because municipalities have not paid their dues regularly. Until 1996, ANAM did not even have its own offices and was housed within the INFOM.

ANAM has been ineffective as a pressure group. In 1990, when the government failed to turn 8 percent of the budget over to municipal institutions, ANAM was unable to exercise any influence over the process (Gálvez Borrell and Mack 1998). It was also silent in constitutional discussions about the percentage of national revenues from the value-added tax that should be allocated to the municipalities. Many mayors are still indifferent toward ANAM and resist its bias toward Guatemala City. As Victor Gálvez Borrell and Luis Fernando Mack (1998) state, "The political influence of the municipality of Guatemala City still weights heavily on ANAM, and although its Presidency has by now been held by mayors from different provinces, all of them have had difficulties establishing their leadership on ANAM."

ANAM, or an institution like it, is necessary to establish a support network that can strengthen the institutional structure and presence of the municipalities. Hence, in spite of its weaknesses, ANAM must focus on defending the global interests of the municipios, and forget about partisan competition and conflict. It must be able to respond quickly to the needs of the municipios.

ANAM's current agenda is dictated by the reforms to the Municipal Code as it was laid out in the peace accords of 1994. It includes several themes. One aim of the reform is to involve the local community more actively in the election of the vice mayors at the community level. Candidates for the position would be proposed at an open meeting of the town council, and the mayor would select a person from this group.

A second part of the reform effort involves the formation of municipal assemblies that would be open to popular participation and tied to the different commissions of the municipality. Commissions responsible for promoting citizen participation, personal security, and human rights have also been created. The Municipal Council is now also authorized to approve the legal constitution of community organizations. This is of particular importance to Mayan communities, since it grants them the ability to bestow a legal basis on Mayan forms of organization. These changes constitute a genuine opening and democratization of the political process at the local level.

Other issues contemplated in the reform of the Municipal Code include increased openness of council meetings, the creation of bridges between municipal authorities, the citizenry, and the private sector that may potentially lead to private-public partnerships, and issues related to taxation and property rights that require public discussion and popular approval.

The government that took over January 14, 2000, has declared a national priority the approval of the Decentralization Law set to be approved in the first months. This legislation had been in Congress for some time sponsored by the *Frente Republicano Guatemalteco* (FRG), which happens to be in power at present. Unofficially, the author had before him this proposal and concluded that it needed substantial revision. It was not ripe to take it to Congress for approval. Nevertheless, the new president has appointed a commissioner on decentralization who is already working on the subject and attending public meetings.

These issues highlight the context in which municipalities now function and the direction in which future reforms must be taken. The principal problem is that the improved fiscal situation of municipalities has not been matched by a strengthening of the normative and institutional structure of the system. The activities of the principal actors—INFOM and ANAM, nongovernmental organizations, and universities—are not united within a single framework that can coordinate and direct actions in the short, medium, and long term. The institutions called upon to provide an institutional framework for technical and financial training either do not have sufficient resources to respond to demand, or have an institutional legacy that does not allow them to identify the needs of the municipalities.

ANAM, which is charged with bringing together the nation's municipal leaders, has only recently begun to project itself as a viable representative of municipal interests. In the past, the institutional framework of ANAM has been unable to incorporate important new actors into the process, such as the private sector, nongovernmental organizations, and the universities, that could assist in and strengthen the reform process. This need has been recognized.

In light of this situation, the budget allocation structure established by constitutional decree is quite troubling. As discussed earlier, 10 percent of the national budget is allocated to the municipalities. Of this 10 percent, 90 percent is earmarked for investment in projects, 10 percent is for current expenditures, mainly bureaucratic costs, and none is allocated to training of municipal personnel. Combined with the existing salary scale, this budget allocation system is an obstacle to the recruitment of more qualified personnel. The demand for training will only be generated from below, as it should be, if it is linked to career promotion and salary improvements. Any action related to institutional development must be accompanied by a change in the structure of incentives to attract the most qualified personnel of Guatemala into positions such as municipal secretary or treasurer. Today, the challenge is to match the budgetary decentralization process, namely the "hardware," with decentralization and strengthening of the municipal structure, the "software."

Restructuring the System of Transfer Payments

In the absence of an effective system for the management and investment of local resources, the sudden increase in transfer payments to the municipalities has sparked tensions and conflicts at the local level. Between 1991 and 1993, close to 15 percent of the nation's municipalities were taken over by the local population, which charged their local municipal councils with mishandling government transfer payments (Luján et al. 1997a; Luján et al. 1997b). Sixty-five percent of Guatemala's municipal corporations are currently under investigation for breach of contract, and 55 percent of the country's mayors have been personally accused of misconduct and mishandling of funds. Finally, 235 municipal functionaries (mayors, treasurers, secretaries, and so on) have been taken to court, and 4 percent of them have received death threats or have been attacked by the local population or forced to go into hiding (Gálvez Borrell, Mack, and Camposeco Hurtado 1997, 323).

As Eduardo Wiesner (1997, 240-41) explains, when a system of transfer payments does not stimulate better local government, then it runs the risk of eroding governance. The simple dispersal of resources without guidelines brings instability and accentuates disputes over the use of resources. For instance, a large part of local funds is invested in infrastructure projects in the urban areas of the municipios (e.g., paving town roads). This has led to a marginalization of the rural areas, where the majority of the population is concentrated, and has created a new form of centralization at the local level.[9] If transfer payments are not designed to act as an incentive for better government and greater efficiency, no central government will be able to moderate the demands and pressures that come with the distribution and transfer of resources.

Table 5.1. Guatemala: Criteria for the Distribution of Local Funds

Decree 52-87

25% in equal parts to all the municipalities

25% proportional to the population of each municipio

25% proportional to the rural population of each municipio

25% directly but inversely proportional to the per capita income of each municipal jurisdiction

Decree 49-88

25% in equal parts to all the municipalities

25% proportional to the population of each municipio

25% directly proportional to the per capita income of each municipal jurisdiction

15% directly proportional to the number of hamlets and *caseríos* (country houses)

10% directly but inversely proportional to the per capita income of each municipal jurisdiction

Decree 49-88 was passed in order to address some of the problems caused by the original guidelines for disbursement and spending of transfer payments established in Decree 52-87. These criteria are presented on table 5.1. The criteria established in Decree 49-88 were designed to reward municipalities that had historically demonstrated proper management of funds. Although there was concern about redistributive issues associated with transfer payments, the shift to these criteria did have a negative effect on the more impoverished municipalities.

It is still unknown whether the incentives contained in Decree 49-88 have functioned as they were designed to do. We also do not know with certainty whether, within each municipio, the transfers have had the hoped-for redistributive effect. It is possible that the poorest populations may be subsidizing the wealthiest persons within the poorest municipios. The concentration of funds within the urban centers of the municipios and the recent protests against municipal leaders suggest that this may indeed have been the case.

A review of the conditions established for the different categories of the municipal transfer payments (see table 5.1) suggests that these are too broad. The criteria are very universal and do not focus specifically on the fight against poverty. There is a need to balance universal concerns and poverty alleviation issues in the budget. One possible solution to this problem is for municipios and the Social Investment Fund to coordinate and cofinance projects and for there to be more detailed criteria for the allotment of transfer payments to specific projects or issues. Universities could collaborate in the study of these problems. The more time that goes by before these issues are addressed, the worse the problems will become.

Biases of the Decentralization Process: Forgetting the Municipios

The process of decentralization in Guatemala faces many Hobbesian monsters, some of which have been conquered in battle, and others that continue to reappear and seem undiminished. In this light, one must be suspicious of public declarations and promises of decentralization, since this is a popular electoral promise that often results in little concrete change.

In the first phase of the democratic transition (1986 to 1991), the SINACODUR and the vice presidency of the Republic launched a plan for the modernization of the central government. The results of this project were limited, and far shy of the original proposal. Serrano's assumption to the presidency in 1991 and the institutional crisis of 1993 first thwarted the development of the original modernization plan, and later prompted its redefinition. One important change in this redefinition was that the presidential secretariats assumed greater relevance. Important changes also took place in the Congress and Supreme Court. The modernization of the state apparatus has become a priority of the administration at present (1996 to the present).

As discussed below, the program to modernize the state has a variety of measures that directly impact the decentralization process. The Arzú administration continues to grant power and resources to the presidential secretariats. The recently approved Law of the Executive Organ calls for a restructuring of several secretariats including the SEP and the newly named Secretariat of Planning and Presidential Programming. New secretarial portfolios have been created and have received full funding, including the Strategic Analysis Secretariat (Congreso de la República de Guatemala 1997, 114-97). At the departmental level, the administrative apparatus has also been strengthened by the Arzú administration. Departmental directors, especially those in Education, have acquired a new status, and salaries have increased notably. Funding decisions for disbursements associated with the Solidarity Fund are also made at the department-level CODURs.

According to the Law of the Executive Organ, the president of the Republic now chooses the governor from a group of candidates selected by the departmental CODUR. This measure is part of the effort to strengthen the CODURs and to encourage citizen participation. This law reinforces management at the same time that it grants citizen participation in a process that, until recently, depended entirely on the will of the executive. This plan has also tried to coordinate the activities of the different institutions engaged in the interaction with INFOM and other governmental organizations.

The decentralization process is also affected by the decision to reduce the state bureaucracy and to privatize state functions and services.[10] These two policy decisions have affected the entire government apparatus and have made significant advances within existing institutional limitations. Whether through sales, concessions, or contracts, the private sector is beginning to undertake activities that were once part of the functioning of the government apparatus. Several government offices have also offered their personnel retirement incentive packages in an effort to reduce the payroll.

In the final analysis, the management policy has opted for a governance structure that coordinates actions between the central government and the departmental level administration, with the result that personnel and funds are concentrated at this nexus. The encounter between the state and civil society therefore takes place at the departmental level, and mainly through the urban and rural development councils. The municipios have been effectively isolated from the centers of power in which policies about the decentralization process are decided. A similar situation in Costa Rica warns us of the consequences of marginalizing the municipio. As Roy Rivera (1997, 34) explains:

> In Costa Rica both citizens and government are interested in a rapid restructuring and modernization of the state apparatus, but the direction of change suggested by the two actors is not complementary. It is difficult to reconcile privatization and reduction of the bureaucracy, the government's agenda, with a return to the strong welfare state of Costa Rica's golden years, the citizen's agenda. In effect, the political agenda does not coincide with the citizen's agenda.

Given the historic failure of the Guatemalan state to invest in social spending, the citizen's agenda in this country, the demand for increased social spending, is even more poignant. It not only challenges the government's agenda, but also highlights a history of state negligence.

Improvements in the department-level management and administration are only one dimension of the reforms needed to achieve greater democracy. There needs to be a coherence of action between accepting the relevance of human development, engaging in social investment to achieve this human development, and the political dimensions of the decentralization process.

Conclusion

This chapter identifies four yet unsolved problems in the triad of decentralization, local government, and citizen participation. The incongruence between the idea and the reality of the National System of Urban and Rural Development Councils (SINACODURs) and how the system has been shaped by policies of three presidencies are discussed. The Cerezo administration (1986 to 1991) compromised and did away with the system's channels for municipal citizen participation and witnessed the erosion of the legal basis for the formation of local councils. Serrano (1991 to 1993) paid little attention to this model and during his presidency focused on the regional and departmental level administrations. By the end of his interrupted mandate, there was little left of the concern with citizen participation. The Carpio administration (1993 to 1996) resurrected the departmental councils and gave strong impulse to the social investment funds, of which seventeen have been approved and thirteen are now financially viable. The Arzú administration (1996 to the present) has followed the policy established under Carpio to privilege the departmental level, and it has strengthened the coordinating role of the Solidarity Fund. The Solidarity Fund is now in regular contact with the CODURs. Whatever direction is taken now, the distance between the ideal and the reality of the SINACODURs continues to be wide. There are still several problems that have not been addressed: the lack of citizen representation in the municipios and villages and a weak representation at the departmental level, and the total absence of citizen participation at the regional and national level.

This chapter also discusses the absence of support systems for the municipal system. The majority of municipios have serious administrative, financial, resource, and personnel problems. There is no system of long-term technical or financial assistance, nor training of personnel that in the medium-term might help fill this void in human resources. The speed with which resources have been channeled to the municipalities is faster than the rate at which they have been able to address their institutional weaknesses. This has created problems of governability as tensions rise due to the mishandling of funds. At the same time, the institutions called upon to lend assistance to the municipalities must deal with an increasingly complex situation in which a growing number of social and political actors—non-governmental organizations, and the private sector in particular—must be incorporated into the political process.

Also examined is the relationship between governability and a transparent and effective design of the budget criteria for transfer payments. On the one hand, the concern for universal access to investments and services financed by the Solidarity Funds and similar schemes make current investment policy imprecise in its focus. Many funds are unnecessarily concentrated on infrastructure projects for the urban areas of the municipality. On the other hand, the demand for social spending can lead to budgetary policies that are too restrictive, focusing on select groups to the detriment of the whole. A second problem with the existing budget allotment system is that, per project, the margin for administrative costs is very small, while the municipalities are in great need of policies that will buttress administrative improvements.

Finally, current management policies that focus on efficiency at the departmental level—shrinking the bureaucracy, cutting public costs, and privatization—neglect the municipios. The citizens' agenda passes primarily through the municipios. To place the municipio at the center of politics is an essential requisite of successful development and democratization of Guatemala.

Notes

1. *Municipio* is a group of inhabitants belonging to a jurisdictional area ruled by a town council *(Ayuntamiento)*. *Municipalidad* is the town council *(Ayuntamiento)* of a municipal area. *Ayuntamiento* is a corporation composed by the mayor and a group that varies in number of councilmen for the administration of the interests of a *municipio*. In English *Ayuntamiento* is equivalent to a town council. See Real Academia Española 1992, *Diccionario de la Lengua Española* (Madrid: Espasa-Calpe).

2. The municipal employees are under the protection of Legislative Decree 4494, a law entitled "Organic Law on the Plan for Social Benefits of the Municipal Employee and its charter"; and other laws such as the Labor Code, the Municipal Service Law, and the Civil Service Law, but their application is precarious at best. See Fundación Incide 1999, *Hacia una Gestión Municipal Democrática para el Nuevo Milenio* (Ciudad Guatemala: Foto Publicaciones-Litografía), 16.

3. All acronyms correspond to the Spanish title of offices and not to the English.

4. In 1997, the FSDC received 39 percent of the total budget assigned to such Funds. Together, the FSDC, FONAPAZ, or the National Fund for Peace, and the FIS, the Social Investment Fund, represented 75 percent of the total budget (Gobierno de la República 1997). These schemes have been launched in most countries of Latin America to mitigate the social effects of structural adjustment reforms. They address poor people who express their needs through specific projects, which are presented to these funds. The innovation is that it is a demand-driven initiative. Usually, projects come from above and are supply-driven.

5. Carlos Quiñones, while being executive sub-director of the Solidarity Fund, confirms that there has been an effort under way to coordinate the primary funds such as the FIS and FONAPAZ, as well as INFOM and the Planning and Programming Secretariat (previously the SEGEPLAN), through the CODURs.

6. There were four questions. The "No" won with 48.5, 53.1, 51.8, and 49.2 percent. The first question refers to multiethnic dimensions; the second one to the Legislature; the third one to the Executive Organ; and the fourth to the Judiciary and the Administration of Justice. All of them contained complex issues. Asociación de Investigación y Estudios Sociales of 1999, "La Consulta Popular y el Futuro del Proceso de Paz en Guatemala," *Momento* 14, no. 5:7.

7. "El lastre de las Finanzas edilicias," *Prensa Libre*, 25 March 2000, p. 12.

8. There are currently four universities in Guatemala that offer programs in technical and financial training that are geared toward municipal personnel. The programs vary in length from technical certificates (two years at the Franscisco Marroquín University) to a master's in development with a concentration in decentralization, local government, and citizen participation (Universidad del Valle).

9. For a detailed examination of this trend for specific municipios, see Amaro 1990; Gutiérrez 1991.

10. For a discussion of how and why privatization of state functions constitutes part of the decentralization process, see Rondinelli, Nellis, and Cheema 1987.

Works Cited

Amaro, Nelson. 1997. La Descentralización en los Países Unitarios de América Latina y El Caribe en la Actualidad: Cuatro Dilemas Gerenciales. *Estudios Sociales* 92, no. 2 (Santiago de Chile): 95-135.

———. 1994. *Descentralización, Gobierno Local y Participación, América Latina-Honduras*. Tegucigalpa: Guaymuras.

———. 1990. *Descentralización y Participación Popular en Guatemala*. Guatemala: INCEP.

Asociación de Investigación y Estudios Sociales. 1999. La Consulta Popular y el Futuro del Proceso de Paz en Guatemala. *Momento* 14, no. 5.

Asociación Nacional de Municipalidades de la República de Guatemala (ANAM). 1997. Centro de Análisis Sociocultural, CASC-UCA y Facultad Latinoamericana de Ciencias Sociales, FLACSO-Programa Guatemala, *Descentralizacion y Desarrollo Municipal en Guatemala: Una Vision desde los Gobiernos Locales*. (Resumen Ejecutivo, Guatemala, Octubre).

Calderón Gonzalez, Arnoldo. 1995. *Desarrollo Municipal*. Guatemala: ASIES.

Coinde, Serjus. 1998. Sector de Mujeres de la ASC, CONIC. DIGI-USAC, Fundación Rigoberta Menchú Tum, CALDH, Menmagua y IEPADES, Participación para el Desarrollo, Una Propuesta a la Sociedad Civil y al Estado. Resumen del Anteproyecto de Reformas a la Ley de los Consejos de Desarrollo Urbano y Rural. Decreto 52-87, Guatemala, Febrero.

Congreso de la República de Guatemala. 1997. *Diario de Centroamérica*, 12 December. Decreto Número 114-97.

El Proyecto del Nuevo Código Municipal. 1998. *Alerta Legislativa* 2, no. 7 (Febrero):12-13.

El Proyecto de Presupuesto 1996, la Modernización y los Fondos Sociales. 1995 *SigloXXI Suplemento de Finanzas Publicas* (Septiembre):4.

Estrada, Luis Everardo, Héctor Ruben Flores, Luis Felipe Linares, and Alvaro Enrique Salguero. 1990. Desarrollo Socio-Económico a Través de Organizaciones Sociales y Gobiernos Locales. Manuscrito. Guatemala: ASIES/ACDI.

FUNCEDE.1997. *Guía Para el Uso de Fondos Sociales*. Manuscrito (Mayo).

FUNCEDE/ASIES. 1997. *Proyecto de Reformas a la Constitución Política de la República. Con Relación al Sistema de Consejos de Desarrollo*. Manuscrito (Marzo).

Fundación Incide. 1999. *Hacia una Gestión Municipal Democrática para el Nuevo Milenio*. Ciudad Guatemala: Foto Publicaciones-Litografía.

Gálvez Borrell, Víctor, and Luis Fernando Mack. 1998. *Descentralización y Movimiento Municipal en Guatemala*. Guatemala: FLACSO-CASC-UCA-Fundación Ford.

———. 1997. Avances, Estancamientos y Retrocesos: El Proceso de Descentralización en Guatemala. *Políticas y Propuestas de Descentralización en Centroamérica*. Ricardo Córdoba Coord. San Salvador: FLACSO.

Gálvez Borrell, Víctor, Luis Fernando Mack, and Roberto Camposeco Hurtado. 1998. *Políticas de Descentralización y Capacidades de Gestión Administrativa y Financiera de las Municipalidades*. El Salvador: FLACSO.

Gobierno de la República de Guatemala. 1997. *Presupuesto General de Ingresos y Egresos del Estado Ejercicio Fiscal 1997*.

Gutiérrez, Edgar. 1991. Estudio Económico-Financiero del 8% Constitucional. *Estudio y Análisis del 8% Constitucional*. IDEAS-Fundación Ford, eds. Guatemala: IDEAS-

Fundación Ford, 1991.
Heiser, Teresita. 1991. *Socio-Economic Development Funds: A Guideline forDesign and Implementation*. Social Dimensions of Adjustment and Development Unit, Africa Region, World Bank, Washington D.C.: African Development Bank, United Nations Development Program (February).
Instituto de Fomento Municipal (INFOM). 1992. *Diagnóstico de la Situación de las Municipalidades*. Guatemala: INFOM.
Larin, Menjivar, and Juan Pablo Perez Sainz. 1989. *Informalidad Urbana en Centroamérica: Evidencias e Interrogantes*. Guatemala: FLACSO/Friedrich Ebert.
Linares Lopez, Luis. 1997. *El Rol del Municipio en la Construcción de la Paz*. Serie Estudios: No. 4. Guatemala: FUNCEDE (February).
Luján, Mario. 1997. *Conflictos Municipales Electorales, Elecciones Generales 12 de Noviembre 1995*. Serie Estudios: No. 5. Guatemala: Konrad Adenauer Stiftung/Funcede.
Luján Mario, et al. 1997. *Los conflictos Municipales en el Periodo Post Acuerdos de Paz*, Serie Estudios. No.6. Guatemala: Konrad Adenauer Stiftung/Funcede.
Nash, Manning. 1959. Relaciones Políticas en Guatemala. *Integración Social en Guatemala*, Vol.2. Guatemala: SISG.
Red Nacional de Formacion, Capacitacion y Asistencia Tecnica Municipal, (RENICAM). 1997. *Plan Nacional de Formacion, Capaticitacion y Asistencia Tecnica Municipal*. Guatemala: RENICAM.
Rondinelli, Dennis A., John R. Nellis, G. Shabbir Cheema. 1987. *Decentralizing Public Services in Developing Countries: A Framework for Policy Analysis and Implementation*. North Carolina: Research Triangle Institute.
Rivera, Roy. 1997. *La Descentralización Real en Costa Rica*. Costa Rica: FLACSO.
Ruiz Calderón, Juan Carlos. 1997. Los Caminos del Desarrollo. *Siglo 21* (8 December): 47.
Sanchez, Jenaro. 1990. El Sistema Municipal en Guatemala. *Desarrollo Local 3*.
Soto Ramírez, Carlos Arturo. 1990. *La Política de Descentralización en Guatemala y su Sistema de Consejos de Desarrollo ¿Solución o Problema?* Manuscrito. Guatemala: FLACSO/Friedrich Ebert (Septiembre).
United States Agency for International Development (USAID). 1998. Request for Proposal 520-98-001. Increased Citizen Participation in Stregthened Local Governments. Downloaded from Internet address belonging to USAID.
Wiesner, Eduardo. 1997. Descentralización Fiscal y Desarrollo Institucional. *Descentralización Fiscal en América Latina: Nuevos Desafíos y Agenda de Trabajo*. Gabriel Aghón y Herbert Edling, eds. Santiago de Chile: CEPAL/GTZ.

6

Demilitarization and Security in El Salvador and Guatemala: Convergences of Success and Crisis

A. Douglas Kincaid

For most of the past quarter century, social scientists endeavoring to analyze the prolonged crises afflicting the Central American region shared a common problematic—how to explain the extraordinary range of variation in political processes within a confined and relatively homogeneous geographic space. For the majority of scholars, independent of their political outlooks, the analytical task was to identify the mix of variables that might simultaneously explain Costa Rica's democratic stability, Nicaragua's revolution, civil war in El Salvador that was not quite a revolution, Guatemala's insurgency and repression that did not quite constitute a civil war, and none of the above in Honduras (see, among others, Brockett 1998; Vilas 1995; Torres Rivas 1993; Williams 1986).

Among the many dramatic changes of the last decade of the twentieth century, therefore, the political panorama of Central America provides another—the challenge of accounting for convergence and similarity rather than divergence and variation. The two exemplary processes in this regard (and for Latin America in general, not just Central America) are democratic transitions and market-oriented economic policies (Korzieniwicz and Smith 1996; Smith, Acuña, and Gamarra 1994). Not that national and local differences in culture and social structure have dissolved or ceased to matter, of course, but in many ways the Central American countries in the 1990s are as noteworthy for what unites them as for what divides them.

The themes of this work, demilitarization and security, fit well within the new context of convergence. Contemporary challenges concerning security are similar from one end of Central America to the other; below I argue that the Salvadoran and Guatemalan cases correspond to a new model of public security that is widely shared across Latin America. Moreover, the more localized processes of demilitarization in the two countries appear to share a similar dynamic, once allowances are made for a five-year offset in the signing of the respective peace accords.

Any effort to examine the reasons for these wider processes of convergence would go well beyond the scope of this work, but they are worth noting as a means of locating a discussion of security issues in close relationship to other aspects of contemporary Central American development. Too often discussions of security issues such as demilitarization or civil-military relations proceed as if they were self-contained dynamics driven solely by the conflicting interests of the immediate actors, rather than as part of more general and complex processes of social change. The first section of this work presents some theoretical considerations and a brief historical summation in order to anchor a comparative analysis of security and demilitarization. The following two sections focus on El Salvador and Guatemala, respectively, in both cases beginning with reforms established in peace accords and then proceeding to a very preliminary evaluation of results. The fourth section proposes an interpretation of these experiences, specifically concerning problems of public security, within a comparative regional framework. The concluding section offers a few observations aimed at promoting debate over possible responses to an emergent security crisis.

Concepts and Antecedents

Both security and demilitarization are widely used terms with multiple meanings and connotations, and thus require some specification before they can be applied to a comparative analysis of specific countries. To begin with, three dimensions of security can be usefully distinguished for the purposes of this chapter—national, public, and citizen. National security, or more precisely the security of the national state, refers to the safeguarding of the state's sovereignty over the territory and population encompassed within its borders, and implies policies to confront any threat to that sovereignty. Public security is here understood as the maintenance of civil order necessary for the execution of basic societal functions (e.g., commercial transactions, transportation, or communication) as well as the upholding of the rule of law. Citizen security refers to the capacity of individuals and groups to enjoy or exercise the political, economic, and civil rights that correspond to the status of citizen in a given society.

Obviously these dimensions of security are interrelated in complex ways. For example, citizens may reasonably expect states to maintain public order (public security) as a prerequisite to the full exercise of their individual rights (citizen security), while governments are routinely confronted with the dilemma of determining when a given exercise of citizen rights turns into an unacceptable alteration of public order. At another moment, the dilemma may be over whether the deterioration of public security has become so severe that it threatens the effective sovereignty of the state—a perceived crisis of national security. In response, governments then commonly suspend or reduce certain rights of citizens, thereby creating a threat to citizen security.

To uphold security in its various dimensions, the state typically counts on a group of specialized bureaucracies and forces—among them, the armed forces or military, police forces, and the organizations responsible for the administration of justice. In modern nation-states, military forces are normally dedicated to the defense of national security, while police forces and the justice system are assigned to guarantee public and citizen security. To carry out these distinctive functions, military and police forces, although sharing the legitimate use of coercive force or violence, are typically differentiated in terms of organization, doctrine, training, and tactics, among other factors.

Nevertheless, inasmuch as the dimensions of security are intertwined, the functions of security forces also may cross these boundaries. In virtually all countries, for instance, there are constitutional or legal provisions allowing for the deployment of military forces in support or substitution of police forces in situations where the capacity of the latter is insufficient to prevent a collapse of public order, or to restore order where it has collapsed. Natural disasters and mass riots are two obvious examples of such situations. On the other hand, it is also common that in situations of large-scale insurrection or civil war, police forces are likely to be subordinated to military authority in contested areas.

If the above set of characteristics can be said to apply to most contemporary nation-states, at the same time it must be recognized that there is great cross-national variation with respect to constitutional bases, political systems, bureaucratic capacities, cultural practices, and other factors that influence the configuration of a particular state's security apparatus. In this respect, without entering into a lengthy historical discussion, we may observe that the majority of Latin American countries are characterized by close structural and functional relations between police and military forces (Bayley 1993).

Within this regional tendency, it is possible to distinguish certain subregional patterns (Kincaid and Gamarra 1994; Kincaid and Juhn 1994). One such pattern can be observed in the northern portion of Central America (Guatemala, El Salvador, and Honduras), where the establishment of national police forces occurred prior to the institutional consolidation of the armed forces. During the early phase of national state formation, toward the end of the nineteenth century, police forces were established to maintain the domination of large landowners associated with agro-export economies, and they subsequently served to uphold dictatorial regimes during the first half of the twentieth century. In this context, after military forces achieved institutional stability beginning around 1930, the military leadership sought formal authority over police institutions as part of its efforts to establish autonomy from partisan civilian political forces. National police forces were transferred to military-controlled defense ministries in El Salvador in 1945 and Honduras in 1963, and in both countries, as well as in Guatemala after 1954, military officers occupied the senior positions of command in the police.

Thus at the outset of the period of authoritarian military regimes, Central America was already characterized by policies that prioritized the security of the national state over public security (or more accurately, that identified public security with the security of the state (Aguilera 1989; Stanley 1996; Williams and Walter 1997). Meanwhile, concerns with citizen security were minimal. The subsequent rise of Cold War doctrines, above all that of the "national security state," only served to strengthen a set of prejudices and practices already in place in the region (see also Huggins 1998).

As a result both of the civil wars and other internal conflicts in Central America during the 1970s and 1980s, and the dramatic changes in the world political context after the 1980s, that national security doctrine has been wholly discredited. The processes of democratization and structural reform of security institutions in El Salvador and Guatemala, along with those of numerous other countries, have involved efforts to detach public security from its subordination to national security, and to valorize and give substance to concepts of citizen security.

One controversial component of these reforms is demilitarization, a term with multiple meanings that range from the simple exit of the military from the presidential palace to the complete abolition of the armed forces as an institution, along the lines of the Costa Rican model of 1948. If we conceive of demilitarization as broadly signifying a transition from the military dictatorships of the past toward a more democratic model of civil-military relations, we can identify several categories of changes applicable to the cases of El Salvador and Guatemala:

- *Peace*. This concerns the implementation of the peace accords that put an end to civil war; it includes the disarmament of guerrilla forces and the demobilization of military combat forces, giving way to the "normal" size and deployment of the armed forces in consonance with their mission.
- *Government*. This refers to the subordination of the armed forces to civilian control, with adequate oversight mechanisms in such areas as doctrine, budget, troop deployment, and so on.
- *Public administration*. This signifies eliminating military control of institutions and enterprises outside the bounds of their operations, and at the same time ending the practice of naming active military officers to head them.
- *Public security*. This implies establishing a clear distinction between the structures and functions of national defense and public security, as well as specifying the emergency circumstances and limits under which military forces may be committed to public security tasks.
- *Justice*. This points to the need to do away with the mechanisms and practices of impunity for the armed forces. Military justice systems will be confined strictly to matters of internal military conduct, again with adequate means of oversight, while crimes and abuses committed by military and police personnel will be prosecuted to the full extent of the law.

Based on the above concepts and theoretical and historical considerations, we may now evaluate the recent experiences of El Salvador and Guatemala.

The Case of El Salvador

The peace agreement signed in Chapultepec in January 1992 by representatives of the Salvadoran government and the Farabundo Martí National Liberation Front (FMLN) established the basis for drastic changes in the Salvadoran security forces. The mission and doctrine of the Salvadoran armed forces were redefined—their primary responsibility would be national defense, and their ability to intervene in matters of public security would be restricted to situations of national emergency, and then only under presidential authorization with prior approval of the legislature (Williams and Walter 1997). Military doctrine was to henceforth reflect democratic values, respect for human rights, and subordination to civilian authority.

Among other provisions, the accord set forth the following:

- Dissolution of a number of security forces, including the National Guard, the Treasury Police, and the National Police, and the creation of the National Civilian Police (PNC) under the authority of the Ministry of the Interior
- Disbanding of various components of the armed forces, specifically the Immediate Reaction Battalions and the civil defense patrols
- Dismantling the military intelligence apparatus and the creation of a new intelligence agency under civilian authority
- A 50 percent reduction in the size of the armed forces, from 63,000 to just over 31,000 persons
- Establishment of a new system of military education that would incorporate programs and mechanisms to promote the revised military doctrine
- Creation of an Ad Hoc Commission to evaluate the military officers corps and recommend the discharge of those individuals guilty of criminal acts, human rights abuses, and other misconduct in the course of the war

A calendar was established for the implementation of these measures, with the majority due to be carried out within a two-year period. During 1992 to 1993, the balance sheet of demilitarization showed both successes and failures. On the positive side, peace was maintained, the FMLN disarmed, and the armed forces demobilized their combat battalions and civil defense patrols—no small accomplishments after more than ten years of war. The army was reduced from 40,000 troops in 1992 to 28,000 in 1994, a diminution which, when combined with the separation of the public security forces from military control, achieved the numeric goal established in the peace accord. It may be noted, however, that even at the reduced level of troop strength, Salvadoran military forces remained at the highest per-capita level in Central America: 5.1 per one thousand inhabitants, compared with figures of 3.4 in Nicaragua and 3.2 in Guatemala and Honduras (Williams and Walter 1997).

On the negative side, there were delays in the dissolution of the old security forces, as well as in the formation and deployment of the new police force

(Washington Office on Latin America 1995; Stanley and Holiday 1996). The government also postponed implementing the recommendations of the Ad Hoc Commission, which had completed its work in September 1992. Various factors explained these delays—military resistance to the loss of control over the institutions and resources of public security, the left's distrust of efforts to incorporate ex-soldiers and members of the old security forces into the PNC, and the government's difficulty in amassing sufficient internal funds and external assistance to deploy the PNC nationwide. In this context, feeling pressured by a rise in criminal activity on the country, President Alfredo Cristiani authorized the participation of the army in patrolling national highways in July 1993.

Almost all of the obstacles to the implementation of the peace accords were resolved in an eighteen-month period beginning mid-1993, when the military high command was restructured in conformity with the recommendations of the Ad Hoc Commission, and the end of 1994, when the dissolution of the old National Police was completed. As a complement to these achievements, analysts of the peace process pointed to improved communication between military officials and civilian leaders, as evidenced in numerous seminars and conferences on security issues.

With respect to other indicators of demilitarization, however, there were a number of military prerogatives (cf. Stepan 1988) that were little affected by the peace accords. The latter made no mention, for instance, of the question of active-duty military officers heading state enterprises or agencies. Thus services such as telecommunications, water, ports, customs, and the post office continued as before under military leadership. The peace accord also did little to concretize the principal of civilian control over the military, since there were no measures specifying that the minister of defense be a civilian, nor giving the legislature effective control over military budgets, nor giving the executive control over the internal promotions of senior military officers. In all of these areas the Salvadoran armed forces were able to conserve a considerable degree of autonomy, even as the scope of their effective power was much reduced in the immediate postwar period.

Debate persists over what activities constitute appropriate military responsibilities in the new democratic context. One such issue concerns the intersection between the core military mission of national defense and the development challenges faced by the country after years of internal strife: Does the concept of national defense permit or imply an active military role in tasks associated with development programs? Spurred on by their U.S. counterparts, the armed forces began civic action programs in the 1960s and significantly increased such efforts during the civil war. In the 1990s, still with the support and participation of U.S. military forces, the Salvadoran armed forces have carried out health, education, and infrastructural repair programs in rural areas of the country, and have broached the possibility of new initiatives in the area of environmental protection. Opposition to such policies, particularly on the left, was quite vocal in the period after the signing of the peace accord, but it appears to have diminished in the late 1990s, perhaps because of a growing confidence in the stability of the peace process and democratic reforms.

Undoubtedly the principal problem affecting security in El Salvador in recent years is the increase of criminal activity and nonpolitical violence. Although reliable statistics on crime are scarce, above all if one wishes to compare current levels with those of wartime or prewar years, a generalized sense of crisis has emerged. According to a 1997 report in the *Miami Herald*, the country's homicide rate (140 per 100,000 inhabitants) was the highest in the world and more than five times greater than the Central American average (Garvin 1997). A year later, official government statistics indicated that the number of homicides was 8,019 in 1996 and 8,281 in 1997, while the number of injuries incurred as a result of reported crimes rose from 14,352 to 15,697 over the same twelve-month period (Guggenheim 1998).

Various reasons have been offered to account for the deterioration of public security (Garvin 1997; Guggenheim 1998; *Proceso* 1998b, 1998c). They include:

- the lack of adequate employment opportunities and concomitant rising poverty;
- the rapid demobilization after the war of combatants from both sides without adequate provisions for productively reintegrating them into society;
- the commercial circulation, legally and illegally, of large quantities of arms, including high-powered weapons; and
- the growth of criminal gangs in the country's principal cities, spurred by the return to the country, either voluntarily or by deportation, of young Salvadorans who had joined gangs in U.S. cities, particularly Los Angeles.

Another likely influence has been the importance of El Salvador (and Central America more generally) as a transshipment site in international drug trafficking, for which criminal networks offer an obvious base of support.

By the late 1990s, the PNC was active throughout the country, with just over 16,000 police personnel deployed in 219 sites as of 1998 (Secretaría de Comunicaciones 1998). Nonetheless, the army has continued to be called on periodically to support the PNC. In 1997 this included small-scale joint police and military deployments to deter crime in coffee-producing regions, and in 1998 the legislature began to debate whether or not to authorize the urban deployment of military forces as well (*Inforpress Centroamericana* 1998e).

The insecurity of the Salvadoran citizenry and their disaffection with government security policies are reflected in the results of a series of polls conducted by the University Institute of Public Opinion at the Universidad Centroamericana. One survey found that a majority of respondents (52 percent) agreed with the statement that individuals have the right to administer justice with their own hands (*Proceso* 1998b). In another survey, nearly three-quarters of the population (72 percent) thought that the government was not resolving the problem of crime; of these, nearly half (49 percent) thought it was because the government was doing nothing, while another 18 percent opined that the government could do nothing. In the same poll, only 29 percent of the 315 people who reported having suffered an assault during the first four months of 1998 said they had filed a complaint with the police (*Proceso* 1998a).

The postwar evolution of the Salvadoran justice system has been complex. The peace accord had relatively little to say about the institutional aspects of the administration of justice. The simultaneous implementation in 1993 of the Ad Hoc Commission's recommendations (retiring military officers involved in serious abusive conduct during the war) and a general amnesty (precluding individuals on both sides from being prosecuted for wartime offenses) made the question of military and police impunity for previous acts largely moot. In the ensuing years, denunciations of the abuse of authority have largely concerned the police, which, since 1994, has meant the civilian police. The 1998 conviction of five PNC agents for the 1995 beating and murder of a medical student in a suburb of San Salvador may be regarded as an important precedent in the effort to end impunity, although it followed a very controversial and drawn-out investigation that included unsubstantiated allegations of the criminal involvement of senior officials, including the Minister of Public Security (*Inforpress Centroamericana* 1998b).

During the same period, a long-delayed overhaul of the country's penal code was worked out and finally approved by the legislature in April 1998. The reform was noteworthy for measures that sought to strengthen the rights of the accused and protect individual citizen rights, such as the sanctity of private homes, from abusive public security practices, such as searches without judicial warrants (*Inforpress Centroamericana* 1998d). Taking effect in the midst of a perceived crime wave, however, the new code was immediately subject to a barrage of criticism from police authorities, private sector organizations, political parties, and other actors, which set in motion new legislative efforts to reform the reform and toughen its anticrime provisions.

The end of the 1990s clearly found El Salvador in a remarkably changed and, in many respects, better situation with respect to demilitarization and security than that of a decade earlier. With respect to negotiated conflict settlements and police-military reforms, the Salvadoran case was regarded by United Nations and other international actors as a major success story (Stanley and Holiday 1996). Yet new challenges had arisen to undermine citizen and public security.

Guatemala

In April 1991, as the Salvadoran peace negotiations neared their end, a similar process began to unfold in Guatemala. Like the civil war, however, which had been carried on with greater or lesser intensity for thirty-six years, the Guatemalan peace process was considerably more difficult and protracted than the Salvadoran case. The final agreement between the government of Guatemala and the Guatemalan

National Revolutionary Unity, signed in December 1996, followed a series of partial accords on specific sets of issues. Perhaps the most difficult set of issues concerned the restructuring of the missions, doctrines, and organization of security forces; the signing of this partial accord in September 1996 paved the way for the concluding document three months later. As in El Salvador, the result was a plan of far-reaching reforms across all three dimensions—national, public, and citizen—of security (Byrne 1996).

With respect to defining the peacetime mission of the armed forces, as well as other significant structural changes, a major obstacle was the country's 1985 Constitution, promulgated under the last military regime prior to the reestablishment of civilian rule. Among other measures, it assigned responsibility to the armed forces for both external and internal security. Thus the peace agreement called for the government to initiate a series of constitutional reforms that would include the redefinition of the military mission as the defense of the sovereignty and integrity of the national territory. A complementary objective would be to assign to the president, in times of emergency, the authority to utilize the armed forces to restore public order.

Other significant measures of the peace agreement affecting the military were a 33 percent reduction in military personnel within one year; the same reduction in the military budget by the end of three years; the closing of military bases and redeployment of troops in conformity with the revised military mission; and the conversion of various military institutions and units to civilian control and use (Byrne 1996; Garst 1997). Another provision called for the formation of a civilian Security Advisory Council to assist the president in setting security policies.

Similarly, the accords provided for a series of major reforms in the institutions and practices of public security. These included:

- the disbanding of rural forces under military control (specifically, the Mobile Military Police and the Voluntary Civil Defense Committees);
- the creation of a new police force, the National Civilian Police (PNC), under authority of the Public Ministry, to replace the existing National Police and other specialized forces;
- an increase in the number of police from 12,000 to 20,000 in the space of three years, along with significant salary increases;
- the participation of local communities in the recruitment and selection of personnel, such that the PNC would reflect the diversity of Guatemalan society;
- the establishment of laws to regulate private security firms and place control of arms possession under police authority;
- the establishment of a civilian intelligence department in the Ministry of the Interior and the creation of congressional oversight mechanisms for all intelligence agencies; and
- the creation of commissions to study the country's system for the administration of justice and make recommendations for its modernization.

Another important component of the peace accords was the stipulation that a Historical Clarification Commission be formed to investigate denunciations of crimes and rights abuses committed during the years of conflict. Unlike its Salvadoran counterpart, however, the Guatemalan commission was not given the right to determine individual responsibilities for any wrongdoing.

As in El Salvador, the first two years following the accords left a mixed record. Most notably, the constitutional reforms were delayed by numerous disagreements over specific provisions and were not approved by the legislature until October 1998. Thus in the interim the armed forces continued to operate under their previous broad mandate, a condition enhanced by the government's reliance on military units for major policing responsibilities, as described below. Interviews with military officers in 1997 revealed divided opinions over both the prospect of reduced roles and the nature of their public security assignments, leading one analyst to express strong skepticism that demilitarization was effectively advancing (Schirmer 1998).

Reports from the United Nations Verification Mission in Guatemala (MINU-GUA) (1998a, 1998b) demonstrated a cautious optimism in this area, noting that a number of mandated changes, such as the reduction of military forces, the disbanding of the Mobile Military Police and the local civilian defense committees, and the establishment of programs for the reintegration of former troops and agents in civil society had fulfilled the requirements of the accords. But they also noted areas where little had been accomplished, including the closure of military bases established for counterinsurgency purposes, redeployment of troops in accordance with the new military mission, and the transfer of intelligence functions from military to civilian hands.

Apart from the delay in amending the constitution, the principal explanation for the slowness of reform was a sense of crisis in the area of public security. Reliable data are again scarce, but the volume and violence of crime have become matters of constant public debate. Organized criminal activity in the areas of drug trafficking, kidnapping, extortion, bank robberies, and car theft, often carried out with the use of high-powered arms, has been especially visible (*Prensa Libre* 1998a). Youth gangs have proliferated in urban areas. According to police reports, some sixty gangs were operating in Guatemala City in mid-1998; among them were several chapters of the largest Salvadoran gang, Salvatruchas, allegedly organized by Salvadoran immigrants (*Prensa Libre* 1998b).

Whatever their true dimensions, there is little doubt that crime and violence have placed severe strains on the process of police reform mandated by the peace accords. Critics have noted a number of weaknesses in the accords with regard to the formation of the new PNC, most notably the absence of the oversight mechanisms and screening procedures for agent recruits that were one of the hallmarks of the Salvadoran police reform. Pressed by the need to respond rapidly to public security problems, the government made its priority the rapid expansion of police numbers, with more than half of the PNC cadres to be drawn from the old

National Police, a force generally acknowledged as corrupt, inefficient, and prone to abusive practices (see Aguilera 1993). By the end of 1998, the PNC numbered about 8,400 agents, of which 75 percent were so-called *reciclados* (personnel previously with the National or Treasury Police), and 25 percent were new recruits (*Inforpress Centroamericano* 1998a). At that point the new force had been deployed in only nine of Guatemala's twenty-two departments.

Elsewhere the old police force remained in place, and throughout Guatemala the government assigned a prominent supporting role to the army. Thus not only did the military retain significant policing responsibilities in rural areas, but it also acquired the task of participating in joint military and police patrols in the cities, for which soldiers often greatly outnumbered police agents (Garst 1997, Schirmer 1998). The Ministry of Defense reported in March 1998 that 11,000 troops were acting in support of the police (*Siglo Veintiuno* 1998). To support this deployment, several military bases scheduled to be closed were allowed to remain open. Military intelligence also continued to be employed in anticrime efforts, particularly through a specialized antikidnapping force.

A notable accomplishment during 1998 was the first step toward a more multi-ethnic police force. A group of agents of Ixil descent, newly graduated from the police academy, were deployed in the largely Mayan department of El Quiché (United Nations Verification Mission in Guatemala 1998a). Though small in proportion to ultimate goals in this area, it was an important symbolic accomplishment in the effort to establish closer police and community relations.

According to MINUGUA's evaluations (United Nations Verification Mission in Guatemala 1998a, 1998b), the process of reform in the administration of justice advanced during 1997 to 1998, albeit slowly. The Commission to Strengthen Justice completed its work and presented its report and recommendations for judicial reform in April 1998. An interagency Coordinating Unit for the Modernization of the Judicial Sector was convened in 1997 and began work during 1998 to develop plans for instituting reforms in the justice-related components of the Judicial Branch, the Public Ministry, and the Ministry of Government. Implementation and substantive results, however, awaited the approval of the constitutional reform package.

With respect to the issue of impunity, the recent record is less promising. As in El Salvador, the combination of the amnesty agreement that accompanied the peace accord and the restrictions placed on the Historical Clarification Commission precluded major prosecutions for wartime military offenses, although the vagueness of the enumeration of crimes covered by the amnesty left open some avenues of legal action. This was demonstrated most convincingly in the December 1998 conviction of three ex-Civil Defense Patrol agents for having participated in the massacre of some two hundred peasants in two separate military actions in 1982, during the height of repressive violence (*Inforpress Centroamericana* 1998c). The three, who received the death penalty from the court, were apparently the only clearly identifiable participants in a combined military and civil defense force unit estimated at three hundred individuals. Their conviction thus simultaneously signifies an important precedent toward ending impunity and the severe constraints impeding efforts to redress historic injustices.

A more immediate test would apply to police and military accountability during the contemporary period. Despite the abolition of the armed forces' *fuero* (immunity from prosecution in civilian courts) in 1996, prosecutions of senior military or police officials remained unknown, although numerous dismissals for suspected involvement in drug trafficking and other criminal activities were reported during 1997 (Garst 1997). More than any other incident, however, the murder of Bishop Juan Gerardi in May 1998 called into question the presumption that the era of impunity had passed. His death, two days after a Church-appointed commission he headed had released a report on human rights abuses during the war, raised widespread suspicion of military involvement, a view subsequently reinforced by the government's inept handling of the investigation (Rohter 1998). Whatever the true circumstances of the crime, the chain of events clearly demonstrated that the reform of Guatemalan security and justice systems remained elusive.

The reform process also had to cope with citizens' efforts to administer justice outside the law. Most notably, the practice of group lynching of suspected criminals became commonplace, especially in rural communities. During 1997, reported deaths by lynching, often for relatively minor offenses, occurred at a rate of one per week (*Inforpress Centroamericana* 1997). During the same period, a new clandestine organization announced its intention to execute kidnappers, thereby resuscitating the specter of the death squads that operated in Guatemala during the decades of conflict.

The Contemporary Challenge of Public Security

A comparison of demilitarization and security reforms in El Salvador and Guatemala in the period following their respective peace agreements shows some interesting differences. In the mechanisms for establishing a new police force, the Salvadoran accords paid much closer attention to the composition, screening, and training of the PNC, in an effort to ensure that the new force would be qualitatively distinct from the old. The Guatemalan accords, on the other hand, went further in specifying processes of judicial and intelligence reforms that would be important complements of police reform. These specific areas of emphasis are likely to influence the directions and rates of change in each case.

The variation is not surprising—though the Guatemalan reform process sought to model itself in part on the Salvadoran experience, each is the product of complex compromises among distinct political, economic, and social actors, both internal and external. In neither case should one expect the outcome to be a purely rational choice of ends and means.

Important similarities are also evident. In each country one may observe a successful redefinition of military and police missions and a significant diminution of military prerogatives, in conformity with a much more democratic model of civil-military relations. It may also be argued that the dynamic of the Salvadoran case offers a more optimistic view of the Guatemalan case than might otherwise be warranted by the events and problems of 1997 to 1998. Two years after the Salvadoran peace accord, numerous obstacles to demilitarization and security reform remained; five years afterward, most of these obstacles had been overcome. Thus, some of the seemingly intractable difficulties observable in Guatemala at the end of 1998 are very likely to fade in the near future. As opposed to an interpretation emphasizing the resourcefulness of the Guatemalan armed forces in defending their longstanding dominance of society (cf. Schirmer 1998), the argument here is that a variety of factors—such as external pressures, generational transitions of leadership, and growing assertiveness among new social actors—will make further demilitarization irresistible.

Nonetheless, a major caveat (and additional point of commonality between the two countries) concerns the contemporary crisis of public security. Quite evidently the demilitarization of politics has brought with it no guarantee of improved public security; rather the perceived rise of crime and violence in the 1990s has resulted in increased citizen insecurity and, as can be seen in both cases, a tendency toward "remilitarization." It is important to place this phenomenon in a wider context, however, because it is not limited to El Salvador and Guatemala. If the same range of problems and the same pattern of responses can be discerned in Brazil, Bolivia, Mexico, and even Costa Rica, then to argue that one or another additional clause in a Central American peace accord might have made a major difference is not convincing. Instead, the Salvadoran and Guatemalan experiences conform to what elsewhere has been described as a new Latin American model of public security (Kincaid and Gamarra 1996). It is better thought of as a modal pattern than a universal reality in the region, but the examples have been more and more frequent in the late 1990s.

The argument is fairly simple. Faced with the incapacity of the police and the justice sector to cope with existing levels of crime and violence, public security systems will fragment. Alongside the institutions formally responsible for public security, three alternative forms of action arise—militarization, informalization, and privatization.

Militarization here signifies the use of military forces in support or in place of the police. This practice began in the early 1990s in both El Salvador and Guatemala and, as was described above, has greatly expanded in recent years. Although it might be argued that this is a provisional measure while the new PNCs acquire full functionality, the frequency with which the same policy has been implemented in other countries raises considerable doubt about how temporary it might be in the cases at hand (see McSherry 1998).

In the same way that the informal sectors of an economy have been defined, the informalization of public security is here taken to mean the emergence of a set of public security services and activities that are unauthorized or unregulated by the state, and may well be explicitly illegal. This category encompasses such diverse phenomena as the formation of neighborhood watch committees, the spontaneous lynching of suspected criminals, the operation of death squads with or without clandestine military or police participation, and even the provision of public security by criminal organizations in urban neighborhoods or rural communities where they may exercise more authority than the state.

The third alternative, privatization, has not been discussed in this chapter but represents another growing dimension of public security. This refers to the growth of a security market, where individuals or organizations with the necessary resources can purchase the degree of security they desire. Obviously this option is not accessible to the majority of the population in countries such as Guatemala or El Salvador.

A variety of factors accounts for the weakened condition of formal public security institutions in Latin America. On the institutional side, the explanation must include ubiquitous deficiencies of police forces (training, organization, equipment, salaries, and so on) and also the institutional deformation of public security enacted by military regimes under the national security state doctrine (Chevigny 1995; Huggins 1998). In Central America, particularly in the cases of El Salvador and Guatemala, additional weight must be given to the consequences of bitter civil conflicts—social dislocations, the demobilization of combatants with few good employment prospects, and widespread black market circulation of military arms.

The roots of the problem run wider than political and institutional legacies, however. Emergent structural factors are also at work. The market-oriented economic policies adopted throughout the region to cope with the economic downturn of the 1980s provided few means of addressing the deterioration of the material welfare of major sectors of the population and a concomitant increase in social inequality. At the same time, the limitations imposed on redirecting (much less increasing) public expenditures and improving the bureaucratic capacity of the state constitute a major brake on a thoroughgoing reform and expansion of its public security institutions. In the view of Guillermo O'Donnell (1994, 1998), the result is that the rule of law does not extend uniformly across national territories or populations in Latin America, democracy is restricted to polyarchy (i.e., its formal political dimension), and citizenship remains incomplete (see also William Robinson 1996).

Another factor impinging on public security is the product of the globalization of crime, manifested in the growth of transnational criminal organizations or cross-border linkages among groups. Susan Strange (1996) argues that in the four structures of power in the international system—production, finance, information, and security—the once-dominant position of national states has been steadily eroding, with the seemingly privileged domain of security just as affected by transnational forces as the others. In the rise of Latin American drug trafficking cartels during the 1980s, the Central American countries became important transshipment points in the South American-U.S. trade routes, and soon suffered the consequences of growing corruption and violence (Linda Robinson 1994). More recently, the operation of chapters of a single youth gang in Guatemala City, San Salvador, and Los Angeles provides another striking example of this development.

Conclusion

There can be little doubt that, no matter how gradual, real progress in demilitarization and democratization has been achieved in the two countries under consideration here. In place of a dominant discourse of national security, which absorbed issues of public security and minimized matters of citizen security, the current discourse of security in Central America is focused on strengthening the structures and practices of citizen security and at the same time promoting new concepts of public security and national defense that reinforce those rights.

Nonetheless, a new crisis has loomed in juxtaposition to these successes. In the midst of real reforms, the deterioration of public security as directly experienced by much of the population is cause for worry. The dangers are not simply a matter of public insecurity, with observable economic and social consequences, but also the risks implied for the other dimensions of security. That is to say, if current tendencies persist or worsen, then the medium-run consequences are likely to be a reduction in the rights of individual citizens as well as a perception of a serious threat to the national state.

It seems appropriate to conclude, therefore, with a brief consideration of alternative strategies and policies for confronting the new crisis. Some, particularly those concerning state policies, are obvious. There is a widespread consensus, for instance, on the necessity of strengthening the police, including the size of the force, salary incentives, and the quality and duration of training. Acceleration of reforms in the administration of justice and increasing the state's capacity to control the circulation and use of arms are other important goals. By contrast, however, the generalized use of military forces to fight crime is a highly questionable long-term strategy, however attractive it may seem to government faced with immediate challenges. Military training is geared neither to investigative techniques nor to the correct forms of interaction with citizens in the course of police duties, so it seems unlikely that the presence of soldiers in the street will deter or reduce criminality or violence except as a deterrent in their immediate vicinity.

Strategies less exclusively centered on state policies should also be explored. Moving downward in organizational terms, the decentralization of the administration and exercise of public security functions—through the promotion of organizations in urban neighborhoods, rural communities, and other collectivities—may offer a double payoff. On the one hand, it might result in patterns of local participation that exercise a preventive impact on some forms of criminal activity, thus producing long-run savings in public budgets in addition to enhanced security.

On the other hand, it may serve to shore up citizen security by inhibiting the temptation to engage in lynchings and other exercises in "popular justice" at the expense of the rule of law. In one sense a decentralization strategy would be the equivalent of "formalizing" the informal sector.

Moving in the opposite direction, that is, strategizing above the state, one may also consider the creation of new forms of cooperation and integration among security forces across national boundaries. This type of collaboration is already well established in the military ambit; examples are the Central American Armed Forces Conference, set up in 1997 to replace the old Cold War-oriented Central America Defense Council, and the coordination of counter-narcotics operations under U.S. tutelage. At the level of police forces, however, such joint efforts are rare. In the present context of economic globalization, where criminal enterprises can avail themselves of the same innovative organizational structures and technologies as transnational corporations, a police response at the same level would seem logical.

In the long run, however, a development-centered strategy is needed. The design and implementation of new strategies for equitable and sustainable economic development will be of fundamental importance to lower the incentives that encourage illegal activities and alter the conditions that promote violent behavior. At the same time, the promising but incomplete reforms of military, police, and justice institutions will have to be deepened. Without such progress, the hard-won gains of peace and democratic citizenship in El Salvador and Guatemala remain at risk.

Works Cited

Aguilera, Gabriel. 1989. *El fusil y el olivo: La cuestión militar en Centroamérica.* San José: DEI.

———. 1993. Función policíaca y transición a la democracia: El caso de Guatemala. Paper presented at the conference Between Public Security and National Security: The Police and Civil-Military Relations in Latin America. Woodrow Wilson Center, Washington, D.C. (21-22 October).

Bayley, David. 1993. What's in a Uniform? A Comparative View of Police-Military Relations in Latin America. Paper presented at the conference Between Public Security and National Security: The Police and Civil-Military Relations in Latin America. Woodrow Wilson Center, Washington, D.C. (21-22 October).

Brockett, Charles. 1998. *Land, Power, and Poverty: Agrarian Transformation and Political Conflict in Central America.* Boluder, Colo.: Westview.

Byrne, Hugh. 1996. The Guatemalan Peace Accords: Assessment and Implications for the Future. *WOLA Briefing Series.* Washington, D.C.: Washington Office on Latin America.

Chevigny, Paul. 1995. *Edge of the Knife: Police Violence in the Americas.* New York: New Press.

Garst, Rachel. 1997. The New Guatemalan National Civilian Police: A Problematic Beginning. *WOLA Briefing Series: The Guatemalan Peace Process.* Washington, D.C.: Washington Office on Latin America.

Garvin, Glenn. 1997. Civil War Over, but Violence Goes On. *The Miami Herald.* <http://www.herald.com/docs/002366.htm>, 4 August.
Guggenheim, Ken. 1998 Ola delictiva ahoga paz salavdoreña. *El Nuevo Herald* (Miami) <http://www.elherald.com/digdocs/040844.htm>, 31 August.
Huggins, Martha K. 1998. *Political Policing: The United States and Latin America.* Durham: Duke University Press.
Inforpress Centroamericana (Guatemala). 1997. ¿Quién se encarga de la seguridad ciudadana? (31 October): 1-3.
———. 1998a. Complicados pasos para reestructurar la policía (6 November): 11.
———. 1998b. Concluye juicio a policías (23 October): 11.
———. 1998c. Condena a ex-PAC: Pequeña fisura en el muro de la impunidad (11 December): 8-9.
———. 1998d. Proponen reformas a Códigos Penal y Procesal Penal (31 July): 14.
———. 1998e. ¿Reformarán leyes penales? (19 June): 6-7.
Kincaid, A. Douglas, and Eduardo Gamarra. 1994. Police-Military Relations. In *Hemispheric Security in Transition: Adjusting to the Post-1995 Environment*, edited by L. Erk Kjonnerud. Washington, D.C.: National Defense University Press, 149-67.
———. 1996. Disorderly Democracy: Redefining Public Security in Latin America. In *Latin America in the World Economy*, edited by Roberto Patricio Korzeniewicz and William C. Smith. Westport, Conn.: Greenwood, 211-28.
Kincaid, A. Douglas, and Tricia Juhn. 1994. La seguridad pública en América Central: Perspectivas sobre las relaciones policía-militares. In *Los retos de la democracia*, edited by Leticia Salomón. Tegucigalpa: Centro de Documentación de Honduras, 33-56.
Korzieniewicz, Roberto Patricio, and William C. Smith. 1996. *Latin America in the World Economy.* Westport, Conn.: Greenwood.
McSherry, Patrice. 1998. The Emergence of "Guardian Democracy". *NACLA Report on the Americas* 33, no. 3 (November-December): 16-24.
O'Donnell, Guillermo. 1994. Delegative Democracy. *Journal of Democracy* 5, no 1: 55-69.
———. 1998. Polyarchies and the (Un)rule of Law in Latin America. Working Paper 254, Helen Kellogg Institute for International Studies, University of Notre Dame.
Prensa Libre (Guatemala). 1998a. Asaltos: bancos deben invertir más en seguridad <http://www.prensalibre.com.gt/noticias.asp?seccion=1&idnoticia=20040&showdate=418>, 30 September.
———. 1998b. Salvatruchas: los cazadores de la noche <http://www.prensalibre.com.gt/noticias.asp?seccion=1&idnoticia=16508&showdate=340>, 5 September.
Proceso (San Salvador). 1998a. La delincuencia y la ineficacia policial. No. 824 <http://www.uca.edu.sv/publica//proceso/proc824.html>, 30 September.
———. 1998b. La seguridad en las armas (I). No. 819 <http://www.uca.edu.sv/publica//proceso/proc819.html>, 26 August.
———. 1998c. La seguridad en las armas (II). No. 820 <http://www.uca.edu.sv/publica//proceso/proc820.html>, 2 September.
Robinson, Linda. 1994. Central America and Drug Trafficking. In *Drug Trafficking in the Americas*, edited by Bruce Bagley and William O. Walker III. New Brunswick: Transaction Publishers, 445-54.
Robinson, William I. 1996. *Promoting Polyarchy: Globalization, US Intervention, and Hegemony.* New York: Cambridge University Press.
Rohter, Larry. 1998. Cover-Up Charged in Killing of Bishop in Guatemala. *The New York Times*, 23 October.

Schirmer, Jennifer. 1998. Prospects for Compliance: The Guatemalan Military and the Peace Accords. *Working Papers on Latin America*, No. 98-99-1. The David Rockefeller Center for Latin American Studies, Harvard University.
Secretaría de Comunicaciones. 1998. Hemos aumentado de 4 mil a 16,181 policías entre 1994 y 1998. Centro de Información Internet, Presidencia de la República de El Salvador <http://www.casapres.gob.sv/newsv/apol8.htm>.
Siglo Veintiuno (Guatemala). 1998. Once mil militares proporcionan seguridad <http://sigloxxi.com/cgi-bin/s22/creator?file=hcgend01>, 7 March.
Smith, William C., Carlos H. Acuña, and Eduardo A. Gamarra. 1994. *Latin American Political Economy in the Age of Neo-Liberal Reform: Theoretical and Comparative Perspectives for the 1990s*. New Brunswick, N.J.: Transaction.
Stanley, William. 1996. *The Protection Racket State: Elite Politics, Military Extortion, and Civil War in El Salvador*. Philadelphia: Temple University Press.
Stanley, William, and David Holiday. 1996. Under the Best of Circumstance: ONUSAL and Dilemmas of Verification and Institution Building in El Salvador. Paper presented to Peacemaking and Democratization in the Western Hemisphere. North-South Center, University of Miami, Miami, Fla. 11-13 April.
Stepan, Alfred. 1988. *Rethinking Military Politics: Brazil and the Southern Cone*. Princeton: Princeton University Press.
Strange, Susan. 1996. *The Retreat of the State: The Difusion of Power in the World Economy*. New York: Cambridge University Press.
Torres Rivas, Edelberto. 1993. *History and Society in Central America*. Austin: University of Texas Press.
United Nations Verification Commission in Guatemala. 1998a. La situación en Centroamérica: Procedimientos para establecer la paz firme y duradera y progresos para la configuración de una región de paz, libertad, democracia, y desarrollo. Tercer informe. Reprinted in documento especial, *Inforpress Centroamericana* (Guatemala), 13 November.
———. 1998b. The Situation in Central America: Procedures for the Establishment of a Firm and Lasting Peace and Progress in Fashioning a Region of Peace, Freedom, Democracy, and Development. Second Report, A/52/757. United Nations, New York.
Vilas, Carlos M. 1995. *Between Earthquakes and Volcanoes: Market, State, and the Revolutions in Central America*. New York: Monthly Review Press.
Washington Office on Latin America. 1995. *Demilitarizing Public Order: The International Community, Police Reform and Human Rights in Central America and Haiti*. Washington, D.C.: Washington Office on Latin America.
Williams, Philip J, and Knut Walter. 1997. *Militarization and Demilitarization in El Salvador's Transition to Democracy*. Pittsburgh: University of Pittsburgh Press.
Williams, Robert G. 1986. *Export Agriculture and the Crisis in Central America*. Chapel Hill: University of North Carolina Press.

7

Democracy and the Market in Guatemala

Edelberto Torres Rivas
(Translated by William Robinson)

The current situation in Guatemalan is marked by a long-overdue process of democratic development and the legacy of an armed conflict that is only now being brought to a close. There are no longer any pretexts for the postponement of peace and democracy, but whether or not these goals can be achieved remains to be seen. Political democracy and economic growth are the issues that require immediate attention now because they go to the heart of the prolonged crisis in Guatemala and have been brandished both as an excuse to wage war and as a goal for achieving peace.

While forces committed to these goals no doubt exist it cannot be said that satisfactory progress is being made toward their achievement. The task of democratic development has been taken up by undemocratic forces. Disillusionment has become the principal obstacle to this complex historic challenge. There was never any doubt that political democracy could not come through the barrel of a gun. But neither could the defeat of popular forces provide an effective basis for political democracy.

If economic development and political democracy are the goals we wish to achieve, what social forces and what resources are available in this effort? To answer this question we need to identify how the conflict came to an end, to determine the social and political forces that emerged victoriously from these long years of conflict. In Guatemala, the country lost the war; the right won peace.

There is no doubt about what happened. All strategies to bring about revolutionary change in society and in politics failed. As a result the rebel forces have fully accepted the status quo. Proposals were included in the peace accords that leave room for certain modification of the status quo. But if these proposals were to be carried out their result would be not the transformation but the modernization of the current order, a strengthening of the "establishment." The end of the armed conflict involved a tacit acceptance of the existing economic and political system and in fact constitutes a contribution to the permanence of that system.

The peace negotiations took place at a very difficult time in which profound structural changes are under way worldwide. The market has been set free to determine growth at a time of expanding democratization and the triumph of liberal democracy, or what may be termed with guarded optimism as the "third wave" of democracy.

Peace Dividends

The problems of Guatemalan society have shifted to a new terrain in the postwar period. Much time has been lost in their resolution, and there are deep deficiencies. The actors are still the same but their role has been modified by the long years of confrontation. Has the landed oligarchy changed its feudal outlook and conduct? Have the middle classes developed a new political and social outlook by becoming modernized? The military retains its arsenal, its internal structure, its ethos as "guardians of the nation," and conserves its monopoly of violence as the state's coercive power. The peasantry remains largely landless. The essential class structure of an agrarian society has changed little.

How do we make sense out of this muddle? Can this constellation of social forces undertake the urgent tasks of modernity? A historic opportunity is before us. International forces have placed political change on the agenda. Yet these forces exercise a contradictory influence, pushing both political democratization and the supremacy of the market. The key now is in the quality of the democratic process and in the political dynamic that can be set in motion in the current conjuncture. Society can be changed despite the inertia that inheres in the class structure in which political actors are embedded, if these actors are willing to act, to see the way forward, to learn the lessons of the conflict, and so on. But this can only occur in a democratic environment.

The End of Counterinsurgency Power

Two analytically distinct processes were brought to a close in Guatemala through the peace accords: the armed conflict that had become a source of ongoing attribution; and a counterinsurgent military dictatorship as an authoritarian power in Guatemala that predated the guerrillas, going back four decades. The peace process in Guatemala is distinct from that of El Salvador, where a decade-long civil war ended because each side became convinced that it could not win the war. In Guatemala a lengthy negotiation process involving four different government administrations was undertaken in the face of the increasingly corrosive effects of a counterinsurgent state. The military state conducted systematic repression not only against the armed and the legal left but against any expression of social discontent, no matter how disorganized or incipient it was.

The inner details of the drawn-out negotiations have been revealed and studied elsewhere and will not be repeated here. After two decades of guerrilla struggle, from the 1960s to the 1990s, the left's ideology and program of revolutionary change underwent successive redefinition as ideals finally gave way to realism in 1997. When an insurgent force *negotiates* it does so within the framework of the enemy's system and therefore without the capacity to negotiate a transgression of the inner logic of the socioeconomic system it set out to transform. In defense of the logic of this system—the continuity of the traditional order, of its key actors, and of its legality—the government and the military at first opposed a political resolution of the conflict and insisted that negotiations were conditional on the guerrillas first laying down their arms. But as time went on, it became clear through dialogue that original positions were untenable and led to increasing convergence around points over which both sides could agree.

Counterinsurgency power as exercised by successive military governments was based on a Cold War conjuncture that facilitated a reactionary holy alliance in the 1960s between the military and the bourgeoisie placed on the defensive by the reformism of the Arbenz period, along with the middle classes, all with the blessing of the Catholic Church hierarchy. This counterinsurgency state began to unravel from 1982 to 1985 through an unusual transition to democracy. The signing of the peace accords put an end to the armed conflict and to the authoritarian model. The accords constitute a coherent program for social change and political modernization in Guatemala and represent, therefore, a historic turning point that cannot be reduced to a pact between the leadership of the Guatemalan National Revolutionary Union (URNG) and the Arzú government. They include a calendar for changes in the political and administrative structure of the state that, if implemented in the coming years, would alter the social and cultural fabric. They call for the modernization of economy and society. And recognition in the accords of the multiethnic and multilingual character of Guatemalan society is a triumph for multiculturalism.

Peace requires strengthening the democratization process that got off to a false start in 1982 and that now faces a new but equally difficult challenge. So long as the armed conflict continued, authoritarian elements saw to it that democratization was extremely limited. Now there are no more pretexts for political exclusion or for human rights violations. Peace and democracy are mutually reinforcing, even if the authoritarian inheritance still weighs heavily over the full enjoyment by all of political liberty and participation.

The Postwar Period: Democratic Consolidation?

The construction of liberal democracy has been coupled with that of unregulated market development. We are emerging from a period of conflicts with a weak state and a corporatist business class that has concentrated wealth and accumulated capital at the expense of the impoverishment of society. The middle classes are more divided than ever due to the economic crisis that has resulted for many in downward social mobility. The segmentation of popular classes has been aggravated by the spread of the informal sector, instability in urban employment, and rising unemployment. The peasantry remains mired in rural misery due to lack of land and is awaiting new opportunities that peace is unlikely to bring.

The greatest challenge is to reorganize and reactivate the domestic economy and reinsert it into the international market. This in turn requires new policies and urgent social reforms that have been postponed during the long years of economic crisis and war. The most urgent task is to reduce the poverty and informality that affect a great majority of the population and that have continued to grow despite an end to the conflict. The problem here is not just lack of resources for satisfying basic and secondary needs. It is as well the cultural backwardness evident in daily life, in interpersonal relations founded on a culture of fear, on a tradition of subordination and despair. It is evident in the state of abandonment of communities in the interior of the country, the complete lack of basic services, the lack of motivation among those who have become accustomed to living in filth and promiscuity. Overcoming the deterioration of social life, the lack of elemental solidarity in social relations, is the greatest challenge to peace and democracy, because both depend on the moral and cultural health of the immense majority.

No government has yet to responsibly face up to the problems of an unjust and authoritarian society since the military order began to crumble. Illusions have grown with each passing election. The impatience of popular sectors has been accumulating and has resulted in the spread of anomic, apolitical, and criminal violence. In any event, a just order cannot simply be willed into existence. The future of democracy depends on economic development, and the obstacles to economic development can only be overcome through an expansion of democratic development. This is the "Gordian knot" that postwar societies in Central America face.

Problems of Democratic Transition

Historic cycles of democratic change in Latin America have almost always come about as a result of the decadence of authoritarian policies rather than of the collapse of authoritarian structures or the definitive withdrawal of authoritarian actors. In Guatemala, the transition is less the result of democratic forces than of the weakening of dictatorial structures. Some speak, therefore, of "cycles" and Huntington has popularized the notion of "waves." Democracy has not developed because avowedly democratic forces and processes have snuffed out dictatorial forces, but rather as part of counterinsurgent strategies that have sought to win civil wars by political means.

When democratic forces are not able to influence or determine substantial political change, the resulting democratization is limited and consolidation of a democratic regime becomes problematic. Currently the electoral game has become an end in itself. It is limited to relatively open competition among political elites little concerned with establishing mechanisms of social representation. This electoralism momentarily satisfies the sense of democratic participation among majorities and stunts the more elemental development of citizenship. The democratic process lacks a solid social foundation capable of weakening authoritarian controls, a sine qua non condition of democracy. Here we need to distinguish, as some have, both democracy by decree, or "from above," and democracy as a result of the active mobilization of social forces "from below."

The weakening of authoritarian forces does not necessarily imply the strength of democratic forces but rather the creation of vacuums that are not easy to interpret. Under such circumstances governments demonstrate a singular weakness vis-à-vis military power or intransigent business sectors that do not like to pay taxes. Historical circumstances have placed at the leadership of the democratization process social forces that are not exceptionally democratic. The right has seized power legitimately for the first time in our history for the simple reason that the left could not win. We thus have the paradoxical situation in which the democratic transition is led by nondemocratic actors who do not believe in democratic values and do not practice them.

This complex scenario is not easily explained by transition theories. Political openings and liberalization occurred in times of war. These conflicts generated the conditions for democratization as a strategy of war. Negotiations and peace were less a result of popular pressure than of strong international pressure, accompanied by offers of financial aid.

A Second Transition to Consolidate Democracy?

Can we speak of a second transition, in the wake of the end of the conflict, in the process of democratization or democratic development? The beginning of the transition, most agree, began when fissures within the military led to the coup d'etat against the Lucas regime. The armed conflict continued, but the military hierarchy from that point on facilitated a certain controlled political opening that involved not only elections but also minimal political freedoms that a vote required, the return of democratic leaders, opposition organizing, open public debate, civil rights, and so on.

These changes are authentic, but the highly visible success of electoral cycles has concealed weaknesses in the democratic process. Political democracy has advanced further than economic democracy. Transitions never occur in isolation, and the transition to democracy has not been as problematic as the transition to a market economy. To the extent that the market has privileged entrepreneurs, the democratic process has turned them into politicians, resulting in a convergence of political and economic elites around corporate interests expressed in the political game. Cristiani, Lacayo, Arzú, Alemana—these Central American heads of state personify the duality of political and economic interests. It is clear that the new dominant groups are attempting to reorganize the nations they lead in their own interests.

This situation is not favorable to democracy, because the corporatist dynamic confuses public with private interests. In agrarian societies market forces are easily manipulated through the exercise of political power for specific economic interests. Democratic culture strengthens the universalist image of state policies as public welfare. This pathological syndrome of power takes may demented forms. One is widespread corruption, or the use of political power for personal gain on the part of those that peddle influence as well as those who purchase it. Corruption is a phenomenon of the market as well as of politics. Behind each corrupt official we invariably find a rogue entrepreneur. Democracy cannot be consolidated so long as corruption is rampant, which sows distrust of public life.

It is not clear that the transition has come to an end and that, therefore, democratic consolidation is now taking place in Guatemala. The rules of the democratic game now occupy the center of debate. The holding of several free and fair elections suggests that the process has become institutionalized. But how many of these elections do we require to reach such a conclusion? The institutionalization of elections is certainly a key marker, as this requires functioning parties, institutions, a citizenship, the ability to mobilize, a capacity for conflict resolution, and so on. Are all these conditions, in fact, in place?

Politics, the State, and the Market

Globalization in the international realm has placed in positions of leadership and control those entrepreneurs closest to finance and speculative capital. In fact, these propertied groups dominate the political and the economic scene in detriment to industrial capital. Let us recall that industrial output has been stagnant for a decade now and investible productive capital is in short supply. We can note the contradiction between the effort to consolidate political democracy at a time when monopolistic speculative and bank/finance capital is consolidating its hegemony.

The proclamation of market freedom and the opportunity to participate in the market in equal conditions have resulted in a discourse among the business elite and the most conservative sectors centered on the rhetoric of political equality and freedom of participation. In the past, democracy and the market never went together, but today it seems that they are compatible so long as the market can maintain its autonomy from politics. The self-regulating market and the corporatist state have converged in a reversal of the traditional pattern that frustrated efforts in the past to achieve democracy and development.

But democratic practice involves a politics that brings a politically active citizenry as subject into a political arena in such a way that it can develop its potential. Democratic consolidation, given the legacies of Guatemalan society, has to occur at different levels. Politics is above all the chance to compete for power, but state power is not the sole end of politics. There are also diverse forms of participation in public life as the pursuit of particular interests that are articulated through an established civil society. And there is also participation in the market, in which people may act as producer and consumers with the understanding that economic growth will generate the conditions for social mobility.

Crucial to the development of a politically active citizenry is the successive broadening of public participation, guided by the constitutional rights and laws that regulate this participation. Citizenship is constructed and a democratic system becomes consolidated to the extent that political institutions and the opportunities are opened up through the exercise of corresponding rights. The peace accords place great emphasize on popular participation in order to consolidate peace and democracy. But little has been achieved.

Democratic development is the creation of a society in which active citizens are free to organize in pursuit of diverse private interests that collective life generates, citizens who are informed, who can express their views, and who can participate in numerous other ways in accordance with the diverse roles involved in cultural, political, and social life. This presupposes a critical public arena in which citizens may influence state policies in conditions of freedom and security for all, without any restrictions other than those established by law and the rights of others. Citizenship, it is clear, is a political phenomenon, and its ultimate point of reference is the state.

Democratic rhetoric, given the authoritarian origins of this postwar society, has focused on the need to increase citizen participation. Participation cannot be reduced to the act of voting, as the instrumental definition of democracy suggests. Suffrage is the most important expression of political participation, but it is not the only. Freedom of expression through the act of voting, of electing, is of decisive importance in establishing the political equality of citizens before the state and in the face of inequalities that the market produces.

As the Central American experience is demonstrating, voting is the easiest form of participation and is, as a result, often the only form that is practiced. And even at that, electoral abstention is a problem. In Guatemala a third of the population does not register to vote, something that has not occurred in the other countries. The number of voters as a percentage of those eligible to vote has declined, as has the number of registered voters who actually turn out to cast a ballot. The 54 percent abstention rate in the last presidential elections in Guatemala was the highest in the region. There is another kind of abstention, which we can call withdrawal from political life: the absence of organizing to make demands and to mobilize in the face of the alarming increase in poverty and inequality. Nicaragua is the exception here, in which electoral abstention is minimal and popular struggles have not diminished.

There are other public spaces in which class inequalities result in an unequal distribution of political roles, of the use of civil rights, and of access to institutions. In societies marked by deep socioeconomic and cultural inequalities and pervasive violence, or with an absence of security, the right to vote loses its importance. Let us recall the demobilizing effects that fear has generated in many communities in the region.

The social structure creates sectors with different levels of interest in democracy and undercuts the development of a democratic center. In democratic development the nature of the state and the market are of decisive importance. We lack an understanding of the role that the state and the market must place in a democratic polity in the development of citizenship and therefore of democracy. This issue has received scant attention in Guatemala.

Is Guatemala progressing toward democracy? There is, without doubt, a process of democratic development in accordance with the particular national legacy upon which it is taking place. There have now been three presidential and parliamentary elections. The institutionalization of elections would suggest that the transition is coming to a close and that the new political regime is becoming stabile. But the institutional stability of this regime is not the same as democratic consolidation.

Democratization is taking place through state structures that in diverse ways reflect the country's cultural limits and possibilities. Democratic development significantly involves the state. Democracy does not necessarily become established from and in society, as if what took place within civil society were the sole determinant of a democratic state. The reverse is true as well. Historically, it is often the case that the state democratizes society. Indeed, there can be no political democracy with a strong and democratic state.

The free market creates highly heterogeneous societies characterized by unequal levels of productive development and technological assimilation and an asymmetric distribution of the social product. This heterogeneous structure, characterized by inequality, polarization, and antagonistic relations, implies an unequal distribution of prospects for political involvement and the exercise of public rights on the part of the citizenry. Most citizens are insolvent consumers, are unable to pay taxes, and do not vote.

In sociological terms, the free market results in the economic and social distortion of the public domain in which juridically equal citizens (as established by the Constitution) operate. Only a part of the population ends up participating in the political and cultural system, and such participation does not involve full equality of opportunity. So long as participation is limited to an elite, the state will be weak and not very democratic. The inverse of this situation is a strong state that limits the anarchy generated by a self-regulated market.

The experience of recent years underscores the importance of a strong state as an integral component of democratization. But the dynamic has resulted in the exact opposite. Since the early 1980s, coinciding with the erosion of authoritarianism, Guatemalan society has undergone a difficult period of macroeconomic adjustment aimed at curbing inflation, fiscal solvency, the liberalization of prices, a reduction in social spending, and deeper reforms, including trade liberalization, market deregulation, privatization, and so forth. The particular manner in which this adjustment has unfolded has resulted in a further weakening of the state, which had already been drained of its vitality by the military conflict.

The most urgent task is the modernization of the state. This necessarily requires, far from a further reduction of its authority and institutionality, that the state be strengthened. We need a power to unify the nation, to integrate it by overcoming the current regional, social, and ethnic segmentation. The authority of the state needs to be respected and backed by solid social support, so that it can collect taxes and impose its measures on the bastions of private power in the country—namely, the military and the giant national and international corporations.

A regression to authoritarianism does not seem likely. Forces favorable to democracy are becoming stronger even though the process is unbalanced. It is of considerable importance in this regard that a fraudulent election or an attempted coup d'etat would run up immediately against the forces of "international accountability," since we all know that clean elections are a condition for international financing. Transitions are accomplished with considerable external support of diverse forms. We might hope that consolidation, if it is to occur, would be achieved through a national effort that provides an internal guarantee of democracy.

8

Coffee and the Guatemalan State

Stephen G. Bunker

The hand of the past sits heavy on Guatemala's present. Incompletely demobilized revolutionary armies must negotiate the implementation of complex peace accords with a national state, a national army, and powerful business and land-owning classes after decades of brutal warfare and aborted promises of economic reform. Implementation of the accords depends ultimately on initiatives by a state notorious for appropriating land and oppressing labor in the interests of a small and powerful oligarchy.

The predilections of the state and of dominant classes for inefficient plantation and ranching systems have concentrated the use of natural resources on two highly opposed poles, one of land-extensive exploitation dependent on seasonal migrant labor, the other of labor-intensive cultivation of small plots on steep slopes and fragile soils. State policies support dominant class control over land and labor; but the state has sometimes attempted to resolve class conflict and deflect protests by grants and concessions of land to various groups. Class struggles over land and labor lead to degradation of the environment both by forcing the majority of the rural population into dependence on insufficient marginal land and by prompting the state to emphasize the political rather than the economic uses of land.

Environmental degradation in Guatemala and the failure of the Guatemalan state to protect the environment are in many ways typical of many countries with mountainous topography, a dense, rapidly growing, and increasingly impoverished rural population, and markedly uneven distribution of land tenure. Like many other such countries, Guatemala has a long history of environmental legislation, dating at least from the 1950s. The state has created numerous agencies to deal with the environment but has given none of them adequate funding, staffing, authority, or continuity. Guatemala has been the target of various international programs and pressures to establish conservation reserves and to include environmental protection in its development programs. Its government is subject to criticism and pressure from local and international nongovernmental organizations (NGOs) to establish and fund new environmental initiatives. Also, like many other such countries, Guatemala experiences multiple powerful claims from different domestic classes and from foreign states and firms for access to environmental resources. Ranchers, loggers, miners, oil companies, tourist agents, and small farmers all make claims to land that environmentalists wish to see protected.

In Guatemala, these very typical problems are compounded by the tremendous ecological diversity of the national territory. Traditional dense occupation of the fertile but fragile mountain slopes contrasts with the much more sparsely populated humid, tropical, relatively flat but quite infertile soils of the Petén. The apparent relative autonomy of the military, whose members have often made their own strong claims to natural resources in environmentally fragile lands, poses further difficulties. Economic crisis, political violence, and the resettlement of refugees intensify the pressure for land, while the state's own fiscal and political weakness limits its will to control access to the environment and its logistical capacity to do so.

The political uses of land and labor that the Guatemalan state has promoted and protected create a serious barrier to integrated management of the environment. Unless the state changes its own political use of land and labor, all environmental programs are doomed to repeat the lack of continuity and sustainability that has characterized these efforts. The fundamental dilemma is that most programs for protecting the environment require that the state deny access to powerful claimants to natural resources, including land. Effective environmental programs would therefore require the state to limit its own potential revenue base, alienate constituents to whom it could otherwise dispense access as a form of patronage, and increase its own administrative costs. The problems of implementation are particularly severe, as much of the international pressure, and a good deal of domestic interest as well, is for preserving sparsely settled land, which has the least developed transport and communication infrastructure and is therefore more costly to administer.

Under these circumstances, the most likely outcome is that only those programs that are externally driven, that is, by the World Bank or the United States Agency for International Development (USAID), will be implemented at all. Such programs tend to be formulated by generic goals and may have relatively little to do with either the most pressing ecological problems of the country or with the ability of the state to carry them out. For example, the most active and certainly the most heavily funded programs in Guatemala now are the Man and the Biosphere programs, which essentially aim to remove all economic activity from reserved areas and to heavily control activity in areas surrounding them. To the extent that these areas are being occupied because of demographic, economic, and ecological problems in other parts of the country, programs that aim to conserve sparsely settled areas may divert attention and resources from the root problems and further discredit the state.

In summary, the circumstances in Guatemala at present seem extremely unfavorable for ecological preservation. First, successful environmental policies are extremely rare in countries like Guatemala. Second, the Guatemalan state has undertaken a series of commitments in the recent peace negotiations that is demonstrably beyond its present fiscal and administrative capacities. Third, the major external, either bilateral or multilateral, agencies with power and resources in Guatemala now are primarily interested in promoting neoliberal political and economic policy; their approach to the environment is to segregate limited areas from economic activity or occupation.

In the face of Guatemala's history of exploitation of both land and labor, and of the present influence of neoliberal ideologies that tend to treat each social and environmental problem as discrete, it probably appears quixotic to even discuss a comprehensive and effective program to deal with the multiple ecological problems the country now faces. There are good reasons to do so, however. The first and most obvious is that, without such a program, Guatemala's environmental problems will only get worse. The second is that the recent peace accords have focused international and national attention on Guatemala's economic and social problems in a context in which violently opposed social classes and groups have surprised themselves and each other by debating and partially accommodating their differences (see Jonas 2001; Warren 2001). The third reason is that the conditionalities imposed on Guatemala by market-oriented donors, creditors, and investors using neoliberal criteria to guide their interventions in the Guatemalan economy might, under the appropriate circumstances, provide effective pressures for more sustainable uses of land available to a much larger proportion of the population. In order to analyze what these circumstances might be, we must examine how the historical struggles of labor and capital over land and production have created the present political economy and whether the neoliberal agenda of international agents currently operating in Guatemala can be manipulated.

Guatemala's environmental crisis is a direct result of conflicts between capitalist and laboring classes and of the ways that the state used access to land to mediate these conflicts. To the extent that negotiations over the implementation of the peace accords have raised the possibility of modifying historic relations of land, labor, capital, and the state, the present moment is as propitious as any for including the integrity of land in the attempts to reorganize these relations. The exogenous agencies most powerful and most active in Guatemala are formally committed to free trade. The logical justification for this commitment lies in Ricardian claims of comparative advantage. The idea of comparative advantage in turn rests on the assumption that nations should exchange those products that they produce best and most cheaply. Agencies committed to maximizing comparative advantage should be willing to provide pressure or resources for changes in land use and in land use policies that limit comparative advantage.

The patterns of land use that have resulted from the state's mediation between labor and capital are antithetical to market-based rationality. If the international agencies working in Guatemala impose conditionalities compatible with free trade, they should also promote allocations of land, labor, and capital responsive to market signals rather than to class privilege and state power. The differentiation of coffee prices, which have been downward for bulk but sharply upward for small batch varietals of high quality, creates a situation in which the neoliberal agenda of the international agencies can be used to foment reforms in land tenure, access to credit, and entry to markets. This favorable conjuncture is specific to Guatemala; soils and climate there are apt for growing excellent coffee, and small family farms with self-disciplining family labor are most appropriate for the close quality control that excellent coffee requires. If successful, such a strategy could simultaneously promote ecological integrity and social equity.

Neoliberal strategies for separating political and economic programs in what William Robinson (2001) calls low-intensity democracy under polyarchy may critically limit the long-range possibilities for equitable development, but these neoliberal strategies are potentially more progressive than the market-insensitive distribution and exploitation of the factors of production that currently structure the economy. The present intersection of global markets and Guatemala's economic structure opens the possibility of new economic forms that would significantly improve the relation between economy and ecology.

Envisioning a comprehensive and integrated program to conserve the environment and to achieve sustainable ways to exploit its resources requires that we imagine new ways of structuring the relations of state and society to land and resources. The lines of tension between landed and laboring classes in Guatemala are currently so charged, and the state remains so enmeshed in its historical relations to these classes, that any effective restructuring probably requires significant pressure from powerful exogenous agencies. If these agencies restrict themselves to ensuring unencumbered flows of capital and commodities across national borders and to generic formulas for limiting the human occupation of select natural sites, the class conflicts at the root of environmental degradation will remain unchanged. It is therefore incumbent on politically engaged actors in both national and international arenas to imagine strategies and projects that simultaneously fit the neoliberal agenda and promote more equitable allocations of land and labor.

Most of the effective impetus for environmental protection comes from external development agencies and from international NGOs. These international agents must be made to see that if they wish to preserve the ecological integrity of Petén and the Sierra de Minas, they must confront as well the social and economic pressure that makes these areas vulnerable to degradation. The question must therefore become: What are the pressures within Guatemala that lead to environmental degradation, and what can be done about them? The answer must consider the nature of the Guatemala state, as it is not only the legitimate implementer of environmental legislation and programs, but is also the ultimate arbiter of claims to resources in the national territory.

Ricardo's dictum that the distribution of control over land, labor, and capital constitutes the study of political economy can also be applied to the study of political ecology, which must be the first step in the assessment of how a nation uses or abuses its physical environment. The Guatemalan state was formed in the crucible of the coffee economy. Even though the central position of coffee in the national economy has diminished as other export crops such as cotton and cattle have expanded, the state continues to use habits, techniques, skills, relationships, and institutions that it learned or invented in the struggles that the coffee economy engendered over land, labor, and capital. Thus, even as the economy changes, coffee continues to mold the institutions and policies that shape social uses of natural resources.

Guatemala is not the only country whose state and policies reflect the peculiar land, labor, transport, or financial requirements of its major raw material export. Recent studies of how dominant export sectors mold the state may be useful to considering what options are available for environmental protection and may be relevant to other issues addressed by the authors in this book. After a lapse of over half a century, a small but persuasive group of political scientists and economists is reconsidering the ways that primary commodity exports may determine the political, economic, and social institutions of the national economies they dominate. The primary stimulus to "commodities-based" or "sectoral" analyses was the remarkably rapid and profound collapse of the principal oil-dependent economies following the exuberant inflow of petrodollars after 1973.

Preliminary, and largely economistic and monetary attention, to the so-called Dutch disease (Corden and Neary 1982) was followed by more institutionally oriented, though still highly monetarist, notions of a "resource curse" and a "staples trap" (Gelb 1986; Auty 1989). Analysts of the Dutch disease have shown that a sudden influx, or windfall, of strong foreign currencies led to extreme overvaluation of domestic currencies, the consequent loss of competitiveness in all sectors outside the booming export, and a tendency for available capital to flee into nontradables, especially real estate, with consequent inflation. The resource-curse and staples-trap analysts have paid more attention to the ways that the multiple demands on the state for the redistribution of more funds than the economy can absorb, or the bureaucracy can manage, corrupt and degrade the state itself, leaving it vulnerable to instability as demands for patronage from different classes and sectors outstrip its own coffers.

Two recent studies of Venezuela (Karl 1997; Coronil 1997) have argued convincingly that the state's inability to buffer the sudden flood of revenues was rooted in the ways that the state was formed. The Venezuelan state emerged from the flows of international revenues that came to a specific place, the place that the oil emerged from the ground. In that sense, the oil as it flows from the ground and oil as it enters international trade provide both the opportunity to form a national state and the source of that state's power, but also set the institutional requirements for the state's collection of revenues, distribution of revenues, and regulation of access to the soil. The state thus is formed in the crucible between the oil in its national soil and the international capital that sought to extract and market it. For both of these authors, the Venezuelan state was significantly the creature of oil, and its institutions reflected not merely its status as rentier state, but also the very nature of oil and of its market.

Path dependencies emerged not simply from vested sectoral and class interests, but also from the limitations of a state bureaucracy whose primary function was the allocation of oil revenues. The state collected these revenues as rents on resources extracted rather than as a share of profits produced. Dependence on rents impeded the state from learning or implementing the disciplines and skills that states dependent on production must use to adjust to new economic circumstances.

The dramatic boom and bust of the oil economies in the 1970s and 1980s made their problems particularly visible, and there is now a robust literature about the impact of oil on state formation. There is also a somewhat more modest literature emerging about the ways that coffee, another widely traded commodity and a black liquid as well, affects political and social institutions.

William Roseberry (1995) claimed that there were so many historical solutions to the problem of "la falta de brazos" (shortage of labor) that no claim could be made for any technical determination of labor relations in the nature of the coffee plant itself. More recent authors have noticed that the peculiarly high and irregular labor demands of coffee, the limited types of soil in which it will yield high-quality cherries, and its long term to mature production set a very narrow range of possible solutions to the relations between land, labor, and capital; and that these solutions seem always to require the active intervention of the state.

While these ideas would not surprise Central American historians and social scientists such as Edelberto Torres Rivas and Severo Martinez, their contemporaneous emergence with parallel analyses of oil- and mineral- exporting national states (see Shafer 1994) may allow a fuller elaboration of their relevance to the Guatemalan state, arguably molded in many of its institutions by its mediation between labor, land, and capital in coffee production as that state confronts a new series of challenges. This chapter considers how these older institutional determinants may affect the state's will and ability to intervene to protect the natural environment, though I believe this is only one sphere in which social and political forms, ideas, and attitudes formed in an earlier time may continue to constrain current policy and implementation options.

Comparative analysis of coffee-dominated economies suggests that both capital and the state are severely constrained by the characteristics of coffee as a crop and as a marketed commodity. Coffee is attractive both because of relatively high prices and because it is only moderately perishable, and so it can be transported considerable distances at a cost that is low relative to value. This allows remote areas to be incorporated into the cash economy in ways that significantly expand the state's revenue base.

The state therefore tends to promote the cultivation of coffee as extensively as possible. High-quality coffee requires certain types of soil, climate, and elevation. It also requires high inputs of labor on a very irregular schedule around the year. These labor inputs must be sustained for up to six years before trees start to produce, so coffee is a peculiar crop in that it imposes high capital barriers to entry and to exit, even though it is labor-intensive. Coffee plantation owners, therefore, require cheap labor available on an intermittent basis. In this sense, coffee tends to immiserate completely any labor force that depends upon it for wages, so the only way to assure access to labor for coffee is either through coercion or through smallholders' control of their own lands.

For this reason, in order to promote the maximum extension of coffee cultivation, most states have intervened to assure access to this labor. State solutions to the problem of labor have varied according to both geography and demography. Brazil, with a vast area of potential cultivation, promoted a liberal immigration policy, in which *colonos* were attracted in part by the possibility of moving on to open new parts of the coffee frontier (Font 1995). In parts of Costa Rica and Colombia, small holders using family labor across multiple crops were a partial solution. In Salvador, land suitable to coffee cultivation was tightly concentrated within a small territory and favored a nearly total expropriation of land from indigenous populations, leading to their fairly complete semiproletarianization.

Guatemala confronted a peculiar combination of relatively scattered areas appropriate to coffee but remote from existing population centers, with large areas available that were not appropriate to coffee but did contain significant indigenous populations (Williams 1994). In Guatemala, the fact that most of the best coffee lands were not those that sustained dense indigenous populations permitted relatively easy establishment of large plantations. Small farms were established, but only in those areas of previous indigo production, where communities integrated into an export economy had developed some transport infrastructure. While the long maturation process required for coffee did promote interests in the alienation of land as private property in order to assure continued control of investment, the major constraint faced by the large plantations was a shortage of labor.

The state responded to this requirement with a series of labor drafts and labor laws that essentially required communities to provide certain amounts of labor and later imposed restraints on "vagrancy." The premium placed on labor, however, did tend to make those coffee-suitable lands closest to indigenous communities more attractive, so that coffee growers sustained pressure for access to those lands as well. The combination of labor coercion and land expropriation prompted widespread and persistent indigenous resistance, while the relative abundance of land outside the coffee-growing areas made indigenous flight or evasion of labor drafts and other coercive forms an option.

Robert Williams (1994) argues that a strong military with considerable administrative authority in rural areas resulted directly from the state's intervention in the struggle between plantation owners and indigenous communities over land and labor. Not only did the state use the military to repress resistance, it also made occasional grants in land to indigenous communities in order to prevent rebellion. In the process, it preempted the municipal authorities that had originally controlled access to land and to labor. Williams argues that the state created itself, its primary institutions, and its own customary attitudes and responses to new opportunities and crises in this process. The state formed a habit of appropriating land to itself and redistributing it to both planters and indigenous communities in order to achieve the expansion of the national economy, to serve the interests of the coffee plantation owners who at first controlled it and then used it to assure their continued control even when they no longer held formal office, and finally to avoid resistance when politically necessary. Williams goes on to show that the patterns of response established during the coffee boom persisted through the twentieth century, in the repression of labor during economic crises, in the state's support for the appropriation of land for sugar, cotton, and beef, and in its sporadic use of small-holder colonization and migration when it perceived threats from peasant resistance.

In marked contrast to El Salvador, growers and the state were apprehensive of indigenous resistance, in part, due to the legacy of Rafael Carrera's successful attack on the Gálvez government and other local rebellions through the nineteenth and early twentieth century (Cambranes 1985; Lynch 1995; McCreery 1995). Correctly or not, Carrera's campaigns of 1838 and 1839 and his subsequent thirty-year dictatorship were seen by ladinos as an indigenous victory. "El Indio" Carrera, even though co-opted by urban and criollo classes during his regime, remained a vivid presence in the minds of later coffee elites and the coffee-dominated state and thus effectively impeded the full implementation of the liberal reforms. Even the second generation of liberal reforms started by Barrios in 1870 moderated the sale of private lands and coercive labor laws with grants of land to indigenous communities.

In some cases, communities were able to buy land back (Goldin and Saenz de Tejada 1993). Thus, the most notorious solutions of the state to the labor problem—a series of coercive labor laws such as the *mandamientos* and vagrancy laws, and effective debt peonage—occurred simultaneously with land grants to indigenous communities and the continued ability of these communities to acquire additional land. The critical point here was that there was additional land to be had, although, as populations increased, this land was increasingly marginal, both spatially and in terms of fertility.

Coffee plantations were larger, and their productivity lower, than elsewhere in Central America, but the availability of land and the fear of indigenous resistance allowed and encouraged the state to sustain large capital's access to land within the context of very incomplete proletarianization. The consequences to the environment were devastating. Land fragmentation and overuse in the Highlands was often a precipitating factor in migration to new areas that required different technologies and understandings of land use. Many officially sponsored as well as spontaneous migrations into empty lands failed because soils and climate were not appropriate to the ways they were used. Failed small holdings often provided the clearing needed for cattle pasture, and the presence of failed small-holders provided the labor required for new clearing. In this sense, the expansion of ranching into new areas continued the peculiar combination of state concessions of land to the rural poor in forms that ultimately served to solve the labor needs of agrarian capital.

The state, in fact, has consistently used empty lands and national lands in its various attempts to avoid rural unrest without compromising agrarian capital's access to cheap labor on an irregular basis. By 1940, labor was formally free of coercive legislation, but by this time the lands available of indigenous populations were insufficient to community needs, so the supply of labor remained adequate even though Guatemala continued to manifest the highest concentration of land tenure and average size of coffee plantation in Central America. The rapid growth in land cultivated for export, in coffee, sugar, and cotton, as well as the doubling of pasture land between 1960 and 1979, was accompanied both by massive migration into the Petén and also by a 50 percent reduction in forest cover. The cattle herd increased by at least three times between 1979 and 1990, with continuing deforestation as a result. In many instances, this expansion was aided by the establishment of logging roads into new areas, the subsequent migration of small settlers along these roads, and their eventual displacement by ranchers who took advantage of the clearing already done to establish a base and then extend their pastures. In these ways, the state continues its long history of using grants of public lands, or in some cases its omission of control over access, to solve capital's labor problem.

The rapid expansion of both cotton and coffee since the 1960s has increased labor demand, while the growth of cattle ranching has reduced the labor absorption on the lands it occupies. The growth of the rural population has in some ways provided a broader labor base, but at the cost of overexploitation of the communal lands and small holdings that sustain labor during the off-season. Most important, though, is that the state has continued to use land as a means to deflect rural unrest. Until 1971, the state sponsored small-holding migration to the Petén.

The state, however, reserved the right to repossess land if the conditions of possession were not met. Despite the end of official colonization projects, spontaneous migration into the Petén has continued. Also, ranchers used various informal means of dispossessing colonists from land they had cleared. The net effect was a continuation of an old policy, one of apparent grants in land to rural labor, but with the effect of providing for the labor needs of capital.

Terry Karl (1997), Fernando Coronil (1997), Michael Shafer (1994) follow the earlier sectoral analysts such as Harold Innis in positing a kind of path dependency in staples exporting economies in which the political institutions, class relations, property rights, and regional power imbalances that emerge around one sector's dominance may persist well beyond their adaptive capability to deal with new economic, political, or environmental requirements. Shafer in particular is highly pessimistic about the possibility of restructuring economic relations with large-scale, capital-intensive enterprises, not just because of the high level of vested interest and power held by sectorally defined capital, but also because of the state's dependence on these sectors for its sources of revenue and stability.

The Guatemalan state learned how to regulate the relations of land, labor, and capital during the growth of the coffee economy. The institutions of the state, and particularly those that deal with taxation, with private and public property, and with the control over labor, were all formed during that period. Unlike many other geographically and demographically similar countries, until recently there was no significant exploitation of subsoil rights that would have encouraged the state to develop institutions for managing publicly held resources, such as copper in Peru and Chile, and oil in Venezuela. Thus the notion of public good is notoriously lacking in Guatemala. The state has restricted itself to grants of land to resolve the intense conflicts that its own labor policies and the control of land involves. One consequence of this was the violent and disorderly manner in which access to the newly discovered mineral wealth of the Franja Transversal del Norte occurred.

Conclusion

An effective environmental policy must have, as its first condition, some notion of the state as steward. Patchwork solutions such as programs to ensure indigenous land rights or programs simply to exclude economic activity from certain areas will only be viable as impositions of donors who make compliance a condition of their grants. Such programs cannot be sustained because the state's own commitment to them is conditional on receiving external funding. International pressure to conserve the environment is useful, but only if it is integrated into a clear and generally held notion that land and resources are part of a national legacy rather than a resource with which the state can partially resolve the problems of its own weakness and lack of authority.

Ideas of path dependence, or of the structural determination of state and society by the production requirements and international market structure of leading staples exports, lead to fundamental pessimism about the possibilities of restructuring economies and polities such as Guatemala's. Pessimism is antithetical to the very essence of planning or reform. Nonetheless, it is essential to avoid overly voluntaristic conceptions of the state and of its capacity to implement new policies. Rather, we must look for ways to change within the boundaries of the possible. In the present conjuncture, we should ask whether global promotion of neoliberal policies and of the market-liberating ideologies that structure international commodity and finance markets might provide leverage to break the particular forms of path dependence that Guatemala seems to embody. The kinds of sectoral analysis that Shafer proposes lead him to focus on relative rigidities, but sectoral analysis can also illuminate sectoral characteristics that allow for positive manipulations.

In the case of coffee, one of the commodity's most notable characteristics is the variety of qualities and prices for which markets exist. Over the past decade, while bulk coffee prices have been falling, niche markets for high-priced varietal coffees have grown enormously. Generally speaking, the best coffees are grown on small farms and processed in small batches. This means that the large plantations harvested by migrant labor have lost market advantage and small-holders have gained advantage.

The first problem to solve would be communication between brokers in small niche markets and small-holding coffee growers. The Guatemalan coffee growers' association, ANACAFE, has long represented the interests of the large plantation growers, but its own interests may, in a more competitive market for coffee, lie more directly with small-holders able to capture more lucrative market positions. Can ANACAFE be persuaded to explore this opportunity? History suggests not, but comparative advantage might provide a serious incentive to do so. If ANACAFE were so persuaded, would it not be in its organizational interests to expedite small-holder access to more lands, or even to expedite small-holder sales of small plots on established large coffee plantations?

Expansion of small-holder coffee growing in response to market changes would indeed break earlier patterns of state activity, allow for more equitable access to land and agricultural markets, and relieve some of the pressure that annual crops put on the most fragile lands of Guatemala. Imposition of free-market trade relations cannot bring about these results alone. It would be necessary to provide credit for small-holder farmers to (1) buy small plots of existing coffee plantations or of other lands, (2) establish curing plants and warehouses competent to promote the processing and storage of high-quality coffee, and (3) for the establishment of transport facilities appropriate to hauling small batches and to keeping them separate. It would probably also be necessary to promote technical knowledge of cultivation, processing, and marketing appropriate to the requirements of the higher value niche markets. All of these projects would require participation of the state and of ANACAFE. If I am correct about the path dependencies that have developed around the oppressive and exploitative regimes of land and labor that the state promoted, and of the market monopoly that the now defunct coffee agreement conferred on ANACAFE and its plantation owning members, none of these proactive policies and budgets can occur without the support and active intervention of the international agencies that promote neoliberal agendas in Guatemala.

Programs to make coffee more responsive to changing global markets would in fact be compatible with the professed policy preferences of the multilateral development agencies. Coordination across international and local agencies to translate global market pressures into positive responses within Guatemala could serve the interests and the programs of multiple previously opposed groups. Path dependencies can be broken if the actors who maintain traditional relationships and antagonisms can be made to see the advantages of doing so. We should remember, however, that these optimistic outcomes of alliances between neoliberal global agents and equity-seeking local actors may be possible only where the characteristics of the dominant export commodity are such as to allow comparative advantage to lie with broader, rather than more restrictive, economic participation. The suggestions here are made specifically for Guatemalan coffee in terms of the separate tendencies for bulk and premium prices, and they work only because of the peculiar topographic, demographic, and political characteristics of the Guatemalan economy.

Works Cited

Auty, Richard M. 1989. The Internal Determinants of Eight Oil-Exporting Countries' Resource-Based Industry Performance. *Journal of Development Studies* 25:3.
Berger, Susan. 1992. *Political and Agrarian Reform in Guatemala.* Boulder, Colo.: Westview.
Cambranes, J. C. 1985. *Coffee and Peasants in Guatemala.* Guatemala: Universidad de San Carlos.
CONAP. 1992. Plan Maestro de la Reserva de la Biosfera Maya. Guatemala: CONAP.
Corden, W. Max, and J. Peter Neary. 1982. Booming Sector and Deindustrialization in a Small Open Economy. *Economic Journal* 92:368.
Coronil, Fernando. 1997. *The Magical State.* Chicago: University of Chicago Press.
Font, Mauricio A. 1995. Labor System and Collective Action in a Coffee Export Sector: Sao Paulo. In *Coffee, Society, and Power in Latin America*, edited by William Roseberry, Lowell Gudmundson, and Mario Samper Kutschbach. Baltimore: Johns Hopkins University Press.
Gelb, Alan. 1986. Adjustment to Windfall Gains: A Comparative Analysis of Oil-Exporting Countries. In *Natural Resources and the Macroeconomy*, edited by J. Peter Neary. Cambridge, Mass.: MIT Press.
Goldin, Liliana R., and Maria Eugenia Saenz de Tejada. 1993. Uneven Development in Western Guatemala. *Ethnology* 32, no. 3:237-52.
Gudmundson, Lowell, and Hector Lindo-Fuentes. 1995. *Central America, 1821-1871: Liberalism before the Liberal Reform.* Tuscaloosa: University of Alabama Press.
Jonas, Susanne. 2001. Democratization through Peace. In *Globalization on the Ground*, edited by Christopher Chase-Dunn, Susanne Jonas, and Nelson Amaro. Boulder, Colo.: Rowman & Littlefield.
Karl, Terry. 1997. *The Paradox of Plenty.* Berkeley: University of California Press.
Lynch, John. 1995. *Caudillos en Hispanoamerica, 1800-1850.* Oxford: Oxford University Press.
McCreery, David. 1995. Wage Labor, Free Labor, and Vagrancy Laws: the Transition to Capitalism in Guatemala, 1920-1945. In *Coffee, Society, and Power in Latin America*, edited by William Roseberry, Lowell Gudmundson, and Mario Samper Kutschbach. Baltimore: Johns Hopkins University Press.
Pasos, Ruben. 1994. *El Ultimo Despale: La Frontera Agricola Centroamericana.* Costa Rica: Fundesca.
Robinson, William I. 2001. Neoliberalism, the Global Elite, and the Guatemalan Transition: A Critical Macrosocial Analysis. In *Globalization on the Ground*, edited by Christopher Chase-Dunn, Susanne Jonas, and Nelson Amaro. Boulder, Colo.: Rowman and Littlefield.
Roseberry, William, Lowell Gudmundson, and Mario Samper Kutschbach, eds. 1995. *Coffee, Society, and Power in Latin America.* Baltimore: Johns Hopkins University Press.
Schwartz, Norman. 1992. *Forest Society: A Social History of Petén, Guatemala.* Philadelphia: University of Pennsylvania Press.

Shafer, Michael. 1994. *Winners and Losers*. Ithaca, N.Y.: Cornell University Press.
USAID. 1993. *Natural Resource Management: Strategy for Guatemala*. Guatemala: Litorama.
Valenzuela, Ileana de Pisano. 1996. *Agricultura y Bosque en Guatemala: Estudio de Case en Petén y Sierra de las Minas*. Guatemala: Ediciones Don Quijote.
Warren, Kay B. 2001. Pan-Mayanism and the Guatemalan Peace Process. In *Globalization on the Ground*, edited by Christopher Chase-Dunn, Susanne Jonas, and Nelson Amaro. Boulder, Colo.: Rowman & Littlefield.
Williams, Robert G. 1994. *States and Social Evolution: Coffee and the Rise of National Governments in Central America*. Chapel Hill: University of North Carolina Press.

Part III:

Indigenous Movements and Social Change

9

Pan-Mayanism and the Guatemalan Peace Process

Kay B. Warren

On December 29, 1996, huge crowds gathered in Guatemala City's central square and cheered representatives of the government, military, and guerrillas as they signed the Accord for a Firm and Lasting Peace.[1] The counterinsurgency war had finally ended, twelve years after the worst of the conflict. In the end, Guatemala's difficult peace negotiations spanned four presidencies, a coup, and many restructurings of the negotiating bodies.[2] While the peace accord represented only the first step in what has been a demanding process of reconciliation and reconstruction, it nevertheless reflected an extraordinary political achievement. This chapter spans the crucial period of 1993 to 1998, during which indigenous rights were debated, an indigenous accord was developed as part of the peace negotiation process, and citizens took part in commissions to think through the implementation of the peace accords. One key element of the behind-the-scenes peace process was the involvement of *popular* left and Mayanist groups, who saw this as a unique opportunity to push for the demilitarization and democratization of the country. Their input not only redefined Guatemalan political culture but also facilitated a rethinking by both groups of their characteristic analyses of inequality. The surprise was that these and other civilian groups gained access to the peace process at all (Cojtí Cuxil 1997).

How was a peace accord achieved in a situation where low-intensity warfare had continued to undercut democracy for more than a decade? How did indigenous issues become central to the peace process when neither of the negotiating parties had a history of commitment to multiculturalism? To answer these questions, it is necessary to retrace the peace process, understand the novel indigenous coalitions it activated, and consider the wide array of national and international actors who found the creation of a more open democracy, however imperfect, an important alternative to military control.

The Seeming Intractability of Conflict

Tidal waves of warfare in the late 1970s and 1980s took a devastating toll on Guatemala, especially in the Western Highlands, where most of the country's indigenous citizens live. During that period alone, an estimated 70,000 to 100,000 people were killed; half a million people out of a national population of eight million became internal refugees; 150,000 fled to Mexico as political and economic refugees; and 200,000 found their way to other countries such as the United States.[3] This was the worst of a series of national crises during the three decades of authoritarian regimes that plagued the country after 1954.

Even after the reduction of mass violence and the turn to civilian rule with the election of President Vinicio Cerezo in 1985, the military had few incentives to negotiate with the Guatemalan National Revolutionary Unity (URNG) guerrilla coalition, which sought an end to armed conflict. It had long been clear that the insurgents would not be able to topple the state and establish a revolutionary socialist government. Their numbers were small—dwindling in 1996 to several thousand rural guerrillas facing an army of forty thousand soldiers—and civilian support had been brutally suppressed. Despite its best efforts, however, the army was unable to extinguish the insurgency or capture its leadership—in contrast to Peru where the Shining Path guerrilla movement had been vanquished with the capture of its leader, Abimael Guzmán, by special forces in 1991. The military resisted peace in Guatemala because it would inevitably bring military downsizing and restrict the army's power to script presidential decision making and national policy. Furthermore, it was feared that negotiations might yet give communist insurgents the victory they had been denied on the field of battle.

Peace negotiations dragged on with few tangible results. The guerrillas searched for political leverage where at first glance it appeared they had very little. The military seemed hesitant to engage a process that could only strip them of their substantial coercive power, and the government struggled with its image as a human-rights violator with little credibility in international circles. Interestingly, in 1997 Minister of Defense Brig. Gen. Balconi Turcios argued that despite these impediments an inner group supportive of peace coalesced early in the negotiations. The challenge was to find a way out of intractable disagreements that had plagued the process between 1987, when President Cerezo created the National Commission for Reconciliation as a forum for civilian discussions of peace, and 1993, when negotiations between the principle antagonists began in earnest, only to be interrupted by a coup.[4]

By the early 1990s, many Guatemalans felt that the time was right for a negotiated peace. After Rigoberta Menchú was awarded the Nobel Peace Prize, international attention turned to human-rights abuses, indigenous issues, and Guatemala's unresolved political conflicts. The *popular* movement—made up of grassroots groups involved in peasant organizing (CUC), war widows support (CONAVIGUA), opposition to civil patrol violence (CERJ), and the exposure of state violence against their families (GAM)—captured the high moral ground by drawing public attention to the tragedies of hundreds of thousands of refugees, forced military recruitment, and clandestine cemeteries.

Members of the Pan-Maya movement—a social movement involved from the early 1980s in indigenous rights and cultural revitalization through national leaders, the creation of Maya schools, and nonformal education programs—saw cultural stakes in the peace process. It was a chance for them to gain recognition of cultural and collective rights and to argue for a state in which Maya communities would have decision-making power over their own destiny. The arguments for Maya recognition and self-determination echoed those articulated by indigenous groups working through the United Nations:

> All people have the right to take part freely in the cultural life of the community, to enjoy the arts and participate in scientific progress and its benefits. The dignity and rights recognized by the Universal Declaration of Human Rights imply the recognition of the person as a social being, affiliated with a community, ethnic group, nation, or state and at the same time as a *distinctive* social being in terms of language, religion, culture, or other pluralizing or diversifying conditions. (ALMG 1997, 1, emphasis mine)

For them, the issue was how to set the framework for asserting commonalities and legitimizing distinctiveness.[5]

Guatemala's economic elites, which had supported authoritarian rule in the past, came to see the pariah status of the country as a liability for their business dealings, especially in the emerging world of global assembly lines, the European Union, and transnational investment opportunities. After years of U.S. sanctions for human rights abuses and European support of grassroots organizing, Guatemala could not reenter the community of nations without a definitive peace. While politically leery of other Guatemalan sectors on many issues, the business community came to recognize the economic interests involved in a move to a more open society.

Finally, the civilian population wanted some sense of closure so that it could turn to other pressing social problems. Citizens had been exhausted by the militarization of daily life; the displacement of so many families from their home communities; the burden of war taxes extorted by underpaid soldiers, guerrillas, and criminals alike; and the fate of family members who had been kidnapped and tortured and had "disappeared" to unknown fates. Without ending the civil war and demobilizing armed forces on both sides, how would Guatemala cope with the legacies of violence, endemic poverty and unemployment, a rapidly growing population, escalating street crime, and the growing use of the country as a transshipment point for international drug cartels?

The power of crosscutting coalitions among politically disparate groups became clear in 1993 when President Serrano Elías attempted a Fujimori-style authoritarian government,[6] instituted media censorship, and attempted to disband Congress, the Supreme Court, and the Constitution. A surprising alliance of business elites, union groups, students, and indigenous leaders convinced the military that such a regime would lack international and national legitimacy. The takeover's failure demonstrated the powerful fluidity of interests and factions in Guatemala and the growing citizen involvement in national politics. The momentum for democratic change was propelled by the overwhelming rejection of the coup by national and international groups. The peace process quickly gained momentum in 1994 with a reorganization that designated the United Nations as the moderator between antagonists, established the Assembly of Civil Society as the forum for indirect civilian input, and created the Group of Friends (including Colombia, Mexico, Venezuela, Spain, Norway, and the United States) to support the process internationally.

Guatemala was surrounded by countries that had recently found ways to end internal wars. Nicaragua and El Salvador, for example, had reincorporated guerrilla forces into civil society and the political party system. In fact, the negotiation of El Salvador's peace accords in 1990 to 1992, brokered by the United Nations, paved the way for Guatemala. This history also provided an important lesson: To be successful, negotiations might well benefit from constructing a mandate beyond the immediate concern of demobilizing armed groups. Some observers felt that the El Salvador process had not gone far enough. A fuller agenda of issues might provide the opportunity to bring wider democratic reforms and address the root causes of violence.[7]

Many Guatemalans found it ironic and disconcerting that antagonistic armed forces with little experience in democracy were negotiating the fate of the nation in distant, secretive talks in Europe and Mexico. In response to these tensions, the Assembly of Civil Society set up consultative discussions with civilian leaders from a variety of social sectors to provide advisory documents for the peace process. The assembly brought together representatives of groups with very different politics and created space for debates and alternative proposals. Maya activists worked through the Coordinator of Organizations of the Maya People of Guatemala (COPMAGUA), which commissioned position papers from different groups and worked toward a consensus on key issues in order to influence the assembly.[8] In this way, *popular* and Maya groups, among others, gained institutionalized representation and the opportunity to organize their own parallel meetings in a process that might otherwise have thoroughly marginalized civilian input.

As a result of pressures, compromise, and consensus building, indigenous rights gained a forum in the negotiations. Grassroots *popular* groups—whose high-profile leaders captured support from their Latin American counterparts, European and North American solidarity movements, international Catholic activists, and liberal Protestant groups—had promulgated human rights discourse in their early days of labor organizing and more recently in responding to military repression. To these concerns, Pan-Mayanists added the issue of cultural rights and self-determination, which they advocated through the Council of Maya Organizations of Guatemala

(COMG), an umbrella group founded in the late 1980s.[9] Pan-Mayanists drew support from discussions at the United Nations on the rights of politically marginalized indigenous groups.[10] The European Economic Community and northern European nongovernmental organizations (NGOs) directly supported projects of cultural reaffirmation in the name of social justice.

In the end, the peace process generated a separate Accord on Identity and the Rights of Indigenous People,[11] signed on March 31, 1995, by the government, military, and URNG high command and put into force at the conclusion of the peace process a year later.[12] (See the appendix for a detailed summary of the four sections of the accords.) The identity accords called on the government to pursue the following commitments and reforms:

- Recognition of Guatemala's indigenous people as descendants of an ancient people who speak diverse, historically related languages and share a distinctive culture and cosmology. Non-Maya Xinca and Garifuna communities are accorded equivalent status.
- Recognition of the legitimacy of using indigenous languages in schools, social services, official communications, and court proceedings.
- Recognition and protection of Maya spirituality and spiritual guides and the conservation of ceremonial centers and archaeological sites as indigenous heritage, which should involve Mayas in their administration.
- Commitment to education reform, specifically the integration of Maya materials and educational methods, the involvement of families in all areas of education, and the promotion of intercultural programs for all children.
- Indigenous representation in administrative bodies on all levels, the regionalization of government structures, and the recognition of localized customary law and community decision-making powers in education, health, and economic development.
- Recognition of communal lands and the reform of the legal system so Maya interests are adequately represented in the adjudication of land disputes. The distribution of state lands to communities with insufficient land.

Despite these achievements, Mayanists hold that the accord process was seriously compromised by secrecy, limited Maya input, and disregard for indigenous norms of consultation with communities and elders. Of great concern is the fact that the final document dealt only obliquely with collective rights. Major issues such as the recognition of regional autonomy, historic land rights, and the officialization of Maya leadership norms were deemed irreconcilable and dropped. In practice, governmental "promises to promote" the various legislative reforms outlined in the accords left many loopholes and ambiguities in a political system where antireform forces were experienced and well organized. Other central issues were eliminated from the agenda when they were transferred for discussion to negotiations for the accord on socioeconomic issues. What could one expect, asked

Mayan editorialists from the indigenous news service *Rutzijol*,[13] given that the formal negotiations were between guerrilla leaders and government representatives?

The decision to make indigenous rights a separate stage in the peace negotiations—which, after all, were explicitly convened to demobilize guerrilla and counterinsurgency forces and establish the framework for political peace—signified a breakthrough for the movement. After summarizing critiques of the assembly's process, Mayanist representative José Serech reported that some Maya groups nevertheless concluded: "The accord widens and opens space in all levels of national life . . . space that until our time has been historically reserved by the colonizers and their descendants. It is a formal instrument to combat racism" (Serech 1995, 7). The document calls for an explicit public acknowledgment of the fierce discrimination that Guatemala's indigenous majority has endured on the basis of their distinctive origin, culture, and language. As a consequence, the document argues, indigenous Guatemalans have often been unable to exercise their rights or gain effective political representation.

Much of the accord's language (see Saqb'ichil/COPMAGUA 1995 and appendix) focuses on the state's *recognition* of indigenous languages, cosmology, spirituality, dress, customary law, and sacred places of worship. For its part, the government repeatedly promised to work with the legislature to promote constitutional reforms to make Guatemala a "multiethnic, culturally plural, and multilingual" nation-state where ethnic discrimination would be prohibited. The government also committed itself to seek institutional reforms in the courts, make sexual harassment a crime, and decentralize and regionalize the school system.

Implementation of the identity accords involved the creation of joint governmental-Maya commissions to make policy recommendations for constitutional and legislative change on highly contentious issues for the country and the movement. Their stress on consensus decision making through frequent meetings and public forums was extraordinarily demanding of time and energy for Mayanists who saw this as a unique opportunity to forge coalitions around controversial issues. Some Ladinos found their participation a consciousness-raising experience, especially when the hearings broke though the accepted compartmentalization of Guatemalan life to reveal hidden injustices.

For instance, during the 1997 Second Congress on Maya Studies, Frederico Fahsen, a member of the European identified elite, epigrapher, and member of the Commission on Sacred Sites, described his group's daunting responsibility to produce in a period of only ten months a comprehensive survey of the country's Maya religious centers, some regionally and nationally famous and others the locus of devotion for particular communities, families, and individuals. In public hearings, the commission, which also involved Mayanist leaders such as Narciso Cojtí, listened to accounts of the efflorescence of Maya spirituality during the violence and painful reports of current religious repression, including the destruction of mountaintop altars by evangelicals, the looting of tombs and archaeological sites for the international market in pre-Columbian artifacts, the blocking of diviners' access to traditional ceremonial centers by property owners, and the hostility of Catholic Action and charismatic groups toward practitioners of Maya spirituality, who they denigrate as witches (*brujos*). Fahsen found these instances of intolerance deeply disturbing, both because of their obvious injustice and because, as a member of the elite, he had been shielded from awareness of these social tensions. On a more optimistic note, he described the recent efforts of some communities to promote the reconciliation of Catholic Action catechists and Maya spiritual guides (*aj q'ijab*).

The peace process has been marked by a shift in Mayanist discourse on sacred cosmology and nation away from a theocratic model, advocated by some activists, in which Maya religion and priests would rule supreme. The emerging ecumenical recognition of Maya spirituality and spiritual guides leaves room for a variety of relations with other religious groups, a multiplicity of individual religious practices, a diffuse understanding of Maya cosmology as crosscutting conventional religious divisions, and secular Mayas whose activism is religiously disinterested. As a result, striking esoteric Maya ceremonies conventionally used to convene public events have been shortened and made more accessible across language divides, while many families continue Mayanist healing and devotional activities along with Catholic masses to celebrate their children's graduations.

Another fruit of the peace process was the Commission on Officialization, organized by the Academy for Maya Languages of Guatemala. Building on the academy's national network of community language committees, the commission convened consultative workshops in each of the country's linguistic communities in July 1997 and a month later held a three-day national congress in the capital to discuss national policy issues (ALMG 1997). Respected elders of the movement, such as Alfredo Tay Coyoy and Martín Chachach, chaired the work groups and encouraged local representatives to air concerns about the role of their own community languages in national policy. All agreed that the fact that Spanish remains the only official language in the country fuels discrimination against the indigenous majority.

One basic goal of this commission was to achieve formal acknowledgment of the multilingual character of the nation through a listing of the country's indigenous languages in the Guatemalan constitution; another was to begin the process of standardizing a written version of each language to take the place of the many ad hoc alphabets currently in use. Participants agreed on the importance of urging government recognition of each regional language group. Yet, it was also evident that community-specific language loyalties within regions raised tricky issues for the selection of a single oral dialect to be transformed into the standard written form for each language, a necessary precursor in the view of Mayanists to a national language policy and the production of administrative and educational materials in Maya languages.

Here knowledge is power in the sense that the movement looked to the expertise of professional linguists to transcend community-centrism by making scientific determinations of the most appropriate dialect. According to Mayanists, the choice of dialect for standardization could be made on several grounds, including which of the many dialects in a given language community incorporated the widest range of early Maya language forms, whether there was regional consensus about a high prestige dialect, or whether it would have been more effective to invent a transcendent dialect that combined features of various spoken versions. In the quest for standardization, scientific knowledge played a key role in the historical reconstruction of tradition and the mediation of what otherwise might have been endless disputes between actual communities based on loyalty to place and ancestors.

Yet, on another level, officialization has been seen as overtly political in that it appeared to force activists to make difficult choices. The most pressing issue became how many of the twenty-three languages, including non-Maya Garífuna and Xinca, needed to be officialized in the practice of state politics and administration. Some activists wanted all languages to operate on a par with Spanish in national and regional affairs. While this might have been appealing in terms of its immediate fairness, many worried that financial constraints—such as the required translation of official documents and proceedings into so many languages—would undermine any real chance that the new policy would be implemented.

Others believed that a *lingua franca*, most likely the numerically dominant K'ichee', would be the best national choice complemented by the use of regional languages for public services, local schools, courts, and administration. There was consensus among the activists that government jobs in education, health, public administration, and the courts should be allocated to those who were fluent in regional languages, whether they were Mayas or nonindigenous Ladinos. This vision produced a clear indigenous alternative to Spanish as the transcendent medium for intergroup and official communication.

Debates over the best model for officialization continued through the commission process and into any call for constitutional and legislative reforms. Neither the Maya commission nor a parallel government body were able to definitively decide among the alternative models for officialization. Although K'ichee'—the largest Maya language community, with more than one million speakers—gained ground over time and became a linguistic front-runner in Maya circles, the final proposal did not pursue co-official status for Spanish and K'ichee' on the national level. A way out of the painful zero-sum dilemma for contending language communities was to avoid the dominance of any one language at the expense of the others. The two commissions struck this balance by supporting co-official status between Spanish and each indigenous language at the appropriate regional level.[14]

Mayanists were active on other aspects of the peace process, including the commissions on democratic participation, land issues in indigenous communities, and the Truth Commission, whose work was phased in at different points during the implementation process. For instance, Otilia Lux de Cotí, a prominent educator, accepted an appointment to the Commission on Historical Clarification, which in August 1997 assumed the controversial task of reconciling the de facto amnesty granted to the soldiers on both sides as part of the peace process with the pressing need urged by many organizations and citizens to document the human rights abuses during the war. At issue were ways to promote reconciliation and healing, to avoid the escalation of old conflicts into new brutality, and to dismantle the mechanisms of terror that engulfed the country for so long. Members were under enormous pressure from the *popular* left to defy the limits on their formal mandate—which severely limited their ability to name protagonists of violence or seek prosecution of human rights violators. From the right they were urged to document that the guerrillas were just as violent in their treatment of civilians as the army. From the Catholic Church, which gathered tens of thousands of personal testimonies of violence through the Project for the Recuperation of Historic Memory (REMHI), they were under pressure to respond to community needs (Oficina de Derechos Humanos del Arzobispado 1997).

Negotiating these political white waters was extraordinarily challenging, as we have learned from the South African Truth Commission. In that instance, the legal process revealed much about the authors of violence and the daily functioning of the state terror apparatus under apartheid. Yet, the Truth Commission embittered civilian victims who in order to testify had to rekindle terrifying memories of abuse only to be denied the concrete personal support they anticipated.

There was tremendous publicity surrounding the February 1999 release of the Truth Commission's summary findings and the impending release of the full nine-volume report. Most telling was the astounding volume of documented violence, the disproportionate government authorship of violence, and the genocidal dimension of the conflict. As documented by the Commission for Historical Clarification, the army committed 93 percent of the violence, guerrillas 3 percent, and the rest is unattributed. An estimated 83 percent of the fully identified victims were Mayan versus the 17 percent who were Ladinos (CEH 1999). Thus, the blame for wartime atrocities has been unequivocally placed at the feet of the army. Yet, the commission also concluded that "the fundamental reasons for the Guatemalan armed confrontation cannot be reduced to the simplistic logic of two armed factions" (*New York Times*, February 26, 1999). Rather the report identified a wide range of structural and political factors—national and international—that influenced the genesis of the war.

In addition to their participation on commissions, Mayanist organizations (such as CEDIM and COCADI) and *popular* organizations (such as the Rigoberta Menchú Foundation) have directed their energies toward rights education. Foreigners, including Europeans, Latin Americans, and North Americans, worked through the United Nations Mission for the Verification of the Peace Accords (MINUGUA) to teach community groups about their identities and rights as recognized by the accords. MINUGUA works to verify cases of discrimination with respect to cultural, political, and civil rights. It has supported research on Maya customary law and programs for bilingual legal translators to assist Mayas in court proceedings. Given the rocky history of recent constitutional reforms, the limited numbers of Mayas in Congress, the absence of governmental norms for local consultation, and the chronic lack of budgetary support to enact legislation, however, serious problems remain concerning the implementation and verification of peace-process reforms.[15]

The movement worked to widen its public appeal and put pressure on the government through publications such as the Mayanist newspaper *Iximulew*, a bimonthly supplement in *Siglo Veintiuno* newspapers, which offered news reports, interviews, and editorials on civic and political participation, the impact of the accords, Maya involvements in the construction of peace, Maya women, Maya and Ladino debates on the significance of their respective identities, language issues, and constitutional reform.

With the identity accords, Cojtí Cuxil and other leaders pressed on with the task of explaining the Mayanist vision of rights as a remedy for ethnic discrimination:

> Almost all the constitutions of Guatemala . . . have established norms which state that all people "should be treated as human beings, should not be discriminated against for any reason," "all human beings are free and equal in dignity before the law," and "discrimination is totally prohibited for reasons of race, religion, sex, origin, or nationality," etc. These norms are excellent when individual rights are discussed . . . but discriminatory when collective rights are treated specifically in terms of ethnic group or community. By dealing with them as equal, community differences are ignored or absorbed.
>
> Ethnic discrimination consists of not recognizing, respecting, and promoting the cultural differences that indigenous communities present in all areas: religion, linguistics, organization, economics, politics, etc. Discrimination is created by disqualifying and inferiorizing people and then by blocking, persecuting, and eliminating indigenous issues and indigenes . . . But this should change. Thus, in the Indigenous Accord, among the government's obligations is to present to the legislature a plan for standardizing ethnic discrimination as a crime. (*El Periódico*, 13 November 1996).

Like the U.S. civil rights struggles in the 1960s, many of the Guatemalan reforms outlined in the indigenous accords are highly controversial. To be successful the accords will have to generate legal reforms, institutional change, wider indigenous representation in national life, and more effective legal means for settling conflicting interests. Such accomplishments will require coalition building across political parties. Recent political history shows the continued strength of patron-client politics. Ríos Montt's rightist party, the Guatemalan Republican Front (FRG), proved well-practiced at the art of derailing indigenous constitutional reforms as they were being debated in the Congress. Tensions persisted between grassroots left civilian groups, which successfully ran congressional candidates through the New Guatemala Democratic Front party (FDNG), and the URNG ex-guerrillas and their supporters, who sought their own political party. In 1997 and 1998 there was clearly much unfinished political business to restructure major institutions and to convince nonindigenous Guatemalans that these reforms would benefit the country as a whole.[16]

Finally, the funding of cultural reforms was a controversial issue in a neoliberal climate where the government was cutting jobs and privatizing government functions and where some economists anticipated that the economy was heading for a recession in 1997. Other economists noted that, despite what turned out to be robust national economic growth, low inflation, and exchange rate stability in that year, the purchasing power of the working classes was seriously compromised by rising transportation costs, stagnant employment, and eroding public services (MINUGUA 1998). Organizations, such as MINUGUA, began to reorient their attention to monitoring the socioeconomic accords, which proved highly controversial in their implementation, especially as they were seen to "universally" affect citizens. Apparently, despite years of effort, the Pan-Maya movement had yet to convince Guatemalans that racism is an issue that affects all citizens.

The first eight months of the implementation process did not focus on indigenous issues. Rather, national priorities concentrated on the more urgent tasks of dismantling civil patrols, disarming and reintegrating the guerrilla combatants, downsizing the army, and removing land mines from the countryside. Attention turned to the many problems faced by internal and international refugees—many of whom found their families dispersed and their homes and lands occupied by others. The *cause célèbre* for grassroots activism has been to challenge what many perceive to be a dangerously comprehensive amnesty program, the impunity enjoyed by those in power given a weak judicial system, and the need to have an effective Truth Commission. Community involvement in teacher selection in local schools has proven to be highly controversial, given the resistance of teachers' unions. Land issues have also been highly politicized. Clearly the changes advocated in the accords created new dilemmas and provoked organized political resistance along many fronts (Jonas 2000). By 1997 Mayanist leaders found themselves active in a wider range of organizations and political settings than ever before. Within Saqb'ichil/COPMAGUA and the indigenous accord commissions, consensus decision making and community consultation were incorporated as Maya models of democratic participation. Important decisions on controversial issues have come from these bodies. Funders (such as USAID, which had been quite critical of Pan-Mayanism) have responded with renewed educational initiatives, including four hundred college scholarships for Mayas studying bilingual education and legal interpreting.

Yet there have also been mismatches between peace-accord organizations and international funders. The fast-paced timetable for accord implementation disadvantaged groups that were not centrally organized and already decisive about their immediate goals. International funders (such as the World Bank, which earmarked $1.9 billion for democratization initiatives in Guatemala) found Maya group process illusive and hard to fathom because it did not conform to the organizational discipline expected of participants in transnational development networks. Funders on this scale appeared not to be interested in peace implementation as a coalitional group process in which discussions and consultations raise important debates, group membership is fluid, and the mechanisms for reaching authoritative decisions situationally dependent.

Many observers agreed that the "best-organized groups" with clear-cut agendas, concrete projects, and track records of working with outside experts to generate concrete proposals made the most headway and reaped the greatest rewards in the implementation process. Thus, while individual Pan-Maya and *popular* organizations with Maya-identified agendas were highly successful in gaining support for their own efforts, especially with educational and community-focused projects, the coalition of representatives of politically diverse Maya organizations created through the accord process played less of a role than groups working in other areas of the accord process.

Without the Mayanist movement, the peace-process reforms might have remained little more than a political gesture in the negotiation process, an opportunity for the guerrillas to show they could be responsive to Maya civilians and activists in the *popular* movement and for the government to appear inclusive and universalistic to the international community. With a decade of organizational experience and their own effective ties to international donors, the European Union, UNICEF, and the UN, however, Pan-Mayanists had already begun projects that flowed from the indigenous accords. They were working most actively to promote Maya schools as forums through which children might gain education supportive of indigenous culture and language. Additionally, they continued to publish a wide variety of educational texts for the schools and scholarship on indigenous issues, and to press for legal recognition of indigenous customary norms and the authority of elders in rural communities. After the signing of the peace accords, Mayanist leaders began advising the government on strategies for decentralization that, consonant with neoliberal reforms, would allow decision-making powers to devolve regionally and locally. Here is where Mayanists hoped to reintroduce the issue of autonomy, which was lost in the accord process. Demetrio Cojtí Cuxil argued:

> Isn't it possible to conceive of Guatemala as a free association of Maya and mestizo communities which undertake common objectives but preserve their respective integrity and identity? Mayanists consider this federal form of political organization an ideal that is still not feasible, and therefore accept the location of their project for national liberation within the framework of the pyramidal State.... In this model, the ethnic diversity and autonomy of each ethnic group would not be complete, but would function at the intermediate level of government. Autonomous regions or microregions would be formed from counties (municipios) composed of the speakers of the same language. (Cojtí Cuxil, in Siglo Veintiuno, 16 February 1995)

There can be no other choice than that the central state apparatus carries out the supraethnic functions that concern all individual and collective members of society (such as national defense, diplomatic relations, common standards), while the particular ethnic region could and should exercise administrative and legislative powers in areas that directly affect its existence and well being (education, culture, social work, police, health, etc.). (Cojtí Cuxil, in Siglo Veintiuno, 28 August 1994)

Officially, the government was committed to legislative and institutional change to create the new multiethnic, multicultural, and multilingual vision of Guatemala in the years 1998 to 2000.[17] In 1997, it was estimated that the implementation of peace in Guatemala would cost $953 million, with the indigenous accords requiring about $88 million, of which $60 million, almost 70 percent, would need to go to educational reform (Colmenares 1997, 31). Clearly, indigenous groups did not wait for the official phasing in of the accords; rather, they began networking internationally and organizing locally in the mid-1990s to pursue their agenda for peace and a more inclusive national society.

Defining Common Purpose across Cleavages

The peace process demonstrated that the divide between the Pan-Maya and *popular* movements, which some commentators portrayed as unbreachable or irreconcilable because of ideological or class differences, was, in fact, bridged quite frequently by individuals who were active in both camps or who borrowed ideas from other groups for their own uses. Thus, in practice there were many instances of cross-fertilization and frequent moments of common purpose between the movements. In responding to *popular* critiques, Mayanists sharpened their class analysis. They came to see Ladino poverty as an important issue that needed to be addressed, and they recognized that the racism of the Ladino underclass is economically fueled. In their reflections on the multiple meanings of racism, they drew on Ladino scholars such as Carlos Guzmán Böckler and Jean-Loup Herbert (1995) who used "internal colonialism" to conceptualize domination and discussed the unstable nature of Ladino identity.[18] They turned to Marta Elena Casaús Arzú's (1992) powerful social history of Guatemala's oligarchy. Of special interest is her lineage-by-lineage documentation of the reproduction since the sixteenth century of Guatemala's microelite through class endogamy, marriage alliances between lineages that controlled vast private resources and public powers, and the racist ideology of "blood purity" (*limpieza de sangre*). In fact, many of these elite lineages see themselves as whites who stand totally apart from and above the indigenous/Ladino divide; none regard themselves as having indigenous blood. These lineages have historically controlled banking, commerce, government, the Catholic Church, and high culture in Guatemala.

For their part, many intellectuals on the left have changed their views on indigenous issues over the years and moved away from total assimilation as the only future for indigenous communities.[19] Mayanists have long admired the courageous work of *popular* human rights activists who publicized human rights abuses at great risk to themselves. They certainly agreed on the importance of demilitarizing civilian life and disbanding civil patrols, which functioned as prime movers in the government's counterinsurgency policy and which parents feared would socialize their sons into violence, corruption, and disrespect for the moral authority of their families.

There were other important experiments—some more promising than others—in institution building across the Pan-Mayanist/*popular* divide. When the *popular* left created a coalitional political party, the New Guatemala Democratic Front (FDNG, or *el Frente*) in 1995, well-known *popular* leaders won six congressional seats. The party, however, was not seen by Mayanists as autonomous from the URNG guerrillas and, thus, had limited appeal across the *popular*/Mayanist divide. Only some were convinced that el Frente would shed its leftist roots, push for the implementation of Pan-Mayanist reforms over other priorities, or develop wider electoral appeal. Nevertheless, many felt and continue to feel that the time is not yet ripe for a Maya political party.

In another experiment before the 1995 elections, a low-key group called K'amalb'e was formed to begin discussions about developing a "Maya way of electoral politics" (*vía maya de política electoral*). The idea was to create not a political party but rather a dialogue in which indigenous leaders from *popular* groups and the Pan-Maya movement would be more than tokens, and Ladinos would listen to their concerns. The group was interested in informing public opinion on the practice of Maya culture. These discussions generated new lines of collaboration across old political divisions.[20]

From the time of the Second Continental Meeting in 1991 to 1997, Mayas active in the grassroots left became increasingly engaged in cultural and ethnic issues, leaving some of their Ladino colleagues wondering about the impact on the left of Maya resurgence and the possibility of new Maya alignments across old political cleavages. Maya members of the Committee for Campesino Unity (CUC), for example, created a splinter organization, the National Indigenous and Campesino Coordinator (CONIC), to focus their efforts more squarely on indigenous land struggles. Mayas from a variety of political backgrounds have begun to evoke Ruwach'ulew (the Earth/the World) or Qate' Ruwach'ulew (our Mother the Earth or Mother Nature) to mark their political discussions culturally. Building on the early work of Mayanist groups such as COCADI, activist organizations used an indigenous ecological discourse in overlapping ways to interconnect Maya cosmology, agricultural rituals, strategies for socioeconomic change, land issues, and rights struggles.

As of 1996 and 1997, some Ladino leaders believed that indigenous *populares* could go either way: toward a cross-movement alliance that would either include Ladinos or perhaps lead in an independent direction with other Mayas. Maya *popular* leaders—some of whom had grown weary of the hierarchies of command in the traditional Left—were considered to be a critical fulcrum point in this process. The militancy of the demobilizing URNG guerrillas who appeared to insist on the preeminence of a ladinoized class-conflict line only heightened the tensions around the issue of realignments.

The missing Ladino voice, one which would publicly condemn Ladino racism and affirm Maya cultural existence, was added to the calculus in August 1996. Casaús Arzú, the analyst of elite hegemony and a member of one of the country's most eminent families, returned to Guatemala after years of exile for her radical politics in the 1970s. For her, this was a crucial historical juncture, an opportunity for Ladino-Maya dialogues to work toward intercultural understanding and the dismantling of racism. She collaborated with Demetrio Cojtí Cuxil and others to promote these exchanges. During the First Congress for Maya Studies in August 1996, she spoke with great urgency in an interview for the country's major newsmagazine *Crónica*:

> The emergence of the Maya movement plays a very important role not only in its capacity to propose change, but also by forcing us, as Ladinos, to think: How do we create our nation from this diversity? ... There are indigenous leaders, like Cojtí, whose project is one of an inclusive political nation (*nación política*), with multiculturalism and ethnic diversity, in which economic and political power are shared. I ask myself and Ladino intellectuals: What kind of a nation do we have? What frame of reference do we use to debate this? (*Crónica*, 16 September 1996, 40)

Casaús Arzú argued that Guatemala must avoid perpetuating either the "*nación étnica*," in which Ladinos continue to rule a homogenous national culture, or the "*nación étnica maya*," in which Mayas seek a separate nation. Instead, her goal was the "*nación política*," which would recognize cultural difference and tackle racism but rule out the formation of separate ethnic nations. In her mind, continuing dialogues were absolutely crucial to avoid future violence:

> In the face of Maya emergence or rebirth, a certain fear has arisen among Ladinos. First, since we have never reaffirmed our identity, we do not strengthen our Ladino culture, and, besides, we never think in terms of the nation since, as the hegemonic class, the Nation-State used to be ours. To the extent another ethnic group formulates a different project in much more inclusive terms, Ladinos go into a panic, manifested in predictions of an ethnic war, but also in a greater interest in discussing Ladino identity. During my stay in Guatemala I encountered this desire among some groups.
> ...
> I have been surprised to find the belief among Ladinos that there could be an ethnic confrontation, or the basis for one, right around the corner. I have heard this among the military and among leftist intellectuals with connections to the Maya movement. The elites in power think less about this than I thought they would. I

believe that it is historic irresponsibility to promote these fears, first, because not even the minimal conditions for this possibility exist, and second, because we have not even signed the peace treaty and we are already talking of another war. We cannot forget that those who feed this myth may provoke a slaughter over some totally subjective incident, just like what happened with the myth of the Jew and the holocaust (*Crónica* 16 August 1996, 39, 40).

In effect, Casaús Arzú offered a reply to Mayan critic Mario Roberto Morales that sought to render problematic Ladino culture and Ladinos' vested interest, however inchoate, in the status quo ante of nation. She reminded her readers that fears are not raw, spontaneous emotion but rather are orchestrated and given narrative form by parties with specific political interests. The implementation of the accords would offer opportunities to rethink national culture and to mobilize around the politics of fear. Renewed interest in intercultural programs and dialogues throughout Guatemalan society was an attempt to bridge these gaps in a potentially volatile situation.

Did the multiple lines of dialogue, collaboration, and self-examination between the Pan-Maya and *popular* movements mean there would be a new unified paradigm, a new synthesis of social movements? Would the early division of labor between collective cultural rights and education, on the one hand, and human rights abuses and agrarian issues, on the other, continue after the accords? The notion of a variety of social movements that pursue their own projects and coalitional opportunities is closer to some European, South Asian, and South African notions of social activism than to the unified paradigm approach that guided the Guatemalan *popular* movement through years of repression and the beginnings of a transition to a yet unfinished democracy.[21]

The issue of forging wider unities and identifications, how these would be labeled, and at whose expense they will be established has been very much on the minds of radical democracy theorists, such as Chantal Mouffe, Ernesto Laclau, and David Trend, who see constructive possibilities in adversarial relations.[22] However, the definition of what is "progressive" in these movements is highly contested in Guatemala, given alternative framings of community and participation. Interestingly, there is still great intellectual nostalgia for the past in much of this political theorizing. As in the *popular* movement, it is marked by the dream of a radical and plural democracy as an enduring project of the left rather than a novel set of struggles that are the legacies of many different histories.

In the years immediately following the 1996 peace accords, the Pan-Maya movement maintained its own language for transcendence—one that promoted ethnic politics as the highest measure by seeking an institutionalized voice for Mayas and structural reforms in power relations. In practice, the impulse toward separatism was moderated by alliances with other groups to transform state and society fundamentally: to change conventional social procedures, renegotiate the terms by which people live, and transform the cognitive structures that shape meanings and identities (see Trend 1996, 105, 110, 161). In their own ways these were thoroughly revolutionary changes, without, however, seeking to topple the state. The failure of several waves of guerrilla opposition since the 1960s had convinced most Guatemalans—including Mayanists who witnessed many deaths in their own communities and lost friends who joined the guerrillas—that nonviolent paths to social change were the only feasible option.

I would agree with Michael Kearney's provocative analysis (1996, 181) that "post-peasant" politics take on an ethnic as opposed to a class character for very specific reasons. In the Guatemalan instance, the boundaries of peasant-like communities have been torn by violence and a land base insufficient for the growing population since the early 1970s. Secondary education and special continuing education opportunities, which often called young adults away from their home communities, increased the internal differentiation of rural communities. Individuals have been recruited by organizations with strong national and international ties: development projects, religious groups, educational programs, and political groups. Increased geographical mobility means that young Guatemalans commonly work in a variety of nonagrarian occupations in towns and cities not only in Guatemala but also in the United States. Yet both societies are ambivalent about indigenous workers.

With its blend of tradition and novelty, the Maya movement offers a language for common identification in the face of fragmentation and dislocation, designs for transcommunity affiliation, and nonmanual job opportunities.[23] The movement is especially attuned to the dilemmas facing post-peasants who have managed to *superarse*, to get ahead, as many agrarian parents wish for their children. In prizing Maya culture, the movement has given educated Mayas a continuing stake in the future of their home communities. With its emphasis on community councils, the movement seeks to include those for whom agrarian life remains central. Maya cosmology—its agrarian ontology, sacred cycles, social preoccupations, and syncretic aesthetics—have been selectively used by a variety of interests as a marker of the intimacy of community in the countryside and as a common moral language for transcommunity movements.[24] Thus, these ethnic "post-peasants" continue to reaffirm religious meaning and cultural distinctiveness through an idiom that reflects their Maya-agrarian roots.[25]

This chapter has traced the interplay of two social movements that began at the margins and moved over time to central stage in Guatemalan postwar national affairs. Across the peace process, especially from the 1993 to 1998 period considered in this analysis, the Pan-Maya and grassroots left movements came together to reshape Guatemalan politics so that it became increasingly responsive to indigenous issues. In the process, the movements mutually influenced each other's political vision, without, however, eroding many of their fundamental political differences. The Maya movement, which had sought cultural rights for the indigenous majority, emerged from this process with a higher public profile and a clearer agenda for institutional reform. The grassroots left, which sought to press for a class-based agenda of economic reforms in support of the country's poor, emerged with a new sense of its own internal ethnic diversity. That politics would take an ethnic turn and focus on racism at this point in history is the telling result of savvy coalitional politics and the consequence of neoliberal economics, which put communities under intense economic pressure, and the international support of democratization. These complex currents of change created the impetus for political participation while denying people access to traditional forums and institutions. As Kearney (1996) and Deborah Yashar (1998, 1997, 1996) have suggested, the result has been a premium on new modes of political organizing and community building. Maya culture has been a powerful source of cultural capital for this political process.

Notes

1. This is a slightly revised and updated version of chapter 2 in *Indigenous Movements and Their Critics: Pan-Maya Activism in Guatemala* (Warren 1998). My thanks to Jessica Mulligan for her editorial assistance with the process.

2. For the details, see Viteri (1997) and Colmenares (1997).

3. See Manz (1988, 30, 209). The toll of thirty years of war is even higher: more than one hundred thousand dead, forty thousand disappeared, and more than a million driven into exile (Schirmer, personal communication). There is a Baudrillard-like aspect to citing one or another set of statistics for the violence in Guatemala. Shifting choices among alternatives may reflect different methods for estimating the terrible slaughter. But the politics of consensus building also means that statistics become a code to represent the political allegiances.

4. He elaborated this point in a presentation on March 14, 1997, at the Woodrow Wilson Center's Conference on Comparative Peace Processes in Latin America.

5. On the indigenous use of the language of human and cultural rights in international forums to advance a rich agenda of issues including cultural recognition, constitutional reform, access to state institutions, land issues, self-administration, and the reconfiguration of national culture and the state, see Stavenhagen (1988, 1992, 1996), Ewen (1994), and the Instituto Centroamericano de Estudios Políticos (1993). On the development of international human rights organizations working in Latin America, see Sikkink (1996) and Cleary (1997), and on rights issues and the discipline of anthropology, see Messer (1995).

6. Fujimori successfully consolidated power in Peru through a dictatorial takeover of his own government, legitimized in part by the failure of earlier counterinsurgency efforts to stamp out the Shining Path guerrilla movement.

7. See Arnson and Quiñones Amézquita (1996).

8. The process and constellation of participating Mayanist and *popular* groups has a particularly complex history, which has been well documented in studies of social movements and the peace process by Guatemalan-based social scientists such as Aguilera, Bran, and Ogaloles (1996) and Bastos and Camus (1995a, 1996). For an insightful comparative study of peace processes in Latin America, see Arnson and Quiñones Amézquita (1996).

9. See COMG (1991, 1995).

10. See Nelson (1999) for the history of ILO Convention 169 in Guatemala.

11. See Saqb'ichil/COPMAGUA (1995).

12. Other accords dealt with the global accord on human rights, the resettlement of populations uprooted by the armed confrontation, the establishment of a commission for historical clarification of human rights violations, socioeconomy and the agrarian situation, the strengthening of civil power and the function of the military in a democratic society, constitutional reform and the electoral system, the definitive cease-fire, and the basis for the legal incorporation of the URNG into civil society (see ASIES 1996).

13. This antagonism played out through a discourse of cultural difference in *Rutzijol*'s first-page editorials on 1-15 November 1994; 16-30 November 1994; 16-31 March 1995; and 16-30 April 1995. See also Cojtí Cuxil (1997) and Serech (1996).

14. My thanks to Timothy Smith in personal communications for updates on the last stage of the debates.

15. On these issues and critiques of the process and substance, see *Rutzijol* (16-30 April: 1), Serech (1995), and Velasco Bitzol (*La República*, 4, 22, and 29 May 1994).

16. The 1999 national referendum (the *consulta popular*) was seen as a dramatic defeat in the court of public opinion for the indigenous accords. Nevertheless, given the wide international support from European and American development funders, the momentum for change kept these issues alive in national politics. As the 1999 general elections neared, there were complex shifts and realignments on the left and on the right. Most surprising was the support of indigenous reforms on the right by winning presidential candidate Portillo from the FRG. See Jonas (2000) for details on this political history.

17. See ASIES (1996) for the phasing of each of the accords.

18. Their analysis, which was first published in 1970, drew on a range of others, including Gonzales Casanova, Stavenhagen, Fanon, and Memmi. In 1995, Mayanists republished the out-of-print Guzmán-Böckler and Herbert book in its first Guatemalan edition through the Maya press, Editorial Cholsamaj.

19. For example, compare Jonas and Tobis (1974) with Jonas (1991) and Jonas and Stein (1990).

20. See Serech (1996) on political versus nonpolitical groups working on Maya issues. As a result of these dialogues, for example, the *Fundación Rigoberta Menchú*, which despite its name was thought of as a Ladino-run institution, funded projects in Maya education, and Demetrio Cojtí Cuxil published with AVANCSO (Asociación para el Avance de las Ciencias Sociales en Guatemala) and FLACSO-Guatemala (Facultad Latinoamericana de Ciencias Sociales-Guatemala), research centers long associated with *popular* issues, though the latter has been very active in research on the Maya movement.

21. The social and historical reasons for the hegemonic, sometimes intolerant nature of the *popular* movement and its scholars are beyond the scope of this paper. The punishing reactions at the 1992 LASA meetings to Carol Smith's (1992) historical analysis of racism in the work of nationally prominent academics on the left and to my own early work (1997, 1998) on the Segundo Encuentro show how difficult it was in the early 1990s to pursue this history. A social history of the full scope of the left and its views of other political tendencies might do much to show how this political vision has been reproduced over time.

22. See Laclau and Mouffe (1985), Mouffe (1992, 1993), and Trend (1996).

23. Of course it is not the only movement to do so. Internationally, religious revivalist movements have had similar agendas. See Denoeux (1993).

24. For important recent work on Maya cosmology in Guatemala, see Hill and Monaghan (1987), Wilson (1995), and Watanabe (1990, 1992).

25. That religious revitalization in other situations has been fraught with tensions, however, should not surprise us, given the diversity of theologies and organizational interests in Guatemala (see chapters 8 and 9 of *Indigenous Movements and Their Critics* [Warren 1998]).

Works Cited

Aguilera, Gabriel, Rosalina Bran, and Claudinne Ogaldes. 1996. *Buscando la Paz: El Bienio 1994-1995*. Debate 32. Guatemala: FLACSO.
ALMG. 1997. Propuesta de Modalidad de Oficialización de los Idiomas Indígenas de Guatemala. Guatemala: Congreso de Oficialización de los Idiomas Indígenas de Guatemala, 12-14 August.
Arnson, Cynthia, and Mario Quiñones Amézquita, eds. 1996. *Memoria de la Conferencia: Procesos de Paz Comparados*. Guatemala: Asociación de Investigación y Estudios Sociales (ASIES) and the Latin American Program of the Woodrow Wilson International Center for Scholars.
ASIES. 1996. *Acuerdo de Paz Firme y Duradera: Acuerdo sobre Cronograma para la Implementación, Cuplimiento y Verificación de los Acuerdo de Paz*. Guatemala: ASIES.
Bastos, Santiago, and Manuela Camus. 1995a. *Abriendo Caminos: Las Organizaciones Mayas desde el Nobel hasta el Acuerdo de Derechos Indígenas*. Guatemala: FLACSO.
———. 1995b. *Los Mayas de la Capital: Un Estudio sobre Identidad Etnica y Mundo Urbano*. Guatemala: FLACSO.
———. 1996. *Quebrando el Silencio: Organizaciones del Pueblo Maya y sus Demandas, 1986-1992*. Guatemala: FLACSO.
Casaus Arzú, Marta Elena. 1992. *Guatemala: Linaje y Racismo*. San José: FLACSO.
CEH. 1999. Guatemalan Commission for Historical Clarification. Guatemala: Memory of Silence Tz'inil Na'tab'al <hrdata.aaas.org/ceh/report>.
Cleary, Edward. 1997. *The Struggle for Human Rights in Latin America*. Westport, Conn.: Praeger.
Cojtí Cuxil, Demetrio. 1997. Unidad del Estado Mestizo y Regiones Autónomas Mayas. Pp. 175-89 in *Guatemala: ¿Oprimida, Pobre o Princesa Embrujada?*, edited by Fridolin Birk. Guatemala: Fundación Friedrich Ebert.
Colmenares, Carmen María de. 1997. La Situación Actual del Proceso de Paz. Pp. 21-33 in *Memoria de la Conferencia: Procesos de Paz Comparados,* edited by Cynthia Arnson and Mario Quiñones Amézquita. Guatemala: ASIES and the Latin American Program of the Woodrow Wilson International Center for Scholars.
Consejo de Organizaciones Mayas de Guatemala (COMG). 1991. Derechos Específicos del Pueblo Maya: Rujunamil Ri Mayab' Amaq'. Guatemala: Editorial Cholsamaj.
———. 1995. *Construyendo un Futuro para Nuestro Pasado: Derechos del Pueblo Maya y el Proceso de Paz*. Guatemala: Editorial Cholsamaj.
Denoeux, Guilain. 1993. Religious Networks and Urban Unrest: Lessons from Iranian and Egyptian Experiences. Pp. 123-56 in *The Violence Within: Cultural and Political Opposition in Divided Nations*, edited by Kay B. Warren. Boulder, Colo.: Westview.
Ewen, Alex, ed. 1994. *Voices of Indigenous Peoples: Native People Address the United Nations*. Santa Fe: Clear Light Publishers.
Guzmán Böckler, Carlos, and Jean-Loup Herbert. 1995 [1970]. *Guatemala: Una*

Interpretación Histórico-Social. Guatemala: Editorial Cholsamaj.
Hill, Robert M., and John Monaghan. 1987. *Continuities in Highland Maya Social Organization: Ethnohistory in Sacapulas, Guatemala.* Philadelphia: University of Pennsylvania Press.
Instituto Centroamericano de Estudios Políticos (INCEP). 1993. *Identidad y Derechos de los Pueblos Indígenas: La Cuestión Etnica 500 Años Después.* Guatemala: INCEP.
Jonas, Susanne. 1991. *The Battle for Guatemala; Rebels, Death Squads, and U.S. Power.* Boulder, Colo.: Westview.
―――. 2000. *Of Centaurs and Doves: Guatemala's Peace Process.* Boulder, Colo.: Westview.
Jonas, Susanne, and Nancy Stein, eds. 1990. *Democracy in Latin America: Visions and Realities.* New York: Bergin and Garvey.
Jonas, Susanne, and David Tobis, eds. 1974. *Guatemala.* Berkeley: North American Congress on Latin America.
Kearney, Michael. 1996. *Reconceptualizing the Peasantry: Anthropology in Global Perspective.* Boulder, Colo.: Westview.
Laclau, Ernesto, and Chantal Mouffe, eds. 1985. *Hegemony and Socialist Strategy; Towards a Radical Democratic Politics.* London: Verso.
Manz, Beatriz. 1988. *Refugees of a Hidden War: The Aftermath of Counterinsurgency in Guatemala.* Albany: SUNY Press.
Messer, Ellen. 1995. Anthropology and Human Rights in Latin America. *Journal of Latin American Anthropology* 1, no. 1:48-97.
MINUGUA (United Nations Verification Mission in Guatemala). 1998. *The Situation in Central America: Procedures for the Establishment of a Firm and Lasting Peace and Progress in Fashioning a Region of Peace, Freedom, Democracy and Development.* A/52/757. New York: United Nations.
Mouffe, Chantal, ed. 1992. *Dimensions of Radical Democracy: Pluralism, Citizenship, Community.* London: Verso.
Mouffe, Chantal. 1993. *The Return of the Political.* London: Verso.
Nelson, Diane. 1999. *The Finger in the Wound: Ethnicity, Nation, and Gender in the Body Politic of Quincentennial Guatemala.* Berkeley: University of California Press.
Oficina de Derechos Humanos del Arzobispado, ed. 1997. *Memoria del Taller Internacional, Metodología para una Comisión de la Verdad en Guatemala.* Guatemala: Oficina del Arzobispado.
Plant, Roger. 1997. Indigenous Identity and Rights in the Guatemalan Peace Process. Paper presented at the Conference on Comparative Peace Processes, the Woodrow Wilson Center, Washington, D.C., 13-14 March.
Saqb'ichil/COPMAGUA (Coordinación de Organizaciones del Pueblo Maya de Guatemala). 1995. *Acuerdo sobre Identidad y Derechos de los Pueblos Indígenas.* Punto 3 del Acuerdo de Paz Firme y Duradera. Suscrito en la Ciudad de México por el Gobierno de la República de Guatemala y la Unidad Revolucionaria Nacional Guatemalteca. Guatemala: COPMAGUA.
Serech, José. 1995. Perspectivas Mayas y Reconstrucción Social Guatemalteca. Paper given at the 19th Congress of the Latin America Studies Association, Washington, D.C.
―――. 1996. Oferta y Aporte de las Culturas Subalternas y Dominadas en el Proceso hacia una Nueva Sociedad. Pp. 109-18 in *Globalización y Diversidad Cultural*, edited by Antonio Gallo. Guatemala: Textos Ak' Kutan.
Sikkink, Kathryn. 1996. The Emergence, Evolution, and Effectiveness of the Latin

American Human Rights Network. Pp. 59-84 in *Constructing Democracy: Human Rights, Citizenship, and Society in Latin America*, edited by Elizabeth Jelin and Eric Hershberg. Boulder, Colo.: Westview.

Smith, Carol. 1992. Marxists on Class and Culture in Guatemala. Paper presented at LASA, September 1992 for the session, 500 years of Guatemalan Mayan Resistance: A Dialogue between Maya and Non-Mayan Scholars. Los Angeles, September.

Stavenhagen, Rodolfo. 1988. *Derecho Indígena y Derechos Humanos en América Latina*. México: Colegio de México.

———. 1992. Challenging the Nation-State in Latin America. *Journal of International Affairs* 45, no. 2: 421-40.

———. 1996. Indigenous Rights: Some Conceptual Problems. Pp. 141-59 in *Constructing Democracy: Human Rights, Citizenship, and Society in Latin America*, edited by Elizabeth Jelin and Eric Hershberg. Boulder, Colo.: Westview.

Trend, David. 1996. *Radical Democracy: Identity, Citizenship, and the State*. New York: Routledge.

Viteri E., Ernesto. 1997. Cinco Años de Negociaciones. Pp. 9-20 in *Memoria de la Conferencia: Procesos de Paz Comparados*, edited by Cynthia Arnson and Mario Quiñones Amézquita. Guatemala: ASIES and the Latin American Program of the Woodrow Wilson International Center for Scholars.

Warren, Kay B. 1998. *Indigenous Movements and Their Critics: Pan-Maya Activism in Guatemala*. Princeton, N.J.: Princeton University Press.

———. 1997. Indigenous Movements as a Challenge to a Unified Social Movement Paradigm for Guatemala. In *Cultures of Politics/Politics of Cultures: Latin American Social Movements Revisited*, edited by Sonia E. Alvarez, Evelina Dagnino, and Arturo Escobar. Boulder, Colo.: Westview.

Watanabe, John. 1990. From Saints to Shibboleths: Image, Structure, and Identity in Maya Religious Syncretism. *American Ethnologist* 17, no. 1: 131-50.

———. 1992. *Maya Saints and Souls in a Changing World*. Austin: University of Texas Press.

Wilson, Richard. 1995. *Mayan Resurgence in Guatemala: Q'echi' Experiences*. Norman: University of Oklahoma Press.

Yashar, Deborah. 1996. Indigenous Protest and Democracy in Latin America. Pp. 87-105 in *Constructing Democratic Government: Latin America and the Caribbean in the 1990s: Themes and Issues*, edited by Jorge I. Dominguez and Abraham Lowenthal. Baltimore: Johns Hopkins University Press.

———. 1997. *Demanding Democracy: Reform and Reaction in Costa Rica and Guatemala, 1870s-1950s*. Stanford, Calif.: Stanford University Press.

———. 1998. Contesting Citizenship: Indigenous Politics and Democracy in Latin America. *Comparative Politics* 31, no. 1 (October).

10

Development of Globalization in the Mayan Population of Guatemala

José Serech

The long discussion about how indigenous peoples should be included (or not) in the process of development has begun to involve the voices of those being discussed. In the countries where there are large indigenous populations, developmental programs have been intended to ensure some benefits for these populations. Efforts have also been made to avoid or mitigate potential adverse effects that might fall upon indigenous peoples. Some technical and legal devices have been created to protect the interests and rights of indigenous peoples over land and other productive resources.

The conceptualization and definitions are important. Terms such as *indigenous populations, indigenous ethnic minorities, tribal groups, registered tribes, indigenous and tribal peoples* are efforts to describe those social groups that have a social and cultural identity distinct from the dominant society (World Bank 1991, 2). The *169th Convention for Indigenous and Tribal Peoples* of the International Labor Organization uses the phrase "indigenous and tribal peoples in independent countries" to describe those with social and cultural identities whose specificity puts them in a vulnerable position and at a disadvantage in the process of development. I use the World Bank's term *indigenous population*, and *Mayan population* for the case of Guatemala.

Development and Indigenous Peoples

Most countries in which indigenous populations have received some sort of recognition have included specific clauses in their constitutions and laws that define a legal framework for identifying and characterizing indigenous peoples. The specific circumstances of indigenous peoples vary. Some possess a strong attachment to ancestral territories or to natural resources. Indigenous peoples often possess their own self-identifications, and others may identify them as members of a distinctive cultural group. They often speak an indigenous language, usually different from the national language. They may have their own social institutions and customary laws. Their production is often oriented primarily toward subsistence, and their economy is usually one of austerity (World Bank 1991, 3).

The Guatemalan Case

In 1985 the Guatemalan Constitution officially recognized that "Guatemala is composed of several indigenous groups of Mayan origin. The State recognizes, respects and promotes their ways of life, customs, traditions, ways of social organization, the use of indigenous clothing by men and women, languages and dialects" (CPRG 1985). The peace accords of 1996 have made explicitly clear that Guatemala is ethnically, linguistically and culturally pluralistic.

This recognition confronts us with our first challenging questions:

- How do we make this state recognition become a state policy while there is little political will on the side of the dominant society, knowing that recognition of an ethnic identity bears an implicit admittance of some specific Mayan rights?
- How do we solidify Mayan ethnic identity while going through the process of development from the local into the national and the worldwide spheres?
- How do we define specific Mayan identity in the context of emerging new models such as globalization of activities, cultures, rules, and norms of behavior and relations?

To keep these questions from being addressed, some invoke the principle of equality under the law and thus disqualify any claim to ethnic identity. In this way, equality is put over and above cultural diversity, while the Mayan population proposes unity in diversity as a characteristic of the Guatemalan society.

Some Approximations to Development

Development policies in countries where different ethnic groups coexist have usually generated great debates regarding the place in development of ethnic minorities, or minimized majorities as in the case of Guatemala. The debates usually revolve around whether to include or to exclude the indigenous populations in the benefits of development; to assimilate or to segregate them in the process of modernization, and social and economic development. These debates have influenced the official development policies of countries such as Guatemala.

The position of exclusion of indigenous peoples from the benefits of modernization and development of the country is based on the rationale that the indigenous populations must be isolated because their cultural and economic practices hinder them in dealing with external powerful groups. In this context, consideration of globalization shines a bright light on the great disparity that exists between the Mayan community, historically excluded (though the majority), and the dominant groups of Guatemalan society. These dominant groups themselves have difficulties catching up with development on world scale, even though they supposedly have great knowledge of the internal logic of global economy and politics.

The consequence of the isolation or exclusion of the indigenous populations from the benefits of development could be their survival, as they would not have difficulties with external powerful groups and perhaps they can receive some special legal protections in order to preserve their cultural characteristics. But the cost of this isolation is exclusion from the benefits of developmental programs (World Bank 1991, 4).

Another position is inclusion, meaning integration and assimilation of indigenous groups into the dominant society. This position is based on the concept that the society in its totality is polarized between a modern sector (in economic terms—industry, commerce, agriculture, services, and so on) and, on the other hand, an obsolete and backward sector made up of peasants, indigenous, and pre-peasant groups. This position holds that this backward sector has to catch up with the so-called modern sector for its own benefit and for the benefit of Guatemalan society as a whole. This allegedly can be attained through accelerating measures such as skill training for certain types of production and consumption.

The consequence of this position of inclusion is supposedly the complete replacement of the productive organization, social policies, and ethnic culture of indigenous people by different variations of a sole model of organization. In this vein, a peripheral kind of capitalism tends to transform the peasantry into a workforce according to the market rules in which producers are slowly alienated from their own means of production, sustenance, and reproduction. The extreme result of this position is the total undoing of an agricultural (peasant) society, the loss of cultural autonomy, and the decline of capacity of self-sustenance, as well as the gradual loss of individual and collective ability to use traditional cultural elements and adaptation strategies (World Bank 1991, 4). Seemingly this position suggests that the indigenous peoples have to acculturate to the values and economic activities of the dominant society in order to be able to participate in national development. In this case, the benefits include the improvement of social and economic opportunities, but the cost is generally the gradual loss of cultural identity.

A middle position intends to seek a pluralistic solution based on the "informed participation" of the indigenous peoples in their process of development. The identification of local needs and interests through direct consultations, the incorporation of indigenous knowledge in the methods of developmental projects, and the involvement of indigenous specialists in the process of development are all key activities for any project that intends to include indigenous peoples. However, it remains problematic as to who decides over the natural and economic resources and who designs the required policies. This model of development would first perform an analysis of the consequences and the costs of a development campaign based on the informed participation of indigenous people (COCADI 1999, 16-27). Lastly, this position implies a practice of democratic participation (or participatory democracy) without which development would be spiritless.

Basic Influences in Developmental Approaches

These alternative methods of development respond to certain basic historical influences. In Guatemala different ideas and projects have influenced the construction of the Guatemalan nation. In the first place, the notion of a "universalistic nation" had taken as central reference the idea of the citizen in which education was thought of as a "civilizing process." In this case the indigenous people, in order to be integrated, must first become citizens. This in turn, is accomplished through the process of a "civilizing education" (García Ruiz 1997, 16).

The Marxist approach to the notion of "nation" has also had an effect on those who have tended to think that the ethnic realities would soon disappear. The idea of the Marxists is that the homogenizing process of proletarianization would be the only alternative for the ethnic groups, and the only viable political alternative would be insertion into the revolutionary processes based on class struggle. From the perspective of class struggle the proponents of indigenous culture tended to be understood as reactionary conservatives. This perspective sees indigenous ethnicities in terms of the idea that "history itself would sweep them away" (García Ruiz 1997, 16).

The culturalist approach usually includes the premise of acculturation and assimilation—the theory of the melting-pot—whose aim is to induce the process of integration of all immigrants.[1] The assimilation process is understood to have five irreversible steps: first contact; competition; conflict; accommodation; and assimilation. In this process, those "assimilated" are supposed to accept the proposed values of the dominant group, and this is supposed to resolve all possible conflicts. Once all participate in the same system of values and norms, all conflicts should be resolved.

All three approaches—the liberals, Marxists, and culturalists—have made a definite impact on the analysis of Guatemalan society, and they have influenced the theories and policies of development for the Mayan people.

Indigenous Peoples and Globalization

From the above views it is apt to infer that the analysis of development in countries with large indigenous groups has been marked by the notion that the awareness of ethnic identity would gradually have to disappear in order to form a single integrated national identity. In the last few decades, with the decline of certain ideologies and the fall of the Berlin wall, there has been a freeing of ethnic and national consciousness and the construction of new dreams from the vague notions of an imperfect past. Though this phenomenon is not new, it has been inspired by dynamic aspects of the present times that have projections for the future. As the Mayan organizations have declared, this makes possible a new effort of "constructing a future for our past" (COMG 1995), while the processes of globalization are clearly emerging all around.

This process of freeing consciousness runs near the course of globalization. Each time we see the world increasingly globalized, the local and regional identities appear as a flood tide of the ocean. Sea flux and reflux come together, but the question is which one is imposing over the other? Are they opposing each other? Or are they complementary? In the Mayan cosmic vision both come together and globalization as a whole includes the awakening of local and ethnic consciousness. Therefore, we risk to ask ourselves whether globalization, among other attributes, is a producer of local, national, and ethnic consciousness.[2]

Some Aspects of Globalization

In the Mayan milieu, some social groups, notably the young productive and intellectual sectors, are met with new questions brought forth by the phenomenon of globalization. In the first place, there is an attempt to understand the social, political, and economic crisis faced in the communities that are attributed to the processes of globalization. On the other hand, those more inclined to intellectual activities are entangled in debates of all sorts, as to whether or not we are still in the period of modernity or a new period of postmodernity. Postmodernism suggests a "rejection of facile certainties, whether of a pseudo-scientific, technological, positivist or ideological stamp; a very favorable attitude to multiculturalism, very much in demand as a consequence of the peace accords, and inter-culturalism; and an attitude of humility in the face of complexity and randomness." On the other hand, some relegate the previous (modernity) to a realm associated with hegemonic and totalizing ideas of the past.

In order to not get lost in an alluring but far-off discussion, suffice it to say that globalization is commonly understood as a synonym for modernity and progress, as well as an affirmation of what the past has constructed. A return to tradition would seem to be a strategy for preparing a less violent entrance into modernity. Thus, tradition not only serves as a conditioning and regulating monitor of change, but it also serves as a feedback to progress. The return to the past and tradition may seem to be backwardness and an affront to modernity and progress. However, as the European Renaissance of fifteenth and sixteenth centuries shows, a return to the ancient classics was needed in order to create a new literary, artistic, and philosophical movement and style.

In the same vein, the retaking of one's own history as a people seems as another face and a concrete expression of globalization. In this sense the construction of individual and collective identity by means of the appraisal of excluded and denied identities is a valid way to support forms of social existence in which individuals can find their collective bonds. Thus, it appears that one of the characteristics of globalization is the localizing of world realities that are also every day more global, integrated, and standardized.

Another commonly identified feature of globalization is the construction of a world-scale market and the massive diffusion of certain products that are bearers of those representations and cultural values that attempt to substitute for local values and cultures. Against this process of the economic space, some identifying reactions of self- defense are being developed and demonstrated in an effort to adapt what is complementary with indigenous culture and reality.

However, it is important to notice that the emergence of ethnic consciousness as a reflux of globalization is not at all free from instrumental manipulation. The revitalization of ethnic sentiments and awareness has been taken as a strategy for meeting the crises of institutions, structures, and ideologies that promote modernity, national progress, and international integration. In contraposition to what has been accepted for a long time, ethnicity is not a passing phenomenon. On the contrary, modernization seems to be a potent catalyst of ethnic resurgence, as a reaction to modernity, or with the aim of creating a new space for specific groups.

We can mention some examples. In Chiapas "the fact is to bet for the Indian cause which increased the legitimacy of the EZLN (Zapatistas) far more than what would have been achieved by a socialist rhetoric" (Baud et al. 1996, 182). Other voices interpret ethnic conflicts such as the present one in the Balkans as having been induced by external forces for ulterior motives.

Globalization as an Attitude

For others, however, globalization has meant the end of developmentalism and progress. For the director of the Institute of Finance of the Ministry of Finance of Japan, "the end of the Cold War is not the end of history, as Fukuyama has popularized. On the contrary, it is the end of a civilization that is based on the indefinite material growth. The civilizing objective of progress that has dominated both the capitalist and the socialist systems has reached an end because of its limits and internal contradictions. The capitalist system looked for an indefinite material growth through the market and private enterprise while the socialist system looked for the same through the State and party with its centralized management (Sakakibara 1996).

Eisuke Sakakibara announces for us the beginning of a non-Western, a non-Eurocentric, civilization that for the first time makes it possible to celebrate the diversity of the long history of humanity. In contrast with the short view of the dominant culture, this long view coming from the East and from the South venerates the complexity of human history while keeping the hope that humanity is not condemned to failure for the majority (Gorostigaga 1996, 11).

Results of Globalization

Some observers claim that globalization presents a threat for the countries of the North while it provides great opportunities for the poor countries. Globalization has increased the power of the big corporations, but, at the same time, it has reduced the authority of the politicians and of the public sector.

On the other hand, other voices continue to affirm that globalization has only positive results—that there are no losers in the process of globalization. They maintain that globalization might have some temporary negative effects. For example, there are people in the North who lose their jobs or their social security. This situation does not happen in the countries of South because the alleged benefits of globalization are directed toward them. These same also admit that certain stronger developing countries can profit from the growth of local and national markets, as well as the expansion of exports. But a great number of developing countries are still unable to compete in the world market. They have been pressured to open their markets to foreign and cheaper products and to foreign investors who, in the long term, can overrun local enterprises and farming (van Rijn 1996).

Still others affirm that the new concepts of globalization and liberalization have been designed in order to be able to do without government help and support for development. In this way, globalization is an instrument that induces "the countries ... to privatize, liberalize, and to reduce their government budgets. Globalization ... converts itself into an instrument of self-help for developing countries. This implies that the North-South dialogue and cooperation are unnecessary for development, and that the cooperation South-South is also unnecessary" (van Rijn 1996). Opinions about the true outcomes of globalization are in dispute.

Conclusion

Globalization is a reality that shortens distances, breaks down boundaries, and quickens the flow of information and communication. The indigenous peoples who were once isolated from the centers of power, as in the case of Huehuetenango, are now closer to the United States, Mexico, and Canada than to Guatemala City. This is because of the new electronic means of communication and information and because of migrations and commercial and economic activities. On the other hand, the chemical products that the farmers use in their farming and the marketing of their products are closely related to other countries of the region and to other continents. All the basic materials for the indigenous clothing, for instance, are largely produced in Northern and Asian countries. It is important to notice that the Asian countries export their mechanical and electronic products without also imposing their cultural values, while the countries of the North introduce their values along with their products. Thus, economic structures and forces are main features and expressions of globalization that indigenous people must confront.

Besides the penetration of the global through economic and cultural activities, the indigenous communities are also related to various international political systems. On one side, they are related to worldwide organizations and governments through the local subsystems that serve as mediators. The presence and activities of international NGOs, as well as religious and missionary groups, are all forms of globalization. One of the oldest known entities of globalization is perhaps the Catholic Church, whose central reference has been and still is the Vatican. In the same vein, the countries of origin of various Protestant congregations and sects have also been important factors in bringing a universal or global interaction with the local.

However, for the indigenous populations, those historically excluded from the benefits of progress, it is difficult to understand how the system and the internal logic of globalization function. It seems that regionalization and globalization as expressions of free commerce are only possible among equals, among partners in equal conditions. But the Mayan people and the other indigenous populations, as part of their survival strategies, will have to look for other mechanisms in order to adapt themselves to the new system. As John Durston says, "In order for a social actor to be successful, determination alone is not enough. Indigenous peoples also need to have four other elements: resources, alliances, a favorable environment and a strategy . . . and perhaps the essential resources to the success of indigenous groups are their own cultures and the appropriation of the universal knowledge which exists in the world as a whole, and that both the favorable conditions and the alliances they need for their success may be generated by the spread of modernity throughout the world" (Durston 1993, 90).

The state, the civil organizations, the educational institutions, the religious entities, the developmental experts and ideologists, the international organizations, and other groups, as intermediaries of the global, could be allies of cooperation toward a viable transition and development in the Mayan communities. However, this process can only be successful in a relationship of equality, and not of paternalism. Moreover, the process of development of globalization in the Mayan populations and in any other indigenous groups throughout the world is only conceivable through a democratic and informed participation of all social actors.

If the Mayan as well as other peoples have to recur to their past cultural identity and values, this should be taken as a contribution to humanize the cruel side that globalization might have, and not as a threat or a backwardness to the progress of humanity.

Notes

1. In the Guatemalan case the Mayan population is not immigrant nor a minority, though it is treated as alien and a minority in its own land.
2. We take as additional examples the ethnic consciousness in Eastern Europe, Asian tribal groups, the peoples of Oceania, and North, South, and Central American ethnic consciousness.

Works Cited

Baud, Michiel, et al. 1996. *Etnicidad como estrategia en América Latina y el Caribe*. Quito, Ecuador: Ediciones Abya-Yala.
COCADI (Coordinadora Cakchikel de Desarrollo Integral). 1999. *Cultura Maya y Políticas de Desarrollo*. 2a. edición. Guatemala.
CPRG. 1985. Constitución Política de la República de Guatemala. Artículo 66.
COMG. 1995. *Construyendo un Futuro para Nuestro Pasado* (April). Guatemala: COMG.
Durston, John 1993. Indigenous People and Modernity. *CEPAL REVIEW* 51. (December).
García Ruiz, Jesús. 1997. Hacia una Nación Pluricultural en Guatemala. Guatemala: CEDIM.
Gorostigaga, Xabier. 1996. Globalización, Educación y Género (July 10). Santiago de Chile: SERNAM.
Sakakibara, Eisuke. 1995. The End of Progressivism: Search for New Goals. *Foreign Affairs* (September-October).
van Rijn, Claudette. 1996. El fin de la geografía: la globalización es como un tren de alta velocidad. *Third World Network Features* 2, no. 4 (August).
World Bank (IBRD). 1991. Directiva operacional concerniente a pueblos indígenas (September 17). Washington, D.C. : World Bank.

11

Linguistic Diversity, Interculturalism, and Democracy

Michael Richards and Julia Richards

Tremendous linguistic diversity exists in Guatemala, where twenty-one Mayan languages, in addition to Xinka (a Nahua language) and Garífuna (an Arawakan-based Creole spoken by Afro-Caribbeans), are spoken. While Spanish is spoken by most Guatemalans, and is the country's official language, nearly half of the nation's population speaks a Mayan language today.

Within the linguistic mosaic of Guatemala, other languages of European origin—English and German particularly, reflecting immigration movements stemming from the late 1800s—are spoken by members of the country's elite. English is spoken increasingly by inhabitants from various social strata, including Mayas, as it is taught as a foreign language in schools, is heard on television, or is introduced by tourists. Languages of Asiatic origin, notably Cantonese and Mandarin spoken by a significant Chinese population, and Korean, introduced by immigration waves beginning in the 1980s, are also heard in the linguistic auditorium of Guatemala's multiethnic society.

Ethnic diversity and multilingualism are key features punctuating the trends of Guatemalan history. The term *interculturalism* more and more is being used to connote the ideal of appropriate forms of interethnic conduct and communication and the pathway to guarantee the modality of democracy outlined in the peace accords that were signed in December 1996 between the Guatemalan National Revolutionary Unity (URNG) and the Guatemalan government.

In the core indigenous population regions of highland Guatemala, the distribution of ethnic and linguistic groups has not changed dramatically during the last three hundred years (Richards and Richards 1993). However, the peripheral zones of the South Coast piedmont zone, the northern region of the Zona Reina/Ixcán, and southern Petén defy this trend of language stability by area. In the Ixcán region of Quiché and the Petén there have been significant changes since the 1960s in language boundaries stemming from colonization movements, a nascent insurgency movement, followed by state-directed counterinsurgency sweeps (see Falla 1992; Manz 1988; Schwartz 1990). Repatriation of refugees, beginning in 1993, and still occurring at the time of this writing, again is molding a new linguistic panorama in these special regions of northern Guatemala.

It is important to note that since the colonial period, however, these northern Guatemalan regions have been precisely the ones most subject to linguistic change. The fight and flight strategies of the recent Guatemala insurgency and the response of the state to reestablish hegemony over the region are not unlike those patterns exercised by recalcitrant indigenous populations and the colonial order of military power and missionary orders entrusted to pacify and Christianize (Richards 1985).

Language and Interculturalism

Although there have been a number of realignments of language boundaries taking place in the peripheral regions of the Maya region, there is another type of linguistic change sweeping the core areas where Mayan languages traditionally have been spoken. In the last twenty-five years or so, widespread language shift has

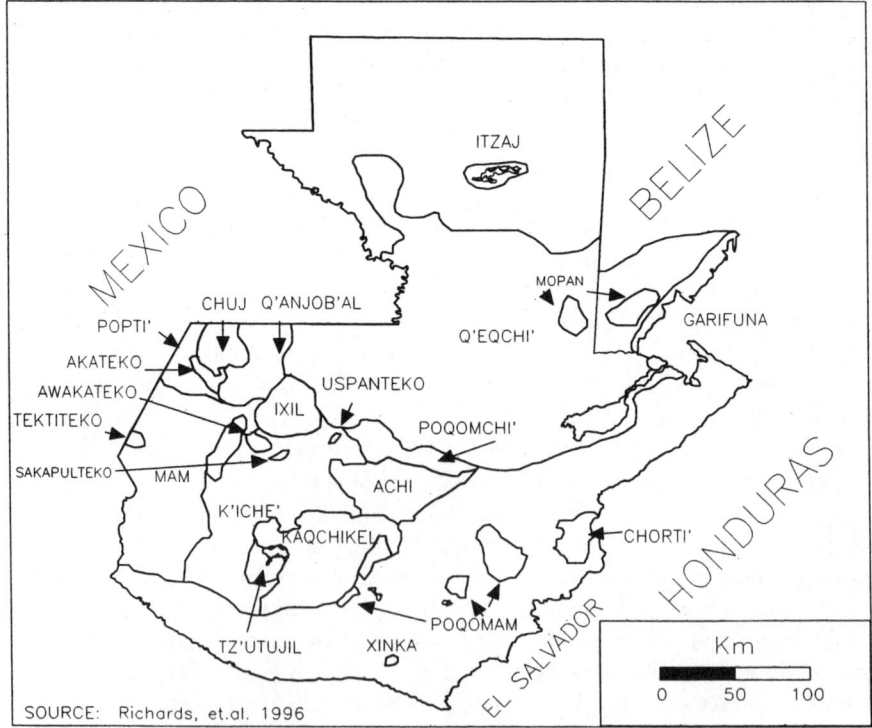

Figure 11.1. Present-Day Amerindian Language Boundaries

occurred, transforming the highland Mayan linguistic region into zones of varying degrees of bilingualism. A generalized tendency for Mayan speakers to want to become bilingual due to perceived real needs to become more competent in Guatemala's code of power is the motivational basis of a language shift phenomenon to Spanish. As Mayas become engaged in the ever-widening sphere of commercial and political interests that accompany globalization trends, language shift leading to widespread bilingualism in Mayan languages and Spanish is an observable fact. In some parts of the country, language shift has evolved to such a degree that there has been total loss of the spoken indigenous language. A language policy of Hispanization, propitiated by design in the colonial period, and continuing throughout Guatemala's history, never really had much measure of success for the Guatemalan state, but exogenous commercial, political, and religious influences certainly are bearing out this process in recent times, to the point that at least a dozen Mayan languages and Garífuna and Xinka today can be considered endangered languages. To say that these factors necessarily emanate from the metropoli to the rural fringes in an inexorable and unidirectional way is to oversimplify processes that fundamentally are much more complex. Nevertheless, from a demographic and spacial perspective, we can conceptualize a process in which cosmopolitan spheres of influence are generating a push toward greater Hispanization in the indigenous rural ambience.

Examining the historical backdrop of societal bilingualism among Guatemala's Maya, before the arrival of the Spanish and the emergent phenomenon of Mayan-Spanish bilingualism, certain members of post-Classic Mayan society undoubtedly could speak more than one language, likely variants of Toltecan and later, Nahua languages, along with their native Maya tongue (Fox 1978; Campbell 1997). When the Spanish arrived and imposed sociopolitical constructs of colonial society upon the indigenous patterns of social organization, members of the subjugated Maya elite quickly learned rudiments of Spanish. In some noteworthy cases, Spaniards learned to speak and even read and write the Mayan languages, such as was the case of certain Catholic friars who encoded Kaqchikel, K'iche', and Q'eqchi' using the Roman alphabet and orthographic conventions (Van Oss 1986, 18).

With the creation of a new Ladino social stratum, bilingualism in the colonial period emerged more prominent. Itinerant Ladinos helped spread Spanish through their mercantile pursuits or through contracting vast numbers of seasonal labor migrants to work in the agro-export industries of first, cacao and sarsparilla, and then indigo, and finally, during the liberal era after independence from Spain, in coffee. Some Ladinos residing in indigenous communities learned to speak the local language. Especially noteworthy is the case of the Verapaz region, where Ladinos (and then later Germans) learned to speak Q'eqchi', which had an equal, if not superior, level of instrumentality as Spanish in this regional context.

The social directionality of Maya-Spanish bilingualism in Guatemala is and always has been one whereby many more members of the indigenous population learn to speak Spanish than do members of the Ladino population learn to speak an indigenous language. Nevertheless, during the colonial period and the early republican period, in absolute terms, the number of Maya who learned to speak Spanish was minimal. In spite of the fact that Spanish functioned as the language of power, and that members of the subordinated indigenous caste group often were inspired to learn it in order to enhance their economic and social possibilities, the context of Spanish language usage was quite restricted, and opportunities to acquire the language were minimal.

Those Maya who did learn Spanish in the colonial period were members of the native elite strata. It was generally the case that the Spanish would situate those who learned the power code in instrumental positions as commercial intermediaries, lower level government functionaries, or as religious assistants. The vast majority of Maya, in contrast, continued speaking their own mother tongue or were bilingual in other indigenous languages with which they came into contact. Incidentally, the phenomenon of intra-Mayan language bilingualism is an area of sociolinguistics that has received little attention, but certainly one that is highly relevant in this era of democratization in Guatemala, where strategies are being sought to enhance language intelligibility across and within languages in order to consolidate the written forms of the Mayan languages.

Guatemala's language profile today is eminently one of widespread bilingualism. In the highland regions, most Maya people are to some degree bilingual in their native tongue and Spanish. Concurrently however, there is an ongoing process occurring in the capital city and in secondary cities wherein many nonindigenous people are also becoming increasingly bilingual, only this time not in Spanish and a Mayan language, but rather in Spanish and another world power language, principally English. Within Guatemala's globalization trend a process of linguistic lag is occurring. For five hundred years the Ladino population has had a linguistic advantage over a subordinated Maya lacking control of Spanish. But now, as Mayas increasingly control Spanish, Ladinos control not only Spanish, but are in command of English or another world language as well. This, of course, allows them to maintain their historic linguistic edge.

Bilingual Education and Interculturalism

Education in Guatemala historically has been underfinanced. Public expenditure in this sector generally has been toted by a series of governing administrations as a symbolic emblem attesting that there indeed is government action to reduce illiteracy and foster numeracy and instill a sense of nationhood among the country's youth. In the Western Hemisphere, Guatemala ranks as one of the lowest investors in human capacity investment. Although school attendance is mandatory (through fourteen years), the provision of educational services remains insufficient, inefficient, and deficient. For indigenous children, the deficit in access and quality formal education is most striking—to illustrate, only 8 percent of the country's

Mayan-speaking school-age children receive instruction in their mother tongue.

Since 1980, the country has had a state-sponsored bilingual education program in Mayan languages and Spanish. Although the program's orientation began with purposeful transition to Spanish, it is now one in which the preservation and strengthening of the indigenous languages is paramount, a so-called maintenance model (see Fishman 1980). The Bilingual Education Project began in 1980 as an initiative proposed and funded by the U.S. Agency for International Development (USAID) in forty pilot schools in the so-called majority languages, K'iche', Kaqchikel, Q'eqchi', and Mam. Demographically speaking, these languages comprise more than 80 percent of the speakers of Mayan languages in Guatemala, hence the designation "majority languages." The National Bilingual Education Program (PRONEBI) was created in 1985 with the Guatemalan government's counterpart contribution complementing continued USAID support. In the "majority language" regions, the forty pilot bilingual school program expanded to four hundred schools (for instruction through fourth grade), and eight hundred additional schools were given transitional bilingual instructional support for the preprimary entry grade for Maya schoolchildren. In 1990, the preprimary level coverage was extended to a number of schools in four additional language regions, although support was rather piecemeal and ad hoc in nature. In 1995, state-funded bilingual education was consigned a higher status as the General Directorate of Intercultural Bilingual Education (DIGEBI). At present, there are 1,470 state schools under the directorate's administration (DIGEBI 1997).

With the designation of an *Intercultural Bilingual* Education Directorate, a formalized use of the term *intercultural* emerged in the official state lexicon. In the Maya Proposal for Educational Reform presented in July 1996, it is argued that "Educational Reform should guide the Guatemalan nation toward *intercultural relations*." In the peace accords, specifically, the Accord on Identity and the Rights of Indigenous Peoples, there are spelled out a number of steps to achieve an authentic bilingual intercultural education in which the government should be proactive. Among others are the following:

- Integrate Maya and other indigenous people's educational concepts, being those of a philosophical, scientific, artistic, pedagogical, historical, linguistic, and political and social nature, as the springboard of a integrated educational reform movement.
- Augment and propel bilingual intercultural education and give value to the study and knowledge base of indigenous languages at all educational levels.
- Include in educational planning content areas that fortify national unity within a context of respect for cultural diversity.

By mandate of the peace accords, the state has a serious obligation to launch an ambitious program of development, democratization, social integration, and political rejuvenation. Being that the "educational system is one of the most important conduits for the transmission and development of values and cultural knowledge," as is stated in the article referring to Educational Reform in the Accord on Identity and the Rights of Indigenous Peoples, "the protection and strengthening of linguistic diversity, both in the development of an intercultural modality for all sectors of the country, are long-term political goals that will only be gained through formal and informal education." Perhaps the most distinguishing aspect of the peace accords is precisely that they focus not so much on how to solve problems in the short run, but that they function as a blueprint to implement a long-term development program to basically transform Guatemalan society. The peace accords framework sets the stage for correcting the injustices that were committed not only throughout thirty-six years of armed conflict, but attempts to resolve injustices and conflicts that are deeply rooted in centuries of history.

The term *intercultural*, apart from its coupled use with the term *bilingual education*, and its appearance in the peace accords, tends to cause some confusion. The manner in which "interculturalism" is proposed to be wedged into the educational arena with the extant model of bilingual education has brought to forth two questions: First, "What really is interculturalism?" and second, "Interculturalism for whom?"

The term *intercultural* is widely used in the context of bilingual education in the Andean countries, Mexico, Nicaragua, to name a few. "Intercultural" connotes tolerant and harmonious interethnic relations, mutual respect, and two-way communication. The concept of interculturalism in the Accord on Identity and the Rights of Indigenous Peoples as does the Mayan Proposal for Educational Reform, clearly puts forth what should be "intercultural," and the meaning is certainly in line with the usage found in other Latin American countries. "Integrative" interculturalism, as opposed to "aggregative" or "confrontative" interculturalism (Zimmermann 1998, 5-12) generally is what is envisioned, whereby meritorious values and concepts of knowledge of both indigenous society and Ladino society are to be put forth in educational formats. The experience of past conflict and the need to change the nature of Maya-Ladino relations suggest to many involved in the process of constructing peace in Guatemala today that something more than watered-down symbols need to spring forth from so-called interculturalism. To be sure, a measure of growing apprehension about the interpretation of the concept of interculturalism and its applicability in the educational arena is surfacing.

Many indigenous persons working in constructing peace in Guatemala, whether it be in education, law, or other fields, know full well that interculturalism is something their people have been putting into practice for centuries and who continue to live it on a daily basis. To them, interculturalism is not viewed as a way of enhancing levels of appreciation for the apparent trappings of Guatemala's linguistic, cultural, and societal diversity. What it does embody is a concept encompassing a set of strategies that has allowed Mayas to survive generation after generation in a societal context in which they have been relegated as members of a caste excluded from any significant participation in the political, economic, and social spheres of the nation.

Some members of the indigenous community view with apprehension the notion of interculturalism, so elegantly stated in the peace accords and the proposal for educational reform, because they fear it may become operationalized in educational strategies as only palliative measures to dilute bilingual educational programs that more aggressively address dimensions of linguistic and cultural rescue and maintenance. As far as educational content is concerned, there is additional apprehension that interculturalism may be reduced to superficial symbolic conveyance in the form of graphic representations of boys and girls from different ethnic groups hand in hand skipping across the schoolyard, the INGUATization of an intercultural vision, to make the analogy with what has already occurred with the Guatemalan tourist bureau's representations of indigenous life. The greatest fear is that individuals working in the production of didactic materials or in teacher training lack the philosophical basis of identity needed to formulate an educational platform that is not based merely on content and form, but rather rooted in process and reason. It is unfortunate that some of the emerging didactic materials typify that superficial manipulation of symbols already mentioned, what Klaus Zimmermann calls an "aggregative modality" (1998, 5-12) of intercultural education, whereby bits and pieces of culture traits from the different societies are simply added without regard to any internal logic of relationships in and among cultural features.

Interculturalism put into practice is a concept that implies a number of actions, and fortunately the time frame stipulated in the peace accords to restructure Guatemalan society in the mold of the principles delineated is ample indeed. Most policy reformers in Guatemala recognize that the start of the activities will depart in a jerky, awkward manner. Although new intercultural relations in Guatemala may experience paroxysmic beginnings, the same indigenous persons who lead the movement to preserve and to fortify linguistic diversity and the intercultural educational modality express their hope that the intercultural vision truly leads to a Mayanization movement within the Guatemalan nation, bringing about positive changes to members of the Ladino spheres so that there is greater tolerance, receptivity, and appreciation for what are indigenous elements.

With regard to the ways to prevent further loss of Guatemala's autochthonous languages, within a national intercultural context, it is hoped that measures can be instituted to genuinely preserve and fortify the country's linguistic diversity. The peace accords stipulate that Maya, Garífuna, and Xinka languages be bolstered in a democratic context of identity and rights of indigenous peoples. In the final recommendations of the Special Parity Commission on Indigenous Language Officialization, three levels of attention to be accorded indigenous languages were identified. In the first group, the so-called "territorial languages," are the four "majority languages" of Kiche', Kaqchikel, Q'eqchi', and Mam—the languages spoken in large regions by numerous people and that are not faced with any dire threat of extinction. For these languages, the recommended educational interventions are that it be bilingual and intercultural through the sixth year of primary, and in certain subject areas (language arts, for example), continue into the secondary level. In matters of health and justice, it is recommended by the Officialization Commission that in these territorial language regions, inhabitants should have access to a professional translator provided by the state, if requested.

The second level of language classification within the Officialization Commission's scheme is called "community languages." There are seventeen languages in this category. The recommended educational treatment of these languages places a bilingual education modality through third grade of primary, the so-called Fundamental Education Cycle (CEF). However, there is no real specificity regarding exactly what should be the nature of formal education beyond third grade other than a vague directive that it should be bilingual.

At the third level are two practically extinct languages—Itzaj and Xinka. These languages are designated as "special" because of their precarious state. The commission calls for extraordinary language rescue measures, including undertaking linguistics research of descriptive nature and the creation of pedagogical grammars, dictionaries, and other classroom aids to reactivate language usage among youth and mounting aggressive campaigns to widen the context of usage of these languages among the Itzaj and Xinka peoples.

There are notorious cases in which language death and loss of language-based cultural identity results in marked transformations of indigenous society. Speaking purely in linguistic terms, the case of Kaqchikel exemplifies a general bilingualization trend, and in some cases, a trend toward a complete shift to Spanish language use. The tendency toward Spanish dominance is quite extreme in some areas, particularly in the Departments of Sacatepéquez and Guatemala. These areas historically acted as the cradle of Spanish language spread. Moving away from Sacatepéquez and the metropolitan area of Guatemala City, toward the Department of Chimaltenango, a tendency toward an intermediate level of bilingualism can be seen. Again, moving more distantly from these core regions, especially in the Department of Sololá, the tendency is for Kaqchikel monolingualism. Kaqchikel poses a case study in a tendency of greater, if not Spanish monolingualism, near the metropolitan core regions, and Mayan language vitality in the peripheral zones, but the trend is not unique in the historical linguistic sequence of all Guatemalan languages.

The peace accords take it as a given that the country is eminently pluricultural and multilingual. However, that all the languages, to one degree or another, are losing their vitality is a fact. Many proposals on how to reinforce the Mayan, Garífuna, and Xinka languages have been set forth, and some strategic rescue actions for the more imperiled languages are currently under way. How effective these efforts will be cannot be predicted at this point in time. None of these activities and proposals lacks in merit, and the fact that there are a multitude of recipes for action attests only to the fact that the languages themselves are diverse in their circumstances of speakers, surrounding populations, and relative interactions with the wider spheres of market and politics. In Guatemala, all the languages are menaced by the threat of language shift or disappearance; there are scenarios ranging from impending language death for Itzaaj and Xinka, for example, to the relative robusticity and likely persistence of K'iche'. Whatever language is examined, a certainty is that global factors increasingly play a role in Mayan language integrity.

What can be interpreted from the peace accords is that, clearly, Guatemalan society needs to embark on a new path of reconciliation and reconstruction. Required elements for a successful path in the peace process are found in the linguistic and ethnic diversity of the country. The Mayan, Garífuna, and Xinka languages need to be revitalized, reinforced, and maintained, and in order to do so, decisive and aggressive postures need to be taken. This certainly does not mean that minimalist translation routines guide a compensatory educational reform, or that lackadaisical lip service be paid to a new intercultural way, or that legislation to protect the use and development of the languages be enacted and no follow-through action is taken.

Decisive revitalization, reinforcement, and maintenance measures for Guatemala's Amerindian languages do mean that serious applied linguistic work has to occur. These activities have to be linked to clearly defined goals to carry out a pedagogical reform of within an educational system that responds to the demands of a multicultural, plurilingual nation within the changing context of a global economy and technological change. In effect, the peace accords basically call for a measure of linguistic reengineering of Guatemala. This is a challenge noted by the only official state institution entrusted to the defense and fortification of Guatemala's Amerindian languages, the Academia de Lenguas Mayas de Guatemala (ALMG).

In Guatemala, sound linguistic policy cannot be formulated and implemented by linguists alone. Nor can good pedagogy for the nation's people be adequately designed and conducted by educators alone. Within the overriding frame of this new era of interculturalism in Guatemala, linguists need to learn some fundamental principles of pedagogy, and commensurately, educators need to learn some measure of linguistics.

The linguistic classification of Guatemala has rested largely on a "splitter" taxonomical approach, creating sometimes highly focalized language designations. This was not done by intent, but more reflects historical trends in the epistemological development of Mayan linguistics. Today, with issues of language rescue and preservation paramount, there is emerging a perceived need that perhaps more encompassing "lumper" taxonomic approaches toward language diversity may be more fitting for meeting the challenges of implementing practical language standardization procedures.

In order to ensure peace and democracy in Guatemala, the peace accords stipulate that mechanisms should be introduced to maintain the pluricultural and multilingual richness of the country. But there will never be enough resources to provide optimum or even adequate treatment to all the languages. However, using applied linguistic techniques, coupled with participatory action from the language/ethnic communities themselves and professional organizations (for example, universities and Mayan organizations) that work in linguistic and cultural revitalization, linguistic diversity will be maintained through strategies oriented toward unifying languages, rather than fragmenting them further. These measures, combined with developing an intercultural modality in social relations, will only enhance the framework to promote democratic processes within a pluricultural and multilingual Guatemala.

Works Cited

Campbell, Lyle. 1997. *Quichean Linguistic Prehistory.* University of California Publications in Linguistics No. 81. Berkeley: University of California Press.
Dirección General de Educación Bilingüe Intercultural (DIGEBI). 1997. *Plan Anual.* Guatemala: Ministerio de Educación. Manuscript.
———. 1997. *Plan Estratégico 1998.* Guatemala Ministerio de Educación. Mimeo.
Falla, Ricardo. 1992. *Masacres de la Selva: Ixcán, Guatemala (1975-1982).* Guatemala: Editorial Universitaria.
Fishman, Joshua. 1980. Language Maintenance and Ethnicity. In *Harvard Encyclopedia of American Ethnic Groups*, edited by S. Thurnstrom. Cambridge, Mass.: Harvard University Press.
Fox, John. 1978. *Quiché Conquest.* Albuquerque: University of New Mexico Press.
Manz, Beatriz. 1988. *Refugees of a Hidden War: The Aftermath of Counterinsurgency in Guatemala.* Albany: State University of New York Press.
Richards, Michael. 1985. Cosmopolitan World View and Counterinsurgency in Guatemala. *Anthropological Quarterly* 3:90-107.
Richards, Michael, and Julia Becker Richards. 1993. Lenguas Mayas y Procesos Históricos en Guatemala. In *Historia de Guatemala.* Vol 2, edited by Luis Luján Muñoz. Guatemala: Asociación de Amigos del País.
Richards, Michael, Julia Richards, Narciso Cojtí, and Technical Members of La Unidad de Planificación Lingüística del DIGEBI. 1996. Mapa de los Idiomas Indígenas de Guatemala. Dirección General de Educación Bilingüe Intercultural. Guatemala: Ministerio de Educación.
Schwartz, Norman. 1990. *Forest Society: A Social History of Petén, Guatemala.* Philadelphia: University of Pennsylvania Press.
Van Oss, Adriaan. 1986. *Catholic Colonialism: A Parish History of Guatemala, 1524-1821.* Cambridge: Cambridge University Press.
Zimmermann, Klaus. 1998. Modos de interculturalidad en la educación bilingüe. Reflexiones acerca del caso de Guatemala. *Revista Iberoamericana de Educación* 13:1-12 (internet version).

Part IV:

Globalization on the Ground

12

Neoliberalism, the Global Elite, and the Guatemalan Transition: A Critical Macrosocial Analysis

William I. Robinson

This chapter discusses the trajectory of social change in Central America and Latin America in recent decades, and beyond that, the transformations in the global system, as the "big picture" that puts into a larger focus issues of democratization and development in Guatemala. I contend that recent change in Guatemala is part of a complex transition that began in Central America in the 1960s and will continue into the twenty-first century, involving the region's ongoing, gradual, highly conflictive and contradictory entrance into emergent global economy and society. I must state as caveat that to compact these issues into the space of a few pages means that we must necessarily simplify complex and open-ended social and historical processes, and risk painting in black and white what is more properly a picture with many shades of gray.

Global Capitalism and the Agenda of the Transnational Elite

Globalization entails the transition from the nation-state phase of capitalism to a qualitatively new transnational phase.[1] Since 1492 the world has been linked together into a single social system by trade and financial flows in an integrated international market. But from the late 1960s and on, and accelerating at the close of the twentieth century, this *world economy* is giving way to a new *global economy*. In this global economy, nations are no longer linked together by external flows and relations but are rather becoming integrated organically through the globalization of the production process itself along with the integration of the whole complex of the social, political, juridical, and cultural superstructure. The emergence of a truly global economy brings with it the material basis for the emergence of a single global society, including the transnationalization of civil society, of political processes, and of cultural life.

The global mobility of capital has allowed for the decentralization and functional integration around the world of vast chains of production and distribution, the instantaneous movement of values, and the unprecedented concentration and centralization of worldwide economic management, control, and decision-making power in transnational capital. Global capitalism is organized in a set of increasingly supra-national institutions. These institutions include the following: the transnational corporations that own and manage the world's resources and appropriate the wealth produced by humanity; the international financial agencies (IFIs, such as the International Monetary Fund [IMF] and the World Bank) that impose the conditions necessary for global capital accumulation to take place; the states of the North, and their junior counterparts of the South, that create the global and the local political, administrative, and legal environment that allow the system to function; and the formal and information transnational elite forums, such as the Groups of Seven, the Trilateral Commission, and the World Economic Forum, that develop strategies for the maintenance and reproduction of the system and supervise its overall operation.

The agent of global economy is a new *transnational elite*. This transnational elite now controls the levers of global decision making and increasingly monopolizes power in global society. It is comprised of the owners and managers of the transnational corporations, and also of the bureaucrats, the cadres, and the technicians, who administer the IFIs, the states of the North and the South, and the transnational forums. And membership in the transnational elite also includes the politicians and charismatic figures, along with select organic intellectuals, who provide ideological legitimacy and technical solutions. Below this transnational elite is a small and shrinking layer of middle classes who exercise very little real power but who, pacified with mass consumption, form a fragile buffer between the transnational elite and the world's poor majority. Globalization dramatically alters the balance of forces among classes and social groups in each nation, and at a level of the global system, away from popular majorities and toward transnational capital and its representatives. National states increasingly respond to the interests of transnationalized fractions of local dominant groups.

The program of the transnational elite, in broad strokes, is to create the conditions most propitious to the unfettered functioning of global capitalism. In promoting this program, this new global elite has been pursuing in every region of the world since the mid-1980s a "transnational agenda" involving concomitant economic and political components (Robinson 1996a, 1996b, 1996c, 1997). The economic component is neoliberalism, a model that seeks to achieve the conditions in each country and region of the world for the mobility and free operation of capital. The neoliberal structural adjustment programs sweeping Latin America and the South seek macroeconomic stability as an essential requisite for the activity of transnational capital. This model seeks to harmonize a wide range of fiscal, monetary, industrial, and commercial policies among multiple nations, as a requirement for fully mobile transnational capital to function simultaneously, and often instantaneously, among numerous national borders. In the neoliberal model, stabilization, or the package of fiscal, monetary, exchange and related measures intended to achieve macroeconomic stability, is followed by "structural adjustment": (a) liberalization of trade and finances, which opens the economy to the world market; (b) deregulation, which removes the state from economic decision making (but not from activities that service capital); (c) privatization of formerly public spheres that could hamper capital accumulation if criteria of public interest over private profit is left operative. This model thus generates the overall conditions for the profitable ("efficient") renewal of capital accumulation through new globalized circuits, and along with it, for social reproduction in the age of globalization. Without a single exception, neoliberal restructuring results in an increase in poverty and inequality in the adjusted country as wealth is redistributed upward and shifted from the domestic market to the external sector linked to the global economy (c.f. Green 1995). The unprecedented growth of inequalities worldwide under globalization, along with the emergence of new social hierarchies and cleavages around these inequalities (see, inter alia, UNDP, various years), is leading to a new global social apartheid and worldwide polarization.

In turn, the political project is the promotion of "democracy," or what is more accurately called *polyarchy*, which refers to a system in which a small group actually rules, and participation in decision making by the majority is confined to choosing among competing elites in tightly controlled electoral processes. This type of "low-intensity democracy" does not involve power (cratos) of the people (demos), much less an end to elite rule or to substantive inequality that is growing exponentially under the global economy. The crisis of elite rule that had developed throughout the Third World in the 1970s and 1980s, in the context of globalization, was resolved through transitions to polyarchies. What transpired in these contested transitions was an effort by transnational dominant groups to reconstitute hegemony through a change in the mode of political domination, from the coercive systems of social control exercised by authoritarian and dictatorial regimes to more consensually based systems of the new polyarchies. At stake was what type of a social order—the emergent global capitalist order or some popular alternative—would emerge in the wake of authoritarianism. Masses push for a deeper popular democratization while emergent transnationalized elites, who have behind them the structural power of the global economy and the inordinate political and ideological influence that this brings, and often count on the direct U.S. political and military intervention, were able to gain hegemony over democratization movements and steer the breakup of authoritarianism into polyarchic outcomes. The transnational elite is now attempting to consolidate fragile polyarchic systems as the political counterpart to neoliberalism. Interaction and economic integration on a world scale are obstructed by authoritarian or dictatorial political arrangements, which are unable to manage the expansion social intercourse associated with the global economy. With its mechanisms for intra-elite compromise and accommodation and for hegemonic incorporation of popular majorities, polyarchy is better equipped in the new global environment to legitimize the political authority of dominant groups and to achieve the political stability necessary for global capitalism to operate. The "democratic consensus" in the new world order is a consensus among an increasingly cohesive global elite on the type of political system most propitious to the reproduction of social order in the new global environment.[2]

Transnational Processes in Central America

The underlying macrostructural dynamic in individual nations and regions of the world over the past few decades has been integration into emergent global society. This has involved the breakup of national economic, political, and social systems reciprocal to the breakup of a pre-globalization nation-state-based world order as globalization has advanced. This process of integration into changing world structures takes place through what elsewhere I have termed *transnational processes* (Robinson 1997, 1998b), which are under way in each country and region of the world. By transnational processes I mean the economic and concomitant social, political, and cultural changes associated with the transition to global capitalism. Transnational processes in Central America should be seen as changes specific to the region that are linked to broader changes in the global system.

What types of changes do we see in each country and region around the world as transnational processes get under way and have a transformative effect? Productive structures are reorganized reciprocal to the reorganization of global production, a process through which each national economy is rearticulated to the global economy as new economic activities linked to globalization come to dominate and as each region acquires a new profile in the global system. There is a complete class restructuring. Domestic classes tend to become globalized, pre-globalization classes such as peasantries and artisans tend to disappear, and new classes and class fractions linked to the global economy emerge and become dominant. The transnational agenda of neoliberalism and polyarchy take hold as the hegemonic project under the guidance of transnationalized fractions of local elites. Local political systems and civil societies become transnationalized, states becomes integrated externally into supranational institutions and forums that gradually assume more and more functions that corresponded to the nation-state in the pre-globalization period. A "global culture" of hyperindividualism, competition, and consumerism has eclipsed nationalist and developmental ideologies.

We see all these changes in Central America, and more broadly throughout Latin America, as transnational processes have taken hold over the past two decades and as a new transnational model of society comes to replace the pre-globalization model. Facilitated by the neoliberal opening to the global economy and the "Export-Led Development" (ELD) strategy, maquiladora production (particularly of garments), tourism, nontraditional agricultural exports, and remittances from emigrant workers have risen dramatically in importance and are coming to eclipse the traditional agro-export model as the most dynamic economic sectors linking Central America to globalized circuits of production and distribution (Robinson 1998b). The Central American peasantry, artisan class, national industrial, and other pre-globalization classes have tended to gradually disintegrate, and three principal globalization groups have come to the forefront: transnationalized fractions of the bourgeoisie tied to the new economic activities; new urban and rural working classes; and a new class of supernumeraries, or superfluous labor pools (a huge portion of the latter has migrated to the United States, where it constitutes a de-nationalized immigrant labor pool). The old authoritarian regimes have crumbled through transitions to polyarchy, and leftist movements that posed in the 1980s an antisystemic alternative to integration in the emergent global order have been defeated or transformed. In each Central American country, a transnationalized "technocratic" or New Right fraction has gained hegemony within the dominant classes and is pushing the transnational agenda of neoliberalism and the consolidation of polyarchies through diverse institutions, including political parties, states, and the organs of civil society.

Neoliberal structuring has resulted in a massive transfer of resources from the public to the private sphere, and within the private sphere, from the domestic to the external sector. The change in the model of accumulation has thus involved a concomitant change from the "developmentalist state" of the national model to the "neoliberal state" of the transnational model. The Central American states have been reduced and transformed, functioning to adjust national structures to emergent global structures. The five Central American states have moved gradually toward supranational integration. This integration is political, taking place through new formal and informal forums, such as the *Sistema de Integración Centroamericana* (SICA), the Central American Parliament (PARLACEN), and regular presidential summits and regionwide ministerial meetings. It is also economic, and includes the negotiation of a new free trade zone based on collective integration into the North America Free Trade Agreement (NAFTA), and beyond it, the global economy. Complex sets of international agreements have opened up the region to transnational capital. If the Central American Common Market (CACM) was a form of "inward" integration, intended to create a regional market for multinational (largely U.S.) capital to take advantage of economies of scale, the type of integration proceeding under globalization is "outward," aimed at creating a single Central American field for the unfettered operation of transnational capital.

The IFIs and diverse United Nations (UN) and Organization of American States (OAS) units and other transnational actors, including the U.S. Agency for International Development (USAID) and numerous international nongovernmental organizations (NGOs) (often linked to core country states), have come increasingly to assume functions of states through the design and imposition of economic policies, management of peace accords, sponsorship of institution building, and so on. In this process, each individual Isthmanian state has been penetrated by two new social forces, one from "within" and the other from "without." From "within," transnationalized fractions of dominant groups vie for, and gain control over, local states, particularly, over key ministries tying the country to global economy and society, such as ministries of foreign affairs, finances, economic development, and central banks. From "without," diverse transnational actors representing an emergent transnationalized state apparatus penetrate local states, liaise with transnationalized fractions therein, and help design and guide local policies.[3]

A Reassessment of the Central American Conflict

These vast and open-ended transformations should be seen as the evolving outcome to the struggle among social forces in Central America as collective agents in dialectic interaction with changes in the global system.[4] In broad strokes, three social forces representing three distinct projects for the region were in dispute during the 1960s to 1990s upheavals. The landed oligarchies and dominant groups tied to the traditional agro-export model sought to sustain and reproduce the old model of capital accumulation, and the particular set of social privileges and relations of domination based on authoritarian political systems.[5] As the "Autumn of the oligarchs" approached, the popular sectors and the mass revolutionary movements sought radical reformism, such as mass land redistribution, as well as more far-reaching revolutionary and socialist-oriented alternatives for the region, that would have deeply undermined the class structure, upset relations of domination, and redistributed power and resources in favor of popular majorities.

As the regional conflict unfolded in the 1970s and 1980s, on the surface it appeared as a bipolar contest between the old oligarchies and the popular revolutionary movements. But, in fact, globalizing dynamics had begun to have a transformative effect on local social forces. A "New Right" gradually cohered in the 1980s, in fits and bouts, into local transnationalized fractions of dominant groups and acquired its own political protagonism. Its project was to advance the agenda of the transnational elite. This transnational fraction was not a group that came into being from outside of the traditional oligarchy but from within, from the same family networks. The prospects of this emerging transnational fraction for accumulating wealth and privilege, however, was less linked to restoring the traditional agro-exports and industries under pre-1980s social relations, as they were to converting the region into a new export platform. It sought to submit backward oligarchic property relations to a capitalist modernization through a program of neoliberal restructuring and to a new "competitive" insertion into the emerging global economy. This New Right project sought to modernize the state and society without any fundamental deconcentration of property and wealth, and without any class redistribution of political and economic power.

It also promoted, together with the United States, transitions from authoritarian to so-called democratic political systems. The immediate aim was to preempt the movements for a more far-reaching popular democratization through immediate reform, such as the replacement of military by civilian personnel and controlled elections. But beyond this conjunctural consideration, the insertion of the region into global capitalism would require a political system with the promise of achieving more lasting social stability through consensual modes of social control rather than the old oligarchic dictatorships. This involved demilitarization, peace negotiations, the institutionalization of procedurally correct electoral processes, states with a functional separation of powers, and so on.

The persistence of an oligarchic political structure combined with rapid capitalist development spurred on by the region's incipient integration into the emergent global economy in the 1960s and 1970s had sparked the revolutionary upheavals by the late 1970s. In the 1980s the revolutionary movements succeeded in breaking the hegemony of the landed oligarchy and rich industrialists and financial groups that had come into existence with the CACM. However, due to a complex confluence of factors, these popular social forces were unable to impose and stabilize their project of a radical redistributive and socialist-oriented reconstruction of the region. One of these factors was massive U.S. intervention. A second was the contradictions and weaknesses internal to the revolutionary project itself, in the context of a changing world order. At the structural level, the emergence of the global economy and the growing power of transnational capital and the world market to impose discipline on antisystemic movements made inviable the revolutionary project. The third factor was the changing composition of the dominant classes, their socioeconomic articulation, and their political-ideological project. The emergence of the neoliberal New Right in the 1980s in each of the Central American countries was, in part, a very result of the revolutionary upsurge, which altered the dominant power blocs in each country. It was also, in part, a result of the changes in the world order with the emergence of the global economy and a transnational elite as both a political and economic protagonist.

These three factors cannot be separated; they are different dimensions of a process whose structural determinacy was the emergence of the global economy and the influence of globalizing pressures on the complex set of regional agents and social, economic, and political structures. It was the threat of revolution from the popular classes that led to U.S. intervention. U.S. policymakers changed the objective of interventionism, from the mid-1980s and on, from a military defeat of revolutionary forces through counterinsurgency to a more thorough political and economic restructuring of the region and its social forces via the linkage of Central America to emergent global structures. This included a shift in policy to "democracy promotion" as a means to neutralize through *incorporation* the threat posed by anti-systemic forces in the region. From the mid-1980s and on, changes in the U.S. strategy and new opportunities, as well as constraints opened by globalization and a changing world order for the distinct social forces in dispute, accelerated the articulation of alternative political-ideological discourse and projects among sectors of the dominant groups that would gradually cohere into a New Right elite. The transnational nuclei of the local elite vied for, and achieved, hegemony over the elite as a whole in the 1980s, and went on in the 1990s to assume state power and to attempt implementation of the program of global capitalism in the region. Political regime change in each country, except Costa Rica, has been one aspect of a broader transition in the nature of political authority and the mode of social control in the region. What took place structurally from the 1960s to the 1990s was the breakup of authoritarian systems on the heels of the mass socioeconomic disruptions and political mobilization caused by the massive entry of foreign capital through the CACM, new economic activities, and social class protagonists, which signaled the beginnings of globalization in the Isthmus. The recomposition of the capitalist order involved a new social structure, based on changes in the economy, state, regime and political system, classes, and so on.

My analysis runs contrary to conventional thinking, according to which, by the end of the 1980s the old oligarchies had virtually disappeared, but neither the popular forces nor their adversaries, the new dominant groups in Central America together with the United States, could prevail. According to this view, a stalemate had been reached that created the conditions for a historic compromise between different class and social forces in favor of a mutual accommodation. A broad consensus was reached through negotiations and peace settlements that shifted the terrain of struggle in the region from the military to the politic-civic arena. In turn, this shift was to be framed within regionwide processes of democratization and demilitarization. Competition between different social projects would now take place through elections and peaceful mobilization.

I do not share this conventional view. The revolutionary upheavals did not end in a regional stalemate leading to a historic compromise among social classes and political groups. Rather, the outcome of the regional conflict was the conditional defeat of the broad popular sectors in Central America and the conditional victory of the new dominant groups.[6] This outcome was formalized in the internationally sponsored peace negotiations of the late 1980s and early 1990s, followed by diverse *concertación* and "reconciliation" forums that transferred social contradictions from the military to the political terrain, and hammered out fragile and temporary pacts, but did not resolve the social contradictions that gave rise to the upheaval.

Synopsis of Change in Each Country

In Nicaragua, the Sandinista triumph of 1979 constituted the seizure of state power in one country by a revolutionary movement and an effort to implement the popular project. The overthrow of the Somocista dictatorship destroyed the traditional oligarchy. However, the structural constraints of globalization and the direct power of the U.S. state conjoined to make unworkable an alternative to polyarchy and global capitalism. Modernizing capitalist fractions had been coalescing since the mid-1960s, and in opposition to Somoza linked with the Sandinistas in 1970s class alliances. These fractions stayed inside Nicaragua following the revolution and retained their links to the international capitalist market. They gradually gained structural strength and political importance in the 1980s, as they increasingly replaced the state as the principal intermediaries between Nicaragua and world markets and developed ties to the emergent U.S.-led transnational elite. In highly simplified terms, a transnationalized fraction took over key institutions of the state following the 1990s elections, even as much of the state, and society at large, was in dispute since 1990. This embryonic transnational nucleus pursued the program of the reinsertion of Nicaragua into the global economy and a far-reaching neo-liberal restructuring.

In El Salvador, a massive popular movement burgeoned in the 1970s and the guerrilla movement had snowballed into a full civil war by the early 1980s. While the revolutionary forces came to threaten state power, the U.S.-led counterinsurgency staved off a triumph similar to that which had taken place in Nicaragua. However, behind the very visible battle between the revolutionary armed movement and the U.S.-supported dominant groups was a more significant process: the reorganization of the Salvadoran state and economy in conjunction with movement at the level of the global economy, a reconfiguration of the dominant groups, and the emergence of a lucid New Right fraction within the ruling party itself, the Nationalist Revolutionary Alliance (ARENA). The transnationalized fraction gained control over the ARENA party—which had ironically first been formed by the most retrograde elements of the oligarchy—and of the state with the election of Alfredo Cristiani in 1988. The insurgency, combined with changes in the dominant project itself, shattered the old oligarchy and its project. This fraction was able to gain hegemony over the elite and over the transition as a whole, and implement sweeping neoliberal transformation since 1988.

In Honduras, both the subordinate and the dominant classes were historically the least developed in Central America. The chaotic disequilibrium among internal social forces for much of the twentieth century into the 1970s created fertile ground for an unstable string of civilian-military regimes responding to competing pressures of a small landed oligarchy, mid-sized ranchers, and bureaucratic elites, and mass peasant and worker mobilizations. The weakness of Honduras social forces and the state allowed for the vulgar domination of the country by foreign companies, making Honduras the quintessential "Banana Republic." A transnational fraction began to cohere in the 1980s in consonance with the virtual U.S. occupation of the country as a staging ground for regional counterinsurgency, and the U.S. sponsorship of economic development and restructuring programs and of a transition to polyarchy. This fraction gained representation in the National Party through Rafael Callejas, who won the 1989 elections and proceeded with sweeping neoliberal reform, a process continued and in fact deepened by the subsequent Liberal Party government.

In Costa Rica, a very different path of twentieth-century development did not deter the outcome in the 1980s and 1990s of integration into the global economy under terms similar to the region as a whole and the characteristic changes in internal social forces. The hegemony of the landed oligarchy was broken in the 1948 civil war and replaced by an alliance of emergent industrial, commercial, and financial capitalists. This united and relatively modernized dominant class was able to incorporate the peasantry and working classes into a stable hegemonic bloc and establish a functioning polyarchic political system. Under the model of import substitution industrialization (ISI) and agro-export expansion with an important redistributive component and significant levels of social welfare spending, Costa Rica experienced levels of development well beyond its neighbors. This model of dependent capitalist development had become exhausted by the late 1970s. The financial crisis of 1981 gave impetus to a gradual restructuring throughout the 1980s and 1990s along with the reinsertion of the country's productive apparatus into the emergent global economy. Under close AID tutelage, successive governments oversaw liberalization, austerity, deregulation, privatization, and the development of a ELD model that began to replace the old ISI model. Socioeconomic restructuring generated new entrepreneurial groups within both parties of the elite, the National Liberation Party (PLN) and the Social Christian Unity Party (PUSC), as transnational nuclei emerged within their ranks, gained control of their parties, and later on, of the state.

And finally we arrive at Guatemala, which we can now assess in comparative and historical perspective. The traditional agro-export oligarchy was the most deeply entrenched and in control of the state—which was administered directly by the military for much of the 1980s—and a transnationalized fraction the weakest. As in El Salvador, the U.S.-supported Christian Democratic project that came to government in the 1980s as part of broader counterinsurgency efforts was intended to defuse the popular movement with reforms and at the head of very visible transitions to (largely dysfunctional) polyarchy. But the Christian Democratic alternatives were not meant to be the bearers of the transnational elite project in the larger scheme of things. With the introduction and expansion of new economic activities in the 1980s, including a powerful new financial sector tied to international banking, incipient export-oriented industry such as maquila textile production, nontraditional agricultural exports promoted by the IFIs, and new commercial groups, a transnationalized fraction of the elite assumed its own profile and clashed with the old state-protected oligarchy over fiscal, tax, liberalization, and related policies.

This tiny and poorly organized fraction articulated in the early 1990s a coherent program for economic and political modernization attuned to the transnational elite agenda, as epitomized, for example, in the policy proposals that flowed out of the influential AID-funded Association for Research and Social Studies (ASIES). Representatives of this transnationalized fraction, after a false start with the election of Jorge Serrano in 1990, assumed the reins of the government with the electoral triumph in 1994 of the National Action Party (PAN), whose leadership included professionals, administrators, and technocrats schooled in neoliberal economics and a modernizing outlook. Unlike El Salvador, where the insurgency actually came to dispute state power and constitute a dual power, the Guatemalan insurgency did not threaten the state. But the movement could continue an indefinite insurgency that would make it impossible to ever pacify the countryside and establish the stability that transnational capital required for the country and the region as a whole. The subsequent New Year's eve 1996 peace accords set the basis for consolidating the transnational elite project for Guatemala. In 1997, the PAN government committed itself to deepening and consolidating a long-term program of neoliberal transformation first launched in 1989 with little success.

The relative strength of the oligarchy and underdevelopment of the transnationalized fraction, rooted in the particular development of the Guatemalan state and social forces, account in part for the tardiness of the transnational project and the severe difficulties in its implementation. The counterrevolution of 1954 followed by a "counterinsurgency state" gave an internal cohesion to the oligarchy that allowed it to resist change in the 1980s (c.f Jonas 1991). In comparative perspective, the particular constellation of social forces and historical events in the other Central American countries generated conditions (relatively) more responsive to the transnational project than in Guatemala. The old oligarchy was crushed in Nicaragua in 1979, displaced in Costa Rica in 1948, and transformed in Honduras by U.S. intervention and regional dynamics. In El Salvador, U.S. and transnational actors promoted tax, land, and other reforms as a component of the counterinsurgency program—in the process, weakening the old oligarchy and strengthening a transnational fraction—in response to the strength of the revolutionary movement. In Guatemala, the counterinsurgency rested on postponing any reform (the IFIs did not impose conditionality on Guatemala, for instance [Jonas 1991, 81, 88]); counterinsurgency was midwife to the transnational project in El Salvador and an obstacle in Guatemala.

Conclusion: Globalization and the Prospects for Democracy and Development in Guatemala

In light of the "big picture" presented here, what are the real prospects for democratization and for development in Guatemala in the current epoch? To phrase the same question in an entirely different manner is to ask, in the current globalized environment, what are the sources of power that the popular Guatemalan majority may be able to develop in order to confront powerful transnational social forces adverse to the kinds of structural transformation that could benefit the poor majority? And what can we say in the way of policy recommendations?

Let us recall, in attempting to answer these questions, that social change is driven by contradictions that make impossible the continuation of an existing set of historic arrangements. I have emphasized above the underlying structural dynamics at play in Central America—a transition to a transnational model of society reciprocal to changes in the global system. This globalization of Central America has not resolved the social contradictions that generated the regional upheaval in the first place, and has simultaneously introduced a new set of contradictions. There has been a continuation—and, in fact, a deepening—from the 1970s to the 1990s, under new circumstances, of an extreme concentration of property and wealth, and of political power, in the hands of tiny minorities, side by side with the impoverishment and powerlessness of a dispossessed majority.[7] The lives of the vast majority of Central Americans have gotten worse, not better.[8] The very conditions that gave rise to the Central American crisis in the first place, therefore, remain for the most part unaltered.

The neoliberal model specifically precludes policies, such as agrarian reform and redistributive measures, that could ameliorate current social conditions. The new model of capital accumulation is not likely to bring about development in the region.[9] For instance, the *maquiladoras* constitute an enclave with little or no backward and forward linkage to host nation economies, very low value added, and are characterized by superexploitation of workers and by conditions of extreme oppression within the free trade zone enclaves. Tourism does stimulate greater local economic activity but it does not generate integrated development. It is generally low-skill and low-wage seasonal employment and is dependent on highly elastic and unstable demand over which host countries have very little control. Neither do NTAEs hold much promise for regional development, as several recent studies have shown (Conroy, Murray, and Rosset 1996; Barham et al. 1992). The transnational model of society in Central America is inherently unstable and indicates contradictions internal to global capitalism, including the worldwide social polarization between rich and poor, the loss of nation-state autonomy and regulatory power, and the deterioration of the social fabric in civil society accompanied by crises of authority and state legitimacy. Resistance of the Guatemalan elite to even the most minimal reforms (e.g, the tax system) creates the image of the transnational project as "progressive" and obscures the essential polarizing and pauperizing consequences of neoliberalism.[10] Let us recall that the transnational elite wants to stabilize its project in Guatemala not in order to democratize and develop the country but in order to secure Central America for global capitalism.

It is not clear to what extent the peace accords in Guatemala will be able to contribute substantively toward democratization and development, if indeed those accords do not actually end up legitimating the emergent neoliberal order by precluding fundamental change in the socioeconomic system and delegitimating opponents of this system (e.g., dispossessed *campesinos* invading land and those who support them) as "extremists who reject peace."[11] We should recall that "success" in a political endeavor is often defined from the summits of power as the extent to which the ruling structures are imposed and reproduced, to which accommodation and conformity around these structures is achieved among the different components of the privileged strata, and to which social control is maintained at the base. Authentic democratization in Guatemala would require the incorporation of the excluded majorities in the vital decisions that affect their lives. It would mean political outcomes in the interests of these majorities predicated on the construction of a democratic socioeconomic system, and therefore a massive redistribution of political power, in Guatemala and in Central America. In turn, political power flows from economic power, and economic power is based on control over society's resources, wealth, and culture. Democratization in Guatemala therefore requires a radical redistribution of wealth and power toward what some have coined "the 87 percent majority" (Jonas 1991).

What about concrete policy recommendations? We could say that, if it is interested in bringing about democratization and development, the transnational elite that controls the levers of global decision making and the gateways to international resources, and its local counterpart among the Guatemalan military, political, and economic elite, "should": promote a far-reaching agrarian reform and income redistribution; organize mass health and educational campaigns and special programs for women and children; encourage independent nationwide trade unionism and social movements; place local, grassroots leaders in position of authority throughout the state's institutions, with special emphasis on the indigenous and women; ban impunity and purge from the state and punish under no uncertain terms all those responsible for human rights violations and for misuse of state institutions; and so on. But such policies will not come about until or unless they are forced on the Guatemalan state and the transnational elite by the "87 percent majority" or unless the elite is removed from positions of institutional power from which it can veto these policies or even suppress them from the discussion of the policy agenda.

Such policy recommendations are seen by many in the policy and academic community as "unrealistic." The current global capitalist order has achieved a remarkable ideological hegemony, in that the structural constraints it sets have become accepted, and the only alternatives put forward as legitimate and "realistic" are those that respect these constraints. We should recall that the extent of social change may be fixed by historic structures, but the outer limits of these structures are always established and reestablished by collective human agency (and our intellectual labor as a form of social action may constrict just as it may extend the proclaimed limits of the possible). Capitalist globalization is the macro-structural-historical backdrop to Guatemala and Central America in the twenty-first century, but this process is not predetermined insofar as structural change is shaped by agents attempting to influence it from below and from above. Varying degrees of ungovernability and crises of legitimacy characterize country after country in Central America and all of Latin America. The crisis and eventual collapse of the neoliberal project may create the regional or transnational conditions and spaces through which to promote an alternative—alternatives to the neoliberal project, alternative viable forms of struggle from civil society, and from the state, if and when the fortress of the neoliberal state is pried open. The real question as regards democratization and development, therefore, is, What are the prospects of the popular majority developing effective new strategies and forms of struggle under the dramatically changed national, regional, and global conditions?

In fact, the dominant groups in Central America have reconstituted and consolidated their control over *political society*, but a new round of popular class mobilization in the early and mid-1990s pointed to their inability to sustain hegemony in *civil society*. Subordinate groups demonstrated a renewed protagonism at the grassroots level, outside of state structures and largely independent of organized left parties. Indigenous, women's, environmental, neighborhood, peasant, worker, and other social movements have flourished in civil society. The failure of the left to articulate a counterhegemonic alternative and to protagonize a process of structural change from political society has helped shift the locus of conflict more fully to civil society. Given the ability of transnational capital to utilize its structural power to impose its project even over states that are captured by forces adverse to that project, perhaps the real prospect for counterhegemonic social change in the age of globalization is a long march through civil society in the Gramscian sense. This march should be part of a globalization-from-below movement to accumulate counterhegemonic forces beyond national and regional borders and to challenge the power of the global elite from within an expanding transnational civil society.[12] Continued change—in Guatemala, in Central America, and in global society at large—will be shaped by conflict and crisis among the summits of power as the hegemonic groups find it increasingly difficult to maintain governability and assure social reproduction, by recomposition of civil society at the base, and by the interplay of the two at the local and the global levels.

Notes

1. For a detailed discussion of the issues summarized here, see Robinson 1996a, 1996b, 1996c, 1997, 1998a; Burbach and Robinson forthcoming.

2. The transitions from authoritarianism to polyarchy in Latin America afforded transnational elites the opportunity to reorganize state institutions and create a more favorable institutional framework for a deepening of neoliberal adjustment. Without a single exception in Latin America, the new polyarchic regimes, staffed by state managers tied to the transnational elite (the new "modernizers" and "technocrats"), have pursued profound neoliberal transformation. The transnational elite has demonstrated a remarkable ability to utilize the structural power of transnational capital over individual countries as a sledgehammer against popular grassroots movements for fundamental change in social structures. Indeed, it is the structural power of global capitalism to impose discipline through

the market that (usually) makes unnecessary the all-pervasive coercive forms of political authority exercised by authoritarian regimes.

3. These transnational actors include the AID and other bilateral agencies and representatives from the IFIs, and multilateral political entities such as UN and OAS units. It is noteworthy that every Central American republic has established, in coordination with the AID and the IFIs, technocratic New Right business associations that have actively engaged in policy development and liaised with local states in promotion of neoliberal restructuring and of the new activities associated with the transnational model (tourism, NTAE, maquila production, and so on). These associations provide leadership to increasingly coherent transnational fractions among local private sectors, help these fractions to shape state policies, and provide a platform for advancing the globalization of Central America. Regarding Guatemala, see inter alia, Escoto and Manfredo 1992.

4. The issues in this section are discussed at more length in Robinson 1998b.

5. Oligarchic domination was the outcome of an intense period of class and social struggle in the region between the two world wars, and particularly the 1930s crisis of world capitalism. These struggles ranged from Sandino's 1926 to 1933 movement in Nicaragua, to the failed 1932 uprising and subsequent *matanza* in El Salvador, and to the CIA-orchestrated overthrow of Jacobo Arbenz in 1954, marking the end of the reformist period in Guatemala.

6. The popular majority was conditionally defeated in what it set about to do—fundamentally alter the social order in its favor. The dominant groups secure the dominance of the project of global capitalism, but they have been unable to stabilize that project and achieve its hegemony, in the Gramscian sense.

7. The only exception was Nicaragua, but these changes have been largely reversed.

8. Poverty and inequality have intensified in every country of the Isthmus. In 1995, 22 percent of the population in Costa Rica lived in poverty, 60 percent in El Salvador, 70 percent in Nicaragua, 77.5 percent in Honduras, and 76.3 percent in Guatemala. In focusing on Guatemala, we should note that social and economic indicators are even *more* alarming than in the other Central American nations. Nearly 40 percent of the population is illiterate, and the average adult has only 3.2 years of schooling. Malnutrition affects one in three children. About 50 percent lack access to electricity, and 64 percent, to running water. Under- and unemployment affect nearly 40 percent of the population, and a full 65 percent of the labor forces is relegated to the informal sector (World Bank 1997). See also, Pico 1997; Jonas 1991, 177-80.

9. We might also note that disruption of traditional established communities and the contraction of domestic demand accompany deeper integration into the global economy, a consequence of the internal concentration of wealth and productive resources toward groups tied to the external sector and transnational economic circuits and a greater transfer of wealth out of the country. This results in a shift in the sources of profitability from productive to commercial and financial activities as outlets for investment. Any prospects of authentic development, barring a break with capitalism, must involve a restoration of the profitability of productive investment. This would likely require a type of state intervention in the accumulation process that is anathema to the neoliberal model.

10. By promoting global capitalism in Guatemala, the transnational elite is anti-oligarchic, but this should not obscure its overarching project of constructing a neoliberal order in Guatemala. The peace accord was the only instrument available for the transnational elite to push forward its agenda. Implementation of the accord, a prerequisite for stability,

sets the entire stage for restructuring the Guatemalan state and society, including relations among dominant groups and fractions, for the larger project of constructing a neoliberal order as part and parcel of the transition. A progressive tax reform could redistribute income downward and finance social spending. But the reform designed by the IFIs proposes indirect taxes levied largely on consumption, in a regressive tax system in which 80 percent of taxes already comes from indirect levies and only 20 percent from direct taxes on income and wealth (Latin America Data Base 1997). The tax reform is seen by the IFIs as an essential macroeconomic instrument for resuming transnational capital accumulation in Guatemala and proceeding with a more sweeping adjustment. "The commitment to raise the tax base is not just a hollow demand or capricious recommendation on the international community," explained the World Bank representative in Guatemala, "but rather a fundamental prerequisite for accelerated and equitable economic growth" (Latin American Data Base 1997). The poor and popular classes are thus being asked to finance through austerity an accord whose purpose, seen from the view of the transnational elite, is to stabilize the country so that a neoliberal order can be constructed. Similarly, by way of further example, the "land reform" (registry and sale of available private lands) is not intended to benefit the dispossessed rural majority, much less achieve social justice. It is a measure that will further facilitate the transition begun several decades ago to a more fully capitalist agriculture, including a market in land and labor, in the countryside.

11. Space constraints preclude discussion, but I should state that, to the extent they end some of the most brutal human rights abuses, open up even partial and limited space (polyarchy *is* preferable to dictatorship), and at least legitimize, if not realize, such demands as indigenous rights, the accords are of major importance. But to argue that in doing these things they pave the way for democracy and development, (they do not in themselves) is tautological: parallel reasoning leads to a conclusion that the old dictatorships really paved the way for democracy and development since they generated the social forces and historical conditions that brought about changes such as those contemplated in the accords.

12. Such discussion is best left for elsewhere, but recent North-South campaigns against maquiladora exploitation, the development of Hemispheric-wide forums for coordination of indigenous and women's struggles, and the creation of unified Central America-wide campesino and popular organizations (e.g., the Central American Agricultural Producers and Cooperation Development [ASOCODE] and the Federation of Community Organizations [FCOC]) are hopeful signs.

Works Cited

Barham, B., M. Clark, E. Katz, and R. Scharman. 1992. Non-Traditional Agricultural Exports in Latin America. *Latin America Research Review* 27, no. 2.
Burbach, Roger, and William I. Robinson. (Forthcoming). The Fin de Siecle Debate: Globalization as Epochal Shift.
Conroy, M. E., D. L. Murray, and P. M. Rosset. 1996. *A Cautionary Tale: Failed U.S. Development Policy in Central America*. Boulder, Colo.: Lynne Rienner.
Escoto, Jorge, and Marroquin Manfredo. 1992. *La AID en Guatemala*. Managua: CRIES/AVANSCO.
Green, Duncan. 1995. *Silent Revolution: The Rise of Market Economics in Latin America*. New York: Monthly Review Press.

Jonas, Susanne. 1991. *The Battle for Guatemala*. Boulder, Colo.: Westview.
Latin America Data Base. 1997. Guatemala: Government Sends New Tax Bill to Congress. *Ecocentral: Central American Economy and Sustainable Development* 2, no. 39 (30 October).
Pico, Juan Hernandez. 1997. Guatemala: Poverty: Protagonist of the Post War. *ENVIO* 16, no. 193:10-15.
Robinson, William, I. 1998a. Beyond Nation-State Paradigms: Globalization, Sociology, and the Challenge of Transnational Studies. *Sociological Forum*.
———. 1998b. Maldevelopment in Central America: A Study on Globalization and Social Change. *Development and Change*.
———. 1997. A Case Study of Globalisation Processes in the Third World: A Transnational Agenda in Nicaragua *Global Society* 11, no. 1: 61-91.
———. 1996a. *Promoting Polyarchy: Globalization, U.S. Intervention, and Hegemony*. Cambridge: Cambridge University Press.
———. 1996b. Globalization, the World System, and "Democracy Promotion" in U.S. Foreign Policy. *Theory and Society* 25, no. 5: 615-65.
———. 1996c. Globalization: Nine Theses of Our Epoch. *Race and Class* 38, no. 2: 13-31.
United Nations Development Program (UNDP). 1992-1997. *Human Development Report*. New York: UNDP/Oxford University Press.
World Bank. 1997. *Poverty and Income Distribution in Latin America: The Story of the 1980s*. Washington, D.C.: World Bank.

13

Globalization from Below in Guatemala

Christopher Chase-Dunn and Susan Manning

This chapter uses a comparative, historical, and macrosociological approach (the world-systems perspective) to analyze the current situation in Guatemala and to consider future possibilities for democracy and development. The historical trajectory of Guatemalan political, social, and economic change is presented in the context of larger structural processes in the Americas and in the global system as a whole. The strategy of *globalization from below* (a populist approach to dealing with corporate globalization) is evaluated in the light of the Guatemalan situation. The contradictions of national and international popular and interclass alliances are discussed.

The trajectory of Guatemalan social change can only be completely understood in the context of the larger world-system within which Guatemalan development has occurred and is occurring. This requires not only a knowledge of the people and institutions of Guatemala, but a historical-structural understanding of Central America, the Americas, and the global political economy.

The theoretical perspective that is best suited to such a temporally deep and spatially broad analysis is the world-systems perspective (Shannon 1996). The world-systems approach looks at human institutions over long periods of time and employs the spatial scale that is necessary for comprehending whole interaction systems. It is neither Eurocentric nor core-centric, at least in principle. The main idea is simple: Human beings have been interacting with one another in important ways over broad expanses of space since the emergence of transoceanic transportation in the fifteenth century. Before the incorporation of the Americas into the Afroeurasian system there were many local and regional world-systems (intersocietal networks) in the Americas (e.g., Blanton, Kowalewski, and Feinman 1992). These were inserted into the expanding European-centered system largely by force, and the surviving populations of indigenous Americans were mobilized to supply labor for a colonial economy that was repeatedly reorganized according to the changing geopolitical and economic forces emanating from the European and (later) North American core societies.

This whole process can be understood structurally as a stratification system composed of economically and politically dominant core societies (themselves in competition with one another) and dependent peripheral and semiperipheral regions, some of which have been successful in improving their positions in the larger core/periphery hierarchy, while most have simply maintained their relative positions.

This structural perspective on world history allows us to analyze the cyclical features of social change and the long-term trends of development in historical and comparative perspective. We can see the development of the modern world-system as driven primarily by capitalist accumulation and geopolitics in which businesses and states compete with one another for power and wealth. Competition among states and capitals is conditioned by the dynamics of struggle among classes and by the resistance of peripheral and semiperipheral peoples to domination from the core. In the modern world-system the semiperiphery is composed of large and powerful countries in the Third World (e.g., Mexico, India, Brazil, China) as well as smaller countries that have intermediate levels of economic development (e.g., the East Asian newly industrialized countries [NICs]). It is not possible to understand the history of social change in the system as a whole without taking into account both the strategies of the winners and the strategies and organizational actions of those who have resisted domination and exploitation.

It is also difficult to understand why and where innovative social change emerges without a conceptualization of the world-system as a whole. As with most earlier regional intersocietal systems, new organization forms that transform institutions and that lead to upward mobility most often emerge from societies in semiperipheral locations. Thus all the countries that became hegemonic core states in the modern system had formerly been semiperipheral. This is a continuation of a long-term pattern of social evolution that Chase-Dunn and Hall (1997) call "semiperipheral development." Earlier semiperipheral marcher states and semiperipheral capitalist city states had acted as the main agents of empire formation and commercialization for millennia. This is a pattern that includes the semiperipheral communist states and probably also future organizational innovations in semiperipheral countries that may transform the now-global system.

This approach requires that we think structurally. We must be able to abstract from the particularities of the game of musical chairs that constitutes uneven development in the system to see the structural continuities. The core/periphery hierarchy remains,[1] though some countries have moved up or down. The interstate system remains, though the internationalization of capital has perhaps further constrained the abilities of states to structure national economies. States have always been subjected to larger geopolitical and economic forces in the world-system, and as is still the case, some have been more successful at exploiting opportunities and protecting themselves from liabilities than others.

In this perspective many of the phenomena that have been called "globalization" correspond to recently expanded international trade, financial flows, and foreign investment by transnational corporations and banks. The globalization discourse generally assumes that until recently there were separate national societies and economies, and that these have now been superseded by an expansion of international integration driven by information and transportation technologies. Rather than a wholly unique and new phenomenon, globalization is primarily international economic integration, and as such it is a feature of the world-system that has been increasing for centuries (Chase-Dunn, Kawano, and Brewer 2000).

As mentioned above, the Great Chartered Companies of the seventeenth century were already playing an important role in shaping the development of world regions. Certainly the transnational corporations of the present are much more important players, but the point is that "foreign investment" is not an institution that only became important since 1970 (nor since World War II). Giovanni Arrighi (1994) has shown that finance capital has been an important component of the commanding heights of the world-system since the fourteenth century. The current floods and ebbs of world money are typical of the late phase of very long "systemic cycles of accumulation."

Types of Globalization

The discourse about globalization has used this term to mean several different things. For some, globalization means a new stage of global capitalism that is qualitatively different from a prior stage that recently ended, though the ways in which it is alleged to be different vary from author to author.[2] We will distinguish between two main meanings of the term *globalization*: (1) international integration and (2) the political-ideological discourse of global competitiveness.

Globalization as international integration needs to be further unpacked as international economic integration, international political integration, and international cultural and communications integration. Of course, each of these subtypes has many aspects. But the point here is that the question of international integration is an objective problem of the extensiveness and intensity of links in a set of global networks of interaction. We can determine empirically how economically integrated were the societies on Earth in the late nineteenth century and how "economically globalized" the world economic network is now (Chase-Dunn, Kawano, and Brewer 2000). This is a question that is separable from the consciousness that people have about their linkages with one another. The question of consciousness regarding linkages (social cosmology) also needs to be studied, and this second main type of globalization is also considered below.

Economic globalization is both a long-term trend and a cyclical phenomenon. If we calculate the ratio of international investments to investments within countries, the world economy had nearly as high a level of "investment globalization" in 1910 as it did in 1990 (Bairoch 1996). A recent study of world trade as a proportion of world GDP (Chase-Dunn, Brewer, and Kawano 2000) also shows that trade integration is both a cycle and a trend (see figure 13.1).

The point here is that globalization needs to be understood as part of a long-term

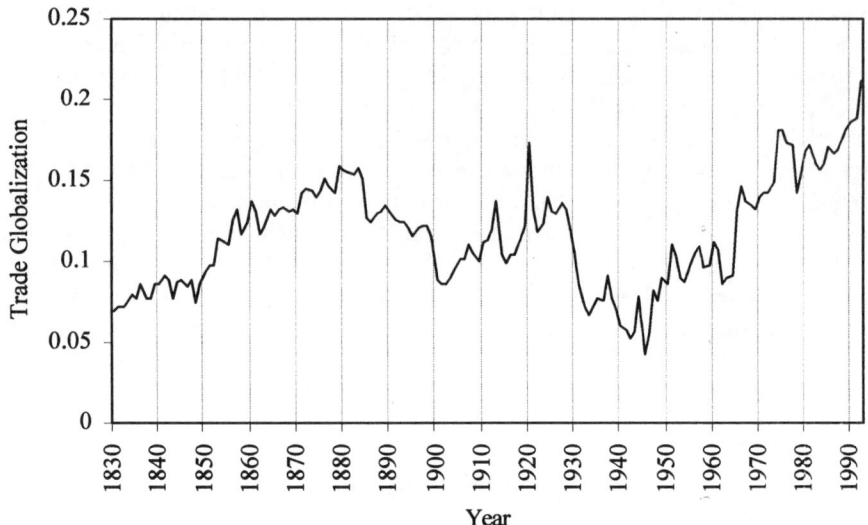

Figure 13.1. Openness Trade Globalization, 1830-1992 (five-year moving weighted average)

set of processes that have characterized the world-system for centuries. These processes can be represented in a model of the structural constants, cycles, and secular trends that constitute the basic and normal operations of the system. We contend that this basic schema continues to describe the system in the current period of global capitalism (Chase-Dunn 1998, xiv-xvi).

The cyclical trend of international economic integration needs to be understood in the context of these other cycles and trends. Of special importance for the topic of Guatemalan development and democracy is the trend toward international political integration—the slow emergence of a world state. Guatemalan democracy cannot come into existence or long survive in a larger system that is undemocratic, and so both national and international politics must be a part of the building of Guatemalan democracy.

The trends and cycles reveal important continuities and imply that future struggles for economic justice and democracy need to base themselves on an analysis of how earlier struggles changed the scale and nature of development in the world-system. While some populists have suggested that progressive movements should again employ the tools of economic nationalism to resist the powers of the "global princes of capital" (e.g., Moore 1996; Mander and Goldsmith 1996), others contend that political globalization of popular movements will be required in order to create a democratic and collectively rational global commonwealth (e.g., Robinson 1998/1999).

The Globalization Project

The term *globalization* has been used in a different way to refer to "the globalization project"—the abandoning of Keynesian models of national development and a new emphasis on deregulation and opening national commodity and financial markets to foreign trade and investment (McMichael 1996). This usage points to the ideological aspects of the most recent wave of international economic integration. The term we prefer for this turn in global discourse is *neoliberalism*. The worldwide decline of the political left may have predated the revolutions of 1989 and the demise of the Soviet Union, but it was certainly also accelerated by these events. The structural basis of the rise of the globalization project is the new level of integration reached by the global capitalist class. The internationalization of capital has long been an important part of the trend toward economic globalization. And there have been many claims to represent the general interests of business before. Indeed every modern hegemon has made this claim. But the real international integration of interests of the capitalists in all parts of the system has reached a level greater than ever before.

This is the part of the model of a global stage of capitalism that must be taken most seriously, though it can certainly be overdone. The world-system has now reached a point at which both the old interstate system based on separate national capitalist classes, and new institutions representing the global interests of capitalists exist and are powerful simultaneously. In this light each country can be seen to have an important ruling class faction that is allied with the transnational capitalist class.

Neoliberalism began as the Reagan-Thatcher attack on the welfare state and labor unions. It evolved into the structural adjustment policies of the International Monetary Fund and the triumphalism of global business after the demise of the Soviet Union. In U.S. foreign policy it has found expression in a new emphasis on "democracy promotion" in the periphery and semiperiphery. Rather than propping up military dictatorships in Latin America, the emphasis has shifted toward coordinated action between the Central Intelligence Agency (CIA) and the U.S. National Endowment for Democracy to promote electoral institutions in Latin America and other semiperipheral and peripheral regions (Robinson 1996). William Robinson points out that the kind of "low-intensity democracy" that is promoted is really best understood as "polyarchy," a regime form in which elites orchestrate a process of electoral competition and governance that legitimates state power and undercuts more radical political alternatives that might threaten the ability of national elites to maintain their wealth and power by exploiting workers and peasants. Robinson (1996) convincingly argues that polyarchy and democracy-promotion are the political forms that are most congruent with a globalized and neoliberal world economy in which capital is given free reign to generate accumulation wherever profits are greatest.

Robinson also discusses a possible new counterhegemony to the globalization project of neoliberal capital. The older organizational strategies of the labor movements and the decolonization movements no longer work very well. Indeed, globalized capital has been explicitly constructed to outmaneuver the institutional contraints that had emerged from labor unions, socialist parties, and welfare states as well as economic nationalism and socialist institutions in the periphery and semiperiphery. Certainly new incarnations of these older strategies will emerge in the future as marginalized, dominated, and exploited peoples learn to resist the new globalized forms of control. Indeed some of the older ideas that may have formerly been ahead of their time may now come into their own. For example, labor internationalism had become a tired phrase used as a fig leaf for Soviet imperialism and so on. But a new wave of labor internationalism will probably be the only rational response to the latest wave of the globalization of capital. The women's movements and the environmental movement have already developed new transnational organizational structures, and such an approach is also emerging among the indigenous peoples of the world (Wilmer 1993).

The term we use for these new transnational antisystemic movements is "globalization from below." Alliances among different groups can organize together across borders based on their common desire to confront neoliberalism and global capital. Thus global capital creates, for the first time, the real historical possibility for an Earthwide antisystemic political alliance for building a more humane and sustainable world society.

The Spiral of Capitalism and Socialism

The interaction between expansive commodification and resistance movements can be denoted as "the spiral of capitalism and socialism" (Boswell and Chase-Dunn 2000). The world-systems perspective provides a view of the long-term interaction between the expansion and deepening of capitalism and the efforts of people to protect themselves from exploitation and domination. The historical development of the communist states is explained as part of a long-run spiraling interaction between expanding capitalism and socialist counterresponses. The Russian and Chinese revolutions were socialist movements in the semiperiphery that intended to transform the global logic of capitalism, but that ended up using socialist ideology to mobilize industrialization for the purpose of catching up with core capitalism.

The spiraling interaction between capitalist development and socialist movements is revealed in the history of labor movements, socialist parties, and communist states over the last 200 years. This long-run comparative perspective enables one to see recent events in China, Russia, and Eastern Europe in a framework that has implications for the future of democratic socialism. The metaphor of the spiral means this: Both capitalism and socialism affect one another's growth and organizational forms. Capitalism spurs socialist responses by exploiting and dominating peoples, and socialism spurs capitalism to expand its scale of production and market integration and to revolutionize technology.

Defined broadly, socialist movements are those political and organizational means by which people try to protect themselves from market forces, exploitation, and domination, and to build more cooperative institutions.[3] The several industrial revolutions, by which capitalism has restructured production and reorganized labor, have stimulated a series of political organizations and institutions created by workers to protect their livelihoods. This happened differently under different political and economic conditions in different parts of the world-system. Skilled workers created guilds and craft unions. Less skilled workers created industrial unions. Sometimes these coalesced into labor parties that played important roles in supporting the development of political democracies, mass education, and welfare states (Rueschemeyer, Stephens, and Stephens 1992). In other regions workers and peasants were less politically successful, but managed at least to protect access to rural areas or subsistence plots for a fallback or hedge against the insecurities of employment in capitalist enterprises. To some extent the burgeoning contemporary "informal sector" in both core and peripheral societies provides such a fallback.

The mixed success of workers' organizations also had an impact on the further development of capitalism. In some areas workers or communities were successful at raising the wage bill or protecting the environment in ways that raised the costs of production for capital. When this happened capitalists either displaced workers by automating them out of jobs, or capital migrated to where fewer constraints allowed cheaper production. The process of capital flight is not a new feature of the world-system. It has been an important force behind the uneven development of capitalism and the spreading scale of market integration for centuries. Labor unions and socialist parties were able to obtain some power in certain states, but capitalism became yet more international. Firm size increased. International markets became more and more important to successful capitalist competition. Fordism, the employment of large numbers of easily organizable workers in centralized production locations, has been partially supplanted by "flexible accumulation" (small firms producing small customized products) and global sourcing (the use of substitutable components from broadly dispersed competing producers). These new production strategies make traditional labor organizing approaches much less viable.

Socialists were able to gain state power in certain semiperipheral states and to create political mechanisms for protection against competition with core capital. This was not a wholly new phenomenon. Capitalist semiperipheral states had done, and were doing, similar things. But, the communist states claimed a fundamentally oppositional ideology in which socialism was allegedly a superior system that would eventually replace capitalism. Ideological opposition is a phenomenon that the capitalist world economy had seen before. The geopolitical and economic battles of the Thirty Years' War were fought in the name of Protestantism against Catholicism. The content of the ideology may make some difference for the internal organization of states and parties, but every contender must be able to legitimate itself in the eyes and hearts of its cadre. The claim to represent a qualitatively different and superior socioeconomic system is not evidence that the communist states were ever able to become structurally autonomous from world capitalism (Chase-Dunn 1982).

The communist states severely restricted the access of core capitalist firms to their internal markets and raw materials, and this constraint on the mobility of capital was an important force behind the post-World War II upsurge in the spatial scale of market integration and a new revolution of technology. In certain areas capitalism was driven to further revolutionize technology or to improve living conditions for workers and peasants because of the demonstration effect of propinquity to a communist state.

U.S. support for state-led industrialization in Japan and Korea (in contrast to U.S. policy in Latin America) is only understandable as a geopolitical response to the Chinese revolution. The existence of "two superpowers"—one capitalist and one communist—in the period since World War II provided a fertile context for the success of international liberalism within the "capitalist" bloc. This was the political and military basis of the rapid growth of transnational corporations and the latest round of "time-space compression" made possible by radically lowered transportation and communications costs (Harvey 1989). This technological revolution has once again restructured the international division of labor and created a new regime of labor regulation called "flexible accumulation." The process by which the communist states have become reintegrated into the capitalist world-system has been long, as described below. But, the final phase of reintegration was provoked by the inability to be competitive with the new form of capitalist regulation. Thus, capitalism spurs socialism, which spurs capitalism, which spurs socialism again in a wheel that turns and turns while getting larger.

The economic reincorporation of the communist states into the capitalist world economy did not occur recently and suddenly. It began with the mobilization toward autarchic industrialization using socialist ideology, an effort that was quite successful in terms of standard measures of economic development. Most of the communist states were increasing their percentage of world product and energy consumption up until the 1980s (Boswell and Chase-Dunn 2000, chapter 1, table 1).

The economic reincorporation of the communist states moved to a new stage of integration with the world market and foreign firms in the 1970s. Andre Gunder Frank (1980, chapter 4) documented a trend toward reintegration in which the communist states increased their exports for sale on the world market, increased imports from the avowedly capitalist countries, and made deals with transnational firms for investments within their borders. The economic crisis in Eastern Europe and the Soviet Union was not much worse than the economic crisis in the rest of the world during the global economic downturn that began in the late 1960s. Data presented by World Bank analysts indicate that GDP growth rates were positive in most of the "historically planned economies" in Europe until 1989 or 1990 (Marer et al. 1991, table 7a).

Put simply, the big regime transformations that occurred in the Soviet Union and China after 1989 were part of a process that had been under way since the 1970s. The regime changes were a matter of the political superstructure catching up with the economic base. The democratization of these societies is, of course, a welcome trend, but democratic political forms do not automatically lead to a society without exploitation or domination. The outcomes of current political struggles are rather uncertain in most of the ex-communist countries. New types of authoritarian regimes seem at least as likely as real democratization (Boswell and Chase-Dunn 2000).

As trends in the last two decades have shown, austerity regimes, deregulation, and marketization within nearly all of the communist states occurred during the same period as similar phenomena in noncommunist states. The synchronicity and broad similarities between Reagan/Thatcher deregulation and attacks on the welfare state, austerity socialism in most of the rest of the world, and increasing pressures for marketization in the Soviet Union and China are all related to the B-phase downturn of the Kondratieff wave,[4] as were the moves toward austerity and privatization in most semiperipheral and peripheral states. The trend toward privatization, deregulation, and market-based solutions among parties of the left in almost every country has been thoroughly documented by Lipset (1991). Nearly all socialists with access to political power have abandoned the idea of doing anything more than buffing off the rough edges of capitalism.

The ways in which the pressures of a stagnating world economy impact upon national policies certainly vary from country to country, but the ability of any single national society to construct collective rationality is limited by its interaction within the larger system. The most recent expansion of capitalist integration, termed *globalization of the economy*, has made autarchic national economic planning seem anachronistic. Yet, political reactions against economic globalization are now under way in the form of revived ex-communist parties, economic nationalism in both the core and the periphery (e.g., Pat Buchanan, the Brazilian military, the Indonesian prime minister), and a growing coalition of popular forces that are critiquing the ideological hegemony of neoliberalism (e.g., Ralph Nader, environmentalists, a resurgent labor movement that defeated the "Fast Track" legislation in the United States, and so on) (see Mander and Goldsmith 1997).

Implications for Guatemala

From the ground in Guatemala it must appear that most of what is written above is a dream of someone who lives on the moon. The enormous problems of everyday life for the vast majority of Guatemalans and the hectic pace of political events in the struggle to implement the peace accords make it difficult to consider the broad sweep of history or the possibilities for constructing a more egalitarian and sustainable world-system. Nevertheless, a historical understanding of the dynamics of global capitalist development is necessary for comprehending current developments and possibilities for the future.

What can we expect of the world-system in the next fifty years that will be of relevance for Guatemala? The world has been in a K-wave downswing (B-phase) since the late 1960s. This has been one of the main causes of the profit squeeze and fiscal crisis of states that have led to the neoliberal attack on labor and the welfare state, as well as debt crisis, restructuring, and privatization in the periphery. It is now going into an A-phase in which relative rates of economic growth will generally be higher. The fiscal pressures on states will be less. Labor will be in demand. The possibilities for mobilizing workers and peasants should be greater than they have been because firms and states will be more willing to make compromises in order to keep things running smoothly.

There are downsides as well. The rate of ecological degradation will increase as more resources are used in production. And late in K-wave upswings, when states have substantial surplus resources, is when wars occur among core states (Goldstein 1988). If the economic hegemony of the United States continues to decline vis-à-vis competing core powers (Germany, Japan, China), the world will enter a dangerous window of vulnerability to core warfare in the 2020s (Chase-Dunn and Podobnik 1999). This is of concern to all peoples, because the advent of a world war with weapons of mass destruction could lead to the annihilation of life on Earth. Another possible doom could result from catastrophic environmental disaster. Progressive movements everywhere need to do all they can to prevent these possible disasters and be ready to pick up the pieces and begin again on a new, more just and sustainable, basis if they should occur.

The slow emergence of a world state will create the possibility for the democratization of global political institutions. Popular movements could act to block global state formation, but they might alternatively struggle to build democratic and collective rationality into the new global institutions. The hypothesis of semiperipheral development suggests that the most transformative institutional innovations and the most powerful challenges to capitalism will come from semiperipheral regions in the world-system. Mexico is the most obvious candidate that has direct relevance for the Guatemalan situation. This said, a country such as Guatemala, with great human and natural resources, could also be a fertile ground for transformational action, especially in an age of global politics. In many ways the smaller countries have a greater interest in the unexplored terrain of globalization from below.[5]

Most recent interpretations of Central American history paint a picture of each country having its own complicated and tumultuous history that has led by different paths to the same happy result: democracy (e.g., Paige 1997). A world-systems perspective produces a different portrait. World market forces and geopolitics have repeatedly restructured all the Central American countries. The landed colonial patricians were displaced by the agro-exporters (who ruled in alliance with the military), and these have in turn been partially supplanted by a new transnational elite of neoliberals who seek to link the national economies more tightly with core capital and global markets. It is fascinating to compare the nineteenth-century liberal ideology and policies of the Central American agro-exporting elites (science, reason, and privatization of communal resources) with more recent neoliberal ideology and policies—competitiveness, fiscal austerity, deregulation, and privatization. Both liberalism and neoliberalism in Central America were (are) combinations of imported ideas and local adaptations that justify and facilitate new forms of exploitation and outmaneuvering of rivals.

Popular movements emerged during the twentieth century in Mexico and Central America in response to authoritarian rule, agrarian restructuring, and grinding poverty, but the timing of these movements has varied from country to country depending on the shifting coalitions of elites and the changing nature of agrarian class relations in different regions. The actions and reactions of local rulers and the interventions of the United States have been influenced by the sequencing of rebellions and revolutions in Central America, Latin America, and the rest of the world. The Guatemalan nationalist movement after World War II and the intervention by the United States to overthrow the elected government of Arbenz in 1954 (Gleijeses 1991) were distinctive regarding their timing. The other Central American countries had their popular upsurges and repressions in the late 1920s and 1930s.

John Markoff's (1996, 1998) studies of waves of democratic movements and institutional inventions show that these occurred on an interactive world stage rather than in isolated trajectories in each country. This also needs to be said of the revolutions of the twentieth century. Both the rebels and the forces that sought to defeat them learned much from previous efforts elsewhere. The world-systems perspective encourages us to see both the uniquenesses of particular political situations and the overall picture of twentieth-century resistance and repression. One irony of the differing sequences is the current situation in Southern Mexico and the quite different situation across the border in Guatemala. After thirty years of civil war, Guatemalans are tired of killing and want to make the peace work, while in Southern Mexico a long-dormant situation has heated up.

I largely agree with the views on Central American social change presented by William Robinson (1996, 1998, and this volume).[6] There are two key aspects of Robinson's depiction that differentiate it from standard views. He sees in each Central American country the emergence of a new ruling-class faction that represents the interests of global capitalism and the recently emerged global capitalist class. This transnational elite promotes neoliberal policies and openness to global investment. Robinson calls this group the "New Right."

The other key difference between Robinson's analysis and the standard depiction of recent Central American history focuses on the outcome of the struggles that occurred in the 1980s. Most observers depict the 1980s struggles as between agro-industrial dynasties in each country and popular forces representing workers and peasants. The outcome of the struggles was, in each case, a stalemate in which neither side could win, and so both sides were forced to compromise in a new democratic regime in which contention was shifted from the military to the political realm. This allegedly led to the establishment of democracy—contested elections in which popular parties compete on a strong footing with the parties of the elites.

Robinson adds the transnational elite to the equation and draws quite different conclusions. Rather than a stalemate, Robinson contends that the popular forces were mainly defeated in each country. The "democracy" that emerged was really polyarchy—a system of elite-controlled elections in which the transnational elite (the New Right) gained the greatest share of power. This analysis is substantially accurate, but there are also important differences between Central American countries that need to be taken into account.

I have already mentioned the differences in movement/repression sequences. But also, as Robinson points out, the strength of the neoliberal factions of the domestic elites varies substantially from country to country, and this faction is perhaps weakest in Guatemala. It is also important to realize that the neoliberal domestic elite may sometimes have interests that are in contradiction with the policies of the neoliberal international organizations such as the World Bank and the International Monetary Fund. And on these issues the domestic neoliberals may join with the older landed elites in a common cause to defend Guatemalan "sovereignty" against the meddling of the international financial institutions (IFIs) and the United Nations (UN).

The Guatemalan case is also different from other Central American countries and Mexico in a number of other important ways. The existence of both poor Ladinos and a large group of indigenous people (indeed a majority of the whole population) has added a strong ethnic dynamic to intraclass and interclass relations in Guatemala. This ethnic division among the poor has made it easy for the rulers to pit exploited groups against one another. This element also operates in Southern Mexico, but is much less important in the other countries of Central America. The possibility of a cross-border (Guatemala/Chiapas) Mayanist alliance that coordinates and cooperates with the global indigenist movement (Wilmer 1993) could be a powerful force in regional politics. But the importance of a strong working alliance between indigenous and Ladino popular groups cannot be overemphasized for Guatemala. The indigenous identity movement has understandably criticized Marxists for ignoring ethnicity and culture, but neo-Mayans will need to define their own version of class analysis so that the common interests between Ladinos and Mayans can be conceptualized and organized.

The Guatemalan revolutionary armed struggle that began in the 1960s was never strong enough to directly threaten the power of the central government, but it did stimulate a huge repressive effort supported by the U.S. Central Intelligence Agency in which the official armed forces received massive resources and recruited large numbers of poor young men from both the Ladino and the Mayan regions. This method of suppressing the revolt provided an avenue of employment and security that is now, ironically, being contracted in the period of the peace accords.

This is probably the most important cause behind the current outbreak of kidnapping and robbery.

As mentioned above, the neoliberal transnational elite in Guatemala, though now in control of the presidency, is not very powerful vis-à-vis the older agro-exporters and the military, at least in comparison with the other Central American countries and Mexico. The original Guatemalan "liberals"—the agro-exporting elite—are reticent to pay income taxes, and so the Guatemalan government must fund itself mainly by extracting revenues from the poor by means of consumption taxes. The old ruling families have been able to find enough allies to prevent a tax reform that would put the state on a firmer fiscal basis. Without this even neoliberal development, projects have little hope of success.

The issue of tax reform is one in which at least some of the domestic neoliberals may have more in common with the landed elites than with their transnational class allies as represented by the IFIs. On a visit to Guatemala in 1997, Michel Camdesus, then head of the International Monetary Fund, explicitly stated the need for tax reform in Guatemala to put the state on a sound fiscal foundation. The Consultative Group (a subcommittee of the Group of Seven) has used its financial leverage (based on a huge commitment of loans and grants for development projects) to try to move the implementation of the peace accords forward (Ruthrauff 1997).

Guatemala in the World Economy

Guatemala is inserted into the core/periphery hierarchy in a position that can be characterized at the upper periphery. Mexico, Brazil, and perhaps Argentina are the classically semiperipheral countries of Latin America. Guatemala's important natural resources and its level of economic development compared to the poorest countries of Latin America justify the notion that it is in the upper tier of the periphery. This location has not changed despite all the ups and downs of Guatemalan history.

This general classification is more finely understood by examining recent trends in the extent to which Guatemala is dependent on foreign capital investment and comparing these with other Latin American countries. Two types of foreign investment have been important for Latin America in recent decades: portfolio investment in which foreigners buy stocks and bonds issued in the home country; and direct investment in which foreign countries invest in subsidiary businesses established in the home country. Foreign investment dependence is the ratio of foreign investment to the size of the national economy as indicated by GDP. Obviously a dollar of foreign investment will have much less significance for a large country than for a small country.

Yearly net flows of portfolio investment and direct investment are provided by the International Monetary Fund (2000). We use these to estimate the stocks of

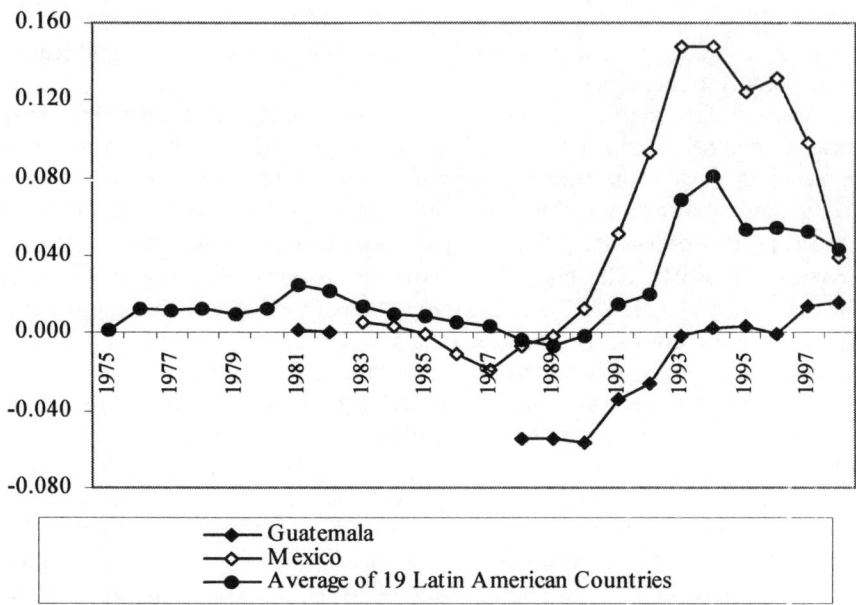

Figure 13.2. Portfolio Investment Dependence, 1975-1998

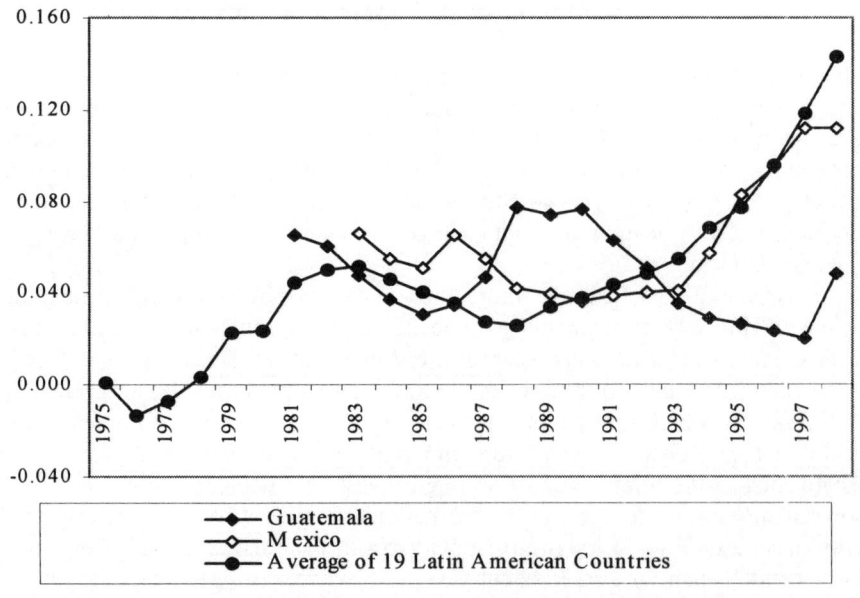

Figure 13.3. Direct Investment Dependence (Net Flows), 1975-1998

investment by summing the flows over a five-year period depreciated by 10 percent per year. Figure 3.2 shows portfolio investment dependence trends from 1975 to 1998 for Guatemala, Mexico, and the average of nineteen Latin American countries.

Figure 13.2 shows that portfolio investment dependence was low in Guatemala compared to other Latin American countries. There was a large expansion of portfolio investment to Latin America from core countries (mainly the United States) in the 1990s, with Mexico becoming more dependent on this kind of foreign investment than most other Latin American countries. Guatemala's negative score is due to the data being net inflows and outflows. Until 1993 there were more portfolio investment outflows than inflows into Guatemala. The upward trend shows that Guatemala has participated in the portfolio investment boom to some extent. And while the 1990s boom of portfolio investment declined in the last five years in the other Latin American countries, Guatemala increased slightly since the signing of the peace accords.

Figure 13.3 compares Guatemala's level of foreign direct investment dependence to Mexico and the average of nineteen Latin American countries. The general Latin American pattern shows an early wave of dependence on foreign direct investment that peaked in 1984, then a decline followed by a new upward surge to 1998 when our data end. Mexico fits this general Latin American pattern closely, but the Guatemalan trajectory is different. While Latin America was experiencing a decline in the late 1980s, Guatemala was reaching a high plateau of direct investment dependence. During the early eighties the Guatemalan level of dependence declined similarly to the other Latin American countries. But the massive genocide of the Maya in the early eighties was followed by a wave of maquiladora investment that was out of sync with the still low levels of direct investment dependence in Mexico and the other Latin American countries. The repression may have created a situation of business confidence that attracted foreign investors. The late eighties wave of investment dependence in Guatemala began to decline in 1990, and that decline lasted until 1997. In 1998, the year of the peace accords, Guatemala experienced a late upturn of foreign investment that may have signaled its belatedly joining the general Latin American upsurge.

Globalization from Below or Delinking?

The strategy of globalization from below means the transnational linking of women's movements, labor struggles, indigenous movements, and agrarian reform movements within regions and globally. Labor movements in Guatemala have already been partially successful in forging new implementations of the old notion of labor internationalism, and in mobilizing support from the United States and other core countries based on concerns about human rights and the labor provisions of international trade agreements (Frundt 1987; Armbruster 1998).

The problems of cross-border labor organizing and international labor solidarity are great, but the new organizational terrain of global capitalism requires new strategies (Stevis 1998). Because the globalization project has abrogated social compacts between business and labor within core countries, especially in the United States, there are new possibilities for cooperation among Latin American and U.S. workers and their organizations. John Sweeney, the president of the U.S. American Federation of Labor-Council of Industrial Organizations (AFL-CIO), visited the leaders of independent unions in Mexico City in 1997. This willingness to look at new alliances is a welcome relief from the long-standing Cold War approach to labor internationalism that was AFL-CIO practice until Sweeney's reform group took the leadership. Armbruster (1998) reports that help from the AFL-CIO was an important factor in the organizing success of the workers at the Phillips-Van Heusen plant in Guatemala. The subsequent withdrawal of Phillips-Van Heusen shows that "job blackmail" is not an empty threat and that the labor movement needs to support the strenthening of labor standards in emerging institutions of global governance.

Women's movements in El Salvador have made important efforts to link their struggles with sympathetic groups in other Central American countries and in the United States. Indeed, these groups have explicitly advocated globalization from below. In Mexico the resurgent electoral left, the agrarian movements in Chiapas and Guerrero, and independent trade unions have found that common opposition to neoliberalism is a uniting force. Some of the popular leaders in Mexico have made an effort to mobilize support from the United States, but not many yet see this as part of a larger effort to democratize both Mexico and the global system.

The emerging popular responses to globalization and neoliberalism face an important and potentially divisive issue. One possibility for mobilizing against global capitalism is "delinking" and self-reliance. Another, and very different, approach is to respond to global capitalism by building global democracy. The world-systems perspective has much to offer regarding the consideration of the value of these options.

The neoliberals have pronounced withdrawal from the capitalist world economy as unthinkable, and many popular leaders seem to agree. The wonders of technology and communications are alleged to be the highest values, and only by playing the game of competitiveness can a developing country have access to these. But some critics are now questioning whether the "necessity" of openness to the global economy is worth the costs. This is a healthy response, because it unmasks many of the ideological presuppositions of neoliberalism. People need housing, clean water, and healthy food. It is not necessary to be able to program your microwave oven from your car radio. The hyperbole of techno-wonders needs be popped, like the financial bubbles that abound in the virtual space of global money. This said, new information technologies in some ways make it easier than ever before to organize transnational movements. Maximum advantage needs be made of these while holding the light to justifications of submission based on alleged economic necessity.

The notion that self-reliance is an anachronism needs to be examined in historical perspective. In long-run panorama, protectionism and national mobiliza-

with O'Donnell, Schmitter, and Whitehead's (1988) conclusion that popular forces should refrain from pressing socioeconomic or political demands until the transition to polyarchy is consolidated. Robinson (personal communication) argues, and we agree, that strong popular movements in Guatemala can provide the support that the global and local neoliberals need to push through peace accord implementation.

Once electoral democracy with popular participation is firmly in place, the campaign against neoliberal policies can commence in earnest. In the mean time the popular movements need to learn about the history of the world-system and the globalization project. This, and the pursuit of further international popular alliances, will make it possible for Guatemalans to benefit from, and contribute to, globalization from below. Global democracy begins at home.

Notes

1. A review of recent studies that measure the position of countries in the core/periphery hierarchy is in Chase-Dunn and Grimes (1995).

2. A review of the literature on stages of capitalism and the alleged most recent stage (global capitalism) is in Chase-Dunn (1998, chapters 3 and 4).

3. The term *antisystemic movements* has also been used to designate this family of popular forms of resistance (Amin et al. 1982; Arrighi, Hopkins, and Wallerstein 1989). The main movements we have in mind are anticolonial and anti-imperial national liberation movements, the global indigenous movement, labor movements, socialist parties, communist states, feminism, and environmentalism. The problem of counterhegemony is how to bring these interests together.

4. The Kondratieff wave (K-wave)—a worldwide economic cycle with a period of from forty to sixty years in which the relative rate of economic activity increases (during "A-phase" upswings) and then decreases (during "B-phase" periods of slower growth or stagnation).

5. What is needed here is a strong linkage between the trajectory of the world-system and the situation in Guatemala today. The theoretical perspective presented above would be much more useful if it were combined with a world-system history and formal comparative analysis that looks at the last 200 years in local, regional, continental and global frameworks from the focal point of the Guatemalan people. This research needs to be done. In its absence we will present a commentary on the current situation that uses insights from the long-term, large scale perspective presented above.

6. Robinson subscribes to the notion of a recently arrived global stage of capitalism that, in my view, needs to be placed in the context of long-run cycles and trends.

Works Cited

Amaro, Nelson. 1990. *Descentralización y Participación Popular en Guatemala.* Guatemala: Panorama Centroamericano.
Amin, Samir. 1990. *Delinking: Toward a Polycentric World.* London: Zed Press.
———. 1992. *Empire of Chaos.* New York: Monthly Review Press.

Amin, Samir, Giovanni Arrighi, Andre Gunder Frank, and Immanuel Wallerstein. 1982. *Dynamics of Global Crisis*. New York: Monthly Review Press.

Armbruster, Ralph. 1998. Cross-Border Labor Organizing in the Garment and Automobile Industries: The Phillips Van-Heusen and Ford Cuautitlan Cases. *Journal of World-Systems Research* 4, 20-24, <http://csf.colorado.edu/ wsystems/ jwsr.html>.

Arnson, Cynthia J. 1999. *Comparative Peace Processes in Latin America*. Palo Alto, Calif.: Stanford University Press.

Arrighi, Giovanni. 1994. *The Long Twentieth Century: Money, Power and the Origins of Our Times*. London: Verso.

Arrighi, Giovanni, Terence K. Hopkins, and Immanuel Wallerstein. 1989. *Antisystemic Movements*. London and New York: Verso.

Bairoch, Paul. 1996. Globalization Myths and Realities: One Century of External Trade and Foreign Investment. In *States against Markets: The Limits of Globalization*, edited by Robert Boyer and Daniel Drache. London and New York: Routledge.

Blanton, Richard, Stephen A. Kowalewski, and Gary Feinman. 1992. The Mesoamerican World System. *Review* 15, no. 3 (Summer): 418-26.

Bornschier, Volker, and Christopher Chase-Dunn, eds. 1999. *The Future of Global Conflict*. London: Sage.

Boswell, Terry, and Christopher Chase-Dunn. 2000. *The Spiral of Capitalism and Socialism: Toward Global Democracy*. Boulder, Colo.: Lynne Rienner.

Chase-Dunn, Christopher. 1998. *Global Formation: Structures of the World-Economy*, 2d edition. Lanham, Md.: Rowman & Littlefield.

———, ed. 1982. *Socialist States in the World-System*. Beverly Hills: Sage.

Chase-Dunn, Christopher, and Peter Grimes. 1995. World-Systems Analysis. *Annual Review of Sociology* 21:387-417.

Chase-Dunn, Christopher, and Thomas D. Hall. 1997. *Rise and Demise: Comparing World-Systems*. Boulder, Colo.: Westview.

Chase-Dunn, Christopher, Yukio Kawano, and Benjamin Brewer. 2000. Economic Globalization since 1795: Waves of Integration in the Modern World-System. *American Sociological Review* 65 (February):77-95.

Chase-Dunn, Christopher, and Bruce Podobnik. 1999. The Next World War: World-System Cycles and Trends. Pp. 40-65 in *The Future of Global Conflict*, edited by Volker Bornschier and Christopher Chase-Dunn. London: Sage.

Evans, Peter. 1995. *Embedded Autonomy: States and Industrial Transformation*. Princeton, N.J.: Princeton University Press.

Frank, Andre Gunder. 1980. *Crisis in the World Economy*. New York: Holmes and Meier.

Frundt, Henry J. 1987. Refreshing Pauses: *Coca-Cola and Human Rights in Guatemala*. New York: Praeger.

Gleijeses, Piero. 1991. *Shattered Hope: The Guatemalan Revolution and the United States: 1944-1954*. Princeton, N.J.: Princeton University Press.

Goldstein, Joshua. 1988. *Long Cycles: Prosperity and War in the Modern Age*. New Haven, Conn.: Yale University Press.

Green, Duncan. 1995. *Silent Revolution: The Rise of Market Economics in Latin America*. London: Cassell.

Harvey, David. 1989. *The Condition of Postmodernity*. Cambridge, Mass.: Blackwell.

———. 1995. Globalization in Question. *Rethinking Marxism* 8, no. 4 (Winter):1-17.

International Monetary Fund. 2000. *International Financial Statistics*. CD-ROM. Washington, D.C.: International Monetary Fund.

Jonas, Susanne. 1991. *The Battle for Guatemala: Rebels, Death Squads and U.S. Power*. Boulder, Colo.: Westview.

———. 1999. Democratization of Guatemala through the Peace Process. Paper presented at the Conference on Guatemalan Development and Democracy, Universidad del Valle, 26-28 March.

Lipset, Seymour Martin. 1991. No Third Way: A Comparative Perspective on the Left. Pp. 183-232 in *The Crisis of Leninism and the Decline of the Left: the Revolutions of 1989*, edited by Daniel Chirot. Seattle: University of Washington Press.

Maddison, Angus. 1995. *Monitoring the World Economy, 1820-1992*. Paris: OECD.

Mander, Jerry, and Edward Goldsmith, eds. 1997. *The Case against the Global Economy: For a Turn toward the Local*. San Francisco: Sierra Club Books.

Manning, Susan. 1999. Introduction. Special Issue on Globalization. *Journal of World-Systems Research*. 5, no. 2, <http://csf.colorado.edu/wsystems/jwsr. html>.

Marer, Paul, Janos Arvay, John O'Connor, and Dan Swenson. 1991. Historically Planned Economies: A Guide to the Data. IBRD (World Bank), Socioeconomic Data Division and Socialist Economies Reform Unit.

Markoff, John. 1996. *Waves of Democracy: Social Movements and Political Change*. Thousand Oaks, Calif.: Pine Forge Press.

———. 1998. From Center to Periphery and Back Again: The Geography of Democratic Innovation. Pp. 229-46 in *Extending Citizenship, Reconfiguring States*, edited by Michael Hanagan and Charles Tilly. Lanham, Md.: Rowman & Littlefield.

McMichael, Philip. 1996. *Development and Social Change: A Global Perspective*. Thousand Oaks, Calif.: Pine Forge Press.

Modelski, George and William R. Thompson. 1994. *Leading Sectors and World Powers*. Columbia, S.C.: University of South Carolina Press.

Moore, Richard K. 1996. On Saving Democracy. A contribution to a conversation about global praxis on the World-Systems Network (WSN), <gopher://csf.Colorado.EDU: 70/00/wsystems/praxis/globprax>.

Murphy, Craig. 1994. *International Organization and Industrial Change: Global Governance since 1850*. New York: Oxford.

O'Donnell, Guillermo, Philip C. Schmitter, and Lawrence Whitehead, eds. *Transitions from Authoritarian Rule*, Vols. 1-4. Baltimore: Johns Hopkins University Press.

Paige, Jeffery M. 1997. Coffee and Power: Revolution and the Rise of Democracy. In *Central America*. Cambridge: Harvard University Press.

Perez-Sainz, Juan Pablo. 1997. Guatemala: The Faces of the Metropolitan Area. Pp. 124-52 in *The Urban Caribbean: Transition to a New Global Economy*, edited by Alejandro Portes, Carlos Dore-Cabral, and Patricia Landolt. Baltimore, Md.: Johns Hopkins University Press.

Petersen, Kurt. 1992. *The Maquiladora Revolution in Guatemala*. New Haven, Conn.: Schell Center, Yale Law School.

Portes, Alejandro, and A. Douglas Kinkaid. 1994. *National Development, Society and Economy in the New Global Order*. Chapel Hill, N.C.: University of North Carolina Press. Spanish translation: *Teorias de Desarrollo Nacional*. San Jose, Costa Rica: Editorial Universitaria Centromericana, 1990, 13-48.

Portes, Alejandro. 1998. Neoliberalism and the Sociology of Development: Emerging Trends and Unanticipated Facts. *Population and Development*.

Robinson, William I. 1996. *Promoting Polyarchy: Globalization, U.S. Intervention and Hegemony*. Cambridge, Mass.: Cambridge University Press.

———. 1997. A Case Study of Globalization Processes in the Third World: A Transnational Agenda in Nicaragua. *Global Society* 2, no. 1:61-91.

———. 1998. Neoliberalism, the Global Elite and the Guatemalan Transition: A Critical Macrostructural Analysis. Presented at NSF-sponsored Conference on Guatemalan Development and Democracy, Universidad del Valle, 26-28 March.

———. 1998/1999. Latin America and Global Capitalism. *Race and Class* 40, no. 2/3: 111-31.

Rueschemeyer, Dietrich, Evelyne H. Stephens, and John Stephens. 1992. *Capitalist Development and Democracy*. Chicago: University of Chicago Press.

Ruthrauff, John. 1997. A Guide to the Inter-American Development Bank and the World Bank: Strategies for Guatemala. Silver Spring, Md.: Center for Democratic Education.

———. 1998. The Guatemala Peace Process, the World Bank and the Interamerican Development Bank. Paper presented at NSF-sponsored Conference on Guatemalan Development and Democracy, Universidad del Valle, 26-28 March.

Shannon, Thomas R. 1996. *An Introduction to the World-Systems Perspective*. Boulder, Colo.: Westview.

Silver, Beverly. 1995. World Scale Patterns of Labor-capital Conflict: Labor Unrest, Long Waves, and Cycles of Hegemony. *Review* 18, no. 1:155-92.

Smith, Carol A. 1993. Local History in Global Context: Social and Economic Transitions in Western Guatemala. Pp. 75-118 in *Constructing Power and Culture in Latin America*, edited by Daniel Levine. Ann Arbor: University of Michigan Press.

Stevis, Dimitris. 1998. International Labor Organizations, 1864-1997: The Weight of History and the Challenges of the Present. *Journal of World-Systems Research* 4: 52-75, <http://csf.colorado.edu/wsystems/jwsr.html>.

Wagar, W. Warren. 1996. Toward a Praxis of World Integration. *Journal of World-Systems Research* 2, no. 2, <http:csf.colorado.edu/wsystems/jwsr. html7>.

Wallerstein, Immanuel. 1995. *After Liberalism*. New York: New Press.

Wilmer, Franke. 1993. *The Indigenous Voice in World Politics*. Newbury Park, Calif.: Sage.

14

Theories of Development and Their Application to Small Countries

Alejandro Portes

Despite its relatively small size, Guatemala has long been the object of disproportionate attention by outsiders. Many foreign academics have made the country the subject of their lifelong intellectual pursuits and some have even taken permanent residence there upon retirement. The natural beauty and climate of the country, no doubt, had much to do with these decisions, but the triggering factor enticing so many researchers and intellectuals down to the lands of the former Mayan empire is its social complexity. In a relatively restricted land mass and with a population of a few million, the country nevertheless features a remarkable variety of languages and cultures, a complex imbrication between what successive foreign influences brought in and what was there from the start (Adams 1970, chapter 2; Amaro 1992). To borrow a page from one of the theories discussed below, Guatemala is its own miniworld system, with sharply delineated cleavages of wealth and power distributed along spacial and ethnic gradients.

It is a land of profound inequality, easily the most so in the Caribbean Basin and, along with Brazil, the most unjust in Latin America. That sorry state of affairs did not happen by chance but is a direct outgrowth of the country's complex ethnic makeup. Just as in the United States, possibly the most unequal of the advanced countries, the basic cleavage of privilege and opportunity follows racial-ethnic distinctions; in Guatemala they flow from the superimposition of the Spanish empire and ensuing European and North American interests on established native civilizations. In both settings, a castelike structure developed, where the subordinate ethno-racial groups—indigenous to the land or brought as slaves—were defined by descendants of Europeans as outside and apart from real civilized society. Spanish-speaking white elites strained to obliterate the indigenous presence from the republic that they had built in Central America, in a manner not altogether different from the exclusion of blacks and Indians by the English-speaking whites who framed the North American Constitution (Appiah and Gutmann 1996). In both settings, the realm of civilized discourse and the scope of legal protections extended just to the edge of European society.

Reduced to a status not too different from that of feudal serfdom (Dobb 1963), the subordinate races represented little more than the "beasts of burden" on which a social order developed. In the American South, as in Central America and in general, in every instance where European settlers have found themselves in the midst of subjugated racial minorities, the dilemma has been how to make use of their labor while pretending that, socially, they do not exist. The most common solution has been a dualistic structure, with the enslaved or indigenous population confined to plantations and mines, while excluded from any presence in legal, cultural, or political institutions. The reactive effect of this structure has been everywhere the same—wars of national liberation and internal rebellions—as the stigmatized masses eventually rejected their invisibility and their role as creators of wealth for others' enjoyment (Wolpe 1975; Paige 1975).

Guatemala was no different. In this sense, the course of its political evolution during the twentieth century is actually closer to that of South Africa, Zimbabwe, and even Algeria than that of neighboring Costa Rica. Relative to its Central American neighbors, Guatemalan underdevelopment possesses certain unique features: the superimposition of a castelike structure on sharp class inequalities, and extreme violence—as the dominant segments of this dualistic structure strove to preserve their privileges (Perez-Sainz 1997). The outcome of these struggles also bears some similarity with those of European settler societies elsewhere and led to a political path at variance with that of other nations in the region.

Despite these key differences, current theories of development led by the omnipresent influence of the neoliberal framework persist in conceptualizing Guatemala as just another small Latin American country, suffering from the same shortcomings and subject to the same remedies as its neighbors. This view is itself part of a new wave of intellectual developments, emanating from the advanced nations, that persists in homogenizing the rest of the world into readily understandable categories for the public, economic advisors, and government officials otherwise ignorant of the nuances of each country's past. The resulting distorted images lead to developmental prescriptions that, when implemented, lead to unexpected outcomes and can, in the extreme, cause serious harm to the fabric of society and its prospects for growth. Reduction of a country to a set of figures is particularly problematic when the very definition of the nation is contested and the limit of its inclusiveness is uncertain (Brubaker 1996; Portes 1997).

Theories of Development in Local Context

Neoliberalism

Almost thirty years ago, I found myself witnessing an animated exchange between a survey interviewer, paid by the U.S. Agency for International Development, and his Mayan respondent in the Highlands surrounding Lake Atitlán. The subject of the study was fertility and birth control, and the Cakchiquel-speaking man had obvious difficulty in grasping the sense of questions posed to him by his Spanish-speaking interlocutor. "Have you or your spouse ever used contraceptive pills? Intrauterine diaphragm? Condoms?" To each and every question, the answer was a silent negative shake of the head. The authors of the survey had one last trump question up their sleeve. "Will you want or need to learn more about these methods?" The reply was an equally silent "no." "But why?" asked the interviewer, beginning to lose his patience. The old Mayan finally broke his mutism to reply in accented, but firm Spanish, "Because these are words, sir, that harm my ears."

Over the years, I have reflected on this encounter as a metaphor for much that is amiss in otherwise well-intentioned efforts to assist poorer societies from the outside. Time and again, the alleged prescriptions for economic growth and social development have clashed with preexisting social structures, leading to unanticipated consequences. These effects can be the actual opposite of those intended or can eventually lead to positive consequences, but for reasons different from those that led to the policy in the first place. In the case of the program of which this contraceptive survey was part, efforts to promote economic development by lowering population growth did not achieve their intended long-term effects; they did register some success in bringing population growth down, but mainly for reasons other than the actual pro-contraceptive campaigns. Urbanization of the population and the rapid disappearance of rural subsistence economies where children represented important economic assets played, in all likelihood, the key role in bringing about this downturn (Stykos 1971; Portes and Walton 1971, chapter 3).

The current neoliberal orthodoxy represents an extreme instance of history-free models of national development. It consists of a series of doctrinal assumptions about the efficiency of free markets for resource allocation, the benefits of the international division of labor, and a derived package of policy prescriptions about how to restore health to national economies. In Latin America, this policy package, promoted by the International Monetary Fund (IMF) and the U.S. Treasury in country after country consists of seven basic steps: (1) unilateral opening to foreign trade; (2) extensive privatization of state enterprises; (3) deregulation of goods, services, and labor markets; (4) liberalization of capital markets, with privatization of pension funds; (5) fiscal adjustment, based on drastic reductions of public outlays; (6) restructuring and downscaling of state-supported social programs; and (7) the end of "industrial policy" and any other form of state capitalism and concentration on macroeconomic management (Diaz 1996; Robinson 1998).

These policies have been applied with mixed results around the hemisphere, generally producing a decline in inflation along with major increases in unemployment and inequality. The latter effects have triggered, in turn, widespread social protests (Filgueira 1996; Berry 1997). The application of neoliberal prescriptions to Guatemala is singularly inappropriate for the following reasons: (1) The country never deviated much from a market model, successively specializing in the production of agricultural commodities in demand in the world market—bananas, coffee, cotton, and so on—and accepting a role as net importer of manufactured goods (Amaro 1992). The import substitution model of industrialization applied for many years in South American countries never made deep inroads in the Guatemalan context. (2) National governments never implemented a consistent industrial policy, nor engaged in the construction of an extensive social safety net. On the contrary, the model of dualistic capitalism practiced in the country was based on exclusion of the majority of the population from such protections and its availability as a mobile labor force for export agriculture. (3) The Guatemalan state had neither the will nor the ability to develop an extensive sector of public-owned enterprises (Adams 1970, chapter 3; Robinson 1998).

By and large, the process of accumulation in Guatemala corresponds fairly well to conditions prevailing under classical nineteenth-century capitalism, as described by Arrighi (1994). Property owners in peripheral countries at the time had the right to accumulate wealth on the basis of primary exports to England and other industrial countries, while excluding the rest of the population from participation except as servile labor. Put differently, Guatemala followed almost by the letter the strictures of the neoliberal program prior to the contemporary period. The state never seriously intervened in the economy, except to protect and extend the rights of property owners; it never sought to implement a program of autonomous development; and it never incorporated the mass of the population into protective social programs. Incipient attempts to move in this direction during the presidencies of Arevalo and Arbens were quickly put to an end (Jonas 1991). This exclusionary and nondevelopmental state did not deviate excessively from neoliberal prescriptions for primary export producers. Simultaneously, it acted consistently to sustain the bases of a castelike social order.

As is well known, the result was not sustained growth, but violent instability along with economic stagnation. Neoliberalism has little to say to Guatemala that the country does not already know and has not already experienced. The state has long been "out of the economy" and indeed out of society altogether, except for systematic repression of the racially stigmatized majority. Recent changes in the nature of exports—from traditional agriculture to low value-added manufactures and some tourist services—change the commodities, but not the overall picture (Perez-Sainz 1997). Clearly, the path for sustained development must be sought elsewhere.

World-Systems Theory

From opposite theoretical quarters comes a perspective that envisions national development as essentially a futile pursuit. The search for economic autonomy and growth, social equality, and participatory politics by peripheral social formations is mostly condemned to failure since they are subject to an overarching system that generally opposes such goals. World capitalism born out of the ashes of feudalism and expanding ceaselessly ever since transcends any national state, and its logic determines the relative position that individual countries occupy in the global hierarchy (Hopkins and Wallerstein 1977; Wallerstein 1974). Peripheral social formations, such as what we call Guatemala today, were created by this global encompassing system in earlier periods of its development and are kept in place by the mechanisms of unequal exchange and unequal political power.

As a backwater of the Spanish empire, a former province of Mexico, and a primary goods producer under U.S. tutelage, the position of Guatemala in the world economy is clearly peripheral and its chances for autonomous development almost nil. Its role as a primary goods producer has barely changed, with little chance of leaving its position on the losing side of the global circles of production and exchange. Under such conditions of subordination, any significant change, political or economic, will most likely come from the outside rather than be generated indigenously.

Although a dismal outlook from the point of view of nationalists, there is a great deal of truth in this perspective. Classical free trade, rather than generating the "wealth of nations," functioned as a key mechanism for keeping former colonies and other subordinate formations in place through both unequally rewarded trade and the local appropriation of any gains from this trade by a restricted class of native property holders. As in Guatemala, the primary role of this dominant class became to control and organize the rest of the population for export production. Although the final commodities entered the circles of capitalist trade, the system that produced them remained semifeudal, depending on coerced labor (Portes and Walton 1971). The combined political and economic imperatives of the world economy generally kept the situation in place, preventing national autonomy or sudden shifts in the global hierarchy of national formations (Hopkins and Wallerstein 1977; Chase-Dunn 1998).

Though accurate in many respects, the key limitation of this theoretical perspective is that its historical generalizations are formulated at a considerable remove from local realities, leading to an excessively schematic picture. The canvas is drawn in broad strokes, with little attention to detail, especially in the most peripheral regions. It is precisely in these areas where differences that count emerge among national formations subject to the same set of external forces. The result is that world-system theorists are often surprised by political and economic events that their perspective could not anticipate, pretty much as neoclassical policy advisers are often taken aback by the real-life consequences of their prescriptions. The world-system approach could no more anticipate the rise of the East Asian economic tigers or the entry of Spain and Portugal into the ranks of the advanced nations than neoclassical doctrine could predict that freeing the markets and "getting the prices right" would lead to street riots and government downfalls in Venezuela and Ecuador, among others (Portes 1997; Echeverria 1994).

The key missing factor is, of course, local history as it has molded the specific contours of the class structure and affected the character and efficiency of national states. In the Caribbean Basin, we find a common pattern of dependency and peripherality corresponding to world-system analysis, but we also find significant variants and departures, most notably the Cuban socialist and anti-imperialist regime, the role of Panama as an international commercial and finance entrepôt, and Costa Rica's stable democracy and relative economic development. Unhappily,

Guatemalan exceptionality runs in the opposite direction. The country is not simply a peripheral primary goods producer, but a mini-world system in which stubbornly resilient pre-Columbian cultures coexist with the equally stubborn resistance of European-origin elites to abandon their exclusionary practices. If English is the language of dominance and oppression among Guatemalan urban groups, Spanish plays a similar role in relations to Mayan communities in the countryside. The country defies easy characterization and fits only in a schematic sort of way into world-system typologies.

Embedded Autonomy

The contours of the Guatemalan social formation and its backwardness even relative to its neighbors cannot be understood without reference to the unique clash that took place in these lands between the colonizing power and a settled and civilized population, subsequently reduced to a servile position. A theory with greater potential to frame these complexities, as well as the diverging national outcomes within the same region, has been proposed by Peter Evans (1995). According to him, chances for sustained economic growth and achievement of other indicators of development depend on the quality of the state and its interactions with civil society. States that are managed by a well-trained bureaucracy relatively autonomous from civil society are, hence, immune to bribe taking, and are better positioned to insert the country advantageously in the circles of world trade. This is especially the case when state agencies selectively nurture private entrepreneurial initiatives and prepare them for global competition. This is the "embedded autonomous" model of developmental states, and Evans offers Taiwan, Singapore, and post-World War II Japan as examples.

On the contrary, states that are effectively penetrated by private interests give rise to "rental havens," enriching these narrow sectors at the expense of the rest of society. Such situations devolve into predatory states that act toward the majority of the population "without any more regard for the welfare of the citizenry than a predator has for the welfare of its prey" (Evans 1989, 562). Zaire under the long reign of Mobutu Sese Zeko is offered by Evans as an archetypical example. In this continuum of state quality and relationships to civil society, it is not difficult to place Guatemala toward the "predatory" end of the continuum. In the Guatemalan case, the state was not so much penetrated by private interests as created and operated by them from the start for the perpetuation of privileges flowing from a dualistic social structure. As seen previously, this situation even had an ideological justification in the alleged racial inferiority of the settled indigenous population and the need to preserve a civilized European enclave in its midst.

The repressive activities of this state were notably effective in demobilizing the subordinate masses and promoting generalized apathy among them. As late as the early 1990s, Perez-Sainz reported in his study of low-income settlements in Guatemala City that political and associational participation was almost nil and that faith in the ability of community organizations to act in behalf of the poor was

Table 14.1. Political Participation and Attitudes in the Caribbean Basin, 1992

Country (%)

	Costa Rica	Dominican Republic	Guatemala	Haiti	Jamaica	Overall
Belongs to a political party	40.0	21.3	4.0	4.0	98.1	47.0
Belongs to a community organization	12.5	11.4	4.5	12.0	2.3	7.3
Supports participation in parties	58.5	59.8	21.3	60.7	41.4	46.6
Believes community organizations accomplish:						
- Nothing	48.5	46.9	71.8	76.0	39.5	52.8
- Something	28.3	36.2	21.0	21.3	44.1	32.9
- A great deal	23.2	16.9	7.2	2.7	16.4	14.3
Best use of free time is:						
- To join a political party	7.5	12.9	3.3	8.0	6.8	7.5
- To join a community organization	62.3	60.3	45.8	54.7	83.8	65.5
- To remain at home	30.2	26.8	50.9	37.3	9.4	28.0
N	400	403	400	300	792	2295

Source: Portes and Itzigsohn 1997, 232.

extraordinarily low. "The demobilization of the city's social actors is essentially absolute; apathy predominates. People find that solutions to problems do not flow from collective action" (Perez-Sainz 1997, 139).

These conclusions are reinforced when results of this study are compared with parallel ones obtained from comparable samples in other cities in the same region.

The Guatemala City study was part of a five-country comparative project of urbanization and political participation in the Caribbean Basin. Identical questions about participation and attitudes toward political parties and community organizations were formulated to samples of low-income residents in the five capital cities selected for this project. Table 14.1 presents the relevant findings. They show that Guatemalans had the lowest levels of political and civic participation among the five countries, the lowest faith in political parties, and, along with Haitians, the most skeptical view of the effectiveness of community organizations. Most telling are responses to a forced-choice question asking respondents about the best use of their free time. Guatemalans are, by far, the most prone to endorse a "do nothing" option as opposed to engaging in any form of political or civic participation, be it at the national or local level. These results provide eloquent testimony of variations among countries that are apparently "the same" in world-system typologies and, more specifically, of the past ability of the Guatemalan state to entirely demobilize its population.

This is not the whole story, however, because along with generalized apathy, the repressive activities of the Guatemalan regime also triggered a resilient insurgency and widespread political instability. The failure of the predatory state to entirely disarticulate all forms of popular mobilization led directly to the civil war and the eventual transformation of the former sociopolitical order. The recent signing of the peace accords between the rebel movement and the government offers a glimpse of hope for moving the country away from its unfortunate past and toward the "embedded autonomy" end in Evans' continuum. For this to occur, however, a number of post-peace transformations in the character of the state and its relation to civil society must take place. Inevitably, these changes will meet strong resistance. It is at this point in which the external forces that steered Guatemala toward its current fragile peace will become once again relevant.

Transnationalism and National Development

In Princeton, the New Jersey town where I live, Guatemalans have become an increasingly visible presence. The migration apparently started with the efforts of churches and other civic groups in the area to help refugees from the civil war and peasant massacres of the 1980s and to prevent their deportation from the United States. Once in Princeton, the original refugees started bringing their kin and friends, to the point that Guatemalans have become the backbone of the town's low-wage and casual labor market. On several occasions, I have addressed one of these distinctly indigenous migrants in Spanish to discover that they had more difficulty understanding me than if I spoke to them in English. Apparently, they effected the transition from their native Cakchiquel or other Mayan languages to English without ever becoming proficient in Spanish.

This experience stands as an illustration of the forces that have an increasingly important bearing on Guatemala from the outside, undermining the stability of its traditional social order. To a large extent, the peace accords were achieved through the pressure and guidance of external actors, and their implementation has been monitored by missions from the United Nations and other international organizations. Simultaneously, external revulsion at the peasant massacres and urban death squads sponsored by the Guatemalan regime in the past led to increasing support of local human rights groups and of refugees abroad. The consolidation of large refugee communities in the United States then played back into the country in the form of economic support for democratic and peace initiatives and massive family remittances. Today, remittances from Guatemala's expatriate communities represent a key source of foreign exchange for the economy (Popkin 1999).

The limitations of world-system theory, discussed above, stem from its excessive remove from local realities and its almost exclusive attention to the logic of dominant geopolitical actors—multinational corporations and states. In addition to these, the contemporary world economy encompasses a number of institutions whose scope of activity has become increasingly transnational and that transnationalize, in turn, the local events on which they focus. These actors range from formal global organizations such as various United Nations agencies and the World Bank to international civil rights, human rights, and ecological groups down to local churches and committees of concerned citizens in the advanced countries. Easy global communications and a world-ranging media bring the initiatives of these various institutions and groups to each other's attention and provide instant coverage of its effects on the ground. Effects on previously isolated local groups are often revolutionary, leading to significant transformations in the balance of domestic political forces.

The emerging transnational perspective in the social sciences seeks to capture these dynamics as a complement, but also a potential counter to theories focused exclusively on the geopolitical logic of markets, capitals, and states. The fundamental ideas are two: First, that the moral authority of organized groups promoting certain values across national borders can have real political consequences and cannot be dismissed as "superstructure." Second, that technological advances in transportation and communications have facilitated the growth of actors and communities that sit astride national borders, commuting across space, and affecting local structures with a significant measure of autonomy (Smith 1995; Portes, Guarnizo, and Landolt 1999).

Thus, along with the "laws" of capitalist accumulation, there have developed in the contemporary world economy a series of parallel dynamics, including those promoting human rights and civil rights on a global scale, those empowering previously oppressed and downtrodden groups, and those initiated by these very groups on the basis of their new transnational linkages. The mobilization of these manifold forces imposes limits on what previously unencumbered national elites can do to their own populations and has given rise to minimum standards of conduct enforced by global opinion. The process affects the conduct of powerful international corporate actors and prompts adaptive changes, both cosmetic and real, in local structures of power.

In the case of Guatemala, the last decade of civil war and the present impasse may be reinterpreted as a contest between entrenched groups bent on maintaining a nineteenth-century structure of privilege and a number of transnationalized actors bent on transforming that structure. Results have been increasing behavioral constraints and defensiveness on the part of ruling elites and the emergence of new modernized sectors of the same elite. As Robinson (1998) points out, this emergent "transnational bourgeoisie" is still acting in defense of its privileges, but it is doing so under new rules of the game largely imposed from the outside. Without such influences, there would have been no fracture in the previously monolithic stance of the elites. Not that violent repression has not continued in Guatemala, but it cannot be implemented with the openness and impunity of the past. Under the glare of world opinion, such actions must be concealed, lest their discovery bring down international disapproval along with very tangible economic and political sanctions.

The presence of transnational actors in alliance with human rights and other domestic groups succeeded in turning the country inside out, "externalizing" the Guatemalan conflict, and taking it out of the protected space of nation-state sovereignty. The question at present is what influence can these actors have in the observance of the peace accords and the emergence of a more inclusive and pluralist nation-state. The externalization of the Guatemalan situation has had so far three main consequences: First, the partial subordination of governmental decision making to external opinion and international monitoring organizations. Such forces will certainly not prevent the continuation of social inequalities nor counter the hegemony of the propertied class, but can put limits to the perpetuation of a dualistic caste structure sustained by violent means. Guatemala will not be developed from the outside, but transnational forces will be instrumental in at least modernizing its dependency.

Second, the externalization of the conflict has helped give greater voice to the indigenous majority. The emergence of a pan-Mayan movement and the growing visibility of its demands would have been inconceivable without the social and political space created by global monitoring. Under previous conditions, such mobilization would not have occurred or would have been ruthlessly repressed. With the sympathy and support of outside groups, Mayan organizations have acquired sufficient voice within the national political space to begin breaking the exclusionary barriers of the past. Third, external actors and events have, in turn, transnationalized the Guatemalan peasantry. The massive refugee flows of the 1980s and their consolidation into immigrant communities abroad have brought in their wake important innovations. Massive remittances of hard currency is one, but so is the capacity of these communities to transmit new ideas and cultural expectations to their hometowns and to alert international opinion about new outbreaks of repression and identify the responsible parties (Popkin 1999; Landolt, Autler, and Baires 1999).

The traditional Guatemalan ruling classes still wield considerable power, but their capacity to enforce their views and maintain the prior exclusionary caste structure is now open to question. This is not because this class has changed of its own accord, but because the world has changed around it. No longer favored with the designation of unconditional U.S. ally in the global anticommunist struggle, it must now confront the force of new morally interventionist global actors and their empowerment of previously silent indigenous masses. More than the logic of global capitalism or the geopolitical interests of core states, for which Guatemala is a remote priority, it is the new interplay between forces fostered by transnationalism in its various forms that holds the potential for moving the nation from its unfortunate past into a more inclusive and equitable society in the coming century.

Works Cited

Adams, Richard N. 1970. *Crucifixion by Power: Essays on Guatemalan National Structure.* Austin: University of Texas Press.
Amaro, Nelson. 1992. *Guatemala: Historia Despiertas.* Guatemala City: IDESAC.
Appiah, Anthony K., and Amy Gutmann. 1996. *Color Conscious: The Political Morality of Race.* Princeton, N.J.: Princeton University Press.
Arrighi, Giovanni. 1994. *The Long Twentieth Century: Money, Power, and the Origins of Our Times.* London: Verso Books.
Berry, Albert. 1997. The Income Distribution Threat in Latin America. *Latin American Research Review* 32:3-40.
Brubaker, Rogers. 1996. *Nationalism Reframed.* Cambridge, UK: Cambridge University Press.
Chase-Dunn, Christopher. 1998. Globalization from Below in Guatemala. Paper presented at the Seminar on Guatemalan Development and Democratization, Universidad del Valle de Guatemala, March.
Diaz, Alvaro. 1996. Chile: Hacia el Pos-Neoliberalismo? Paper presented at the Conference on Responses of Civil Society to Neo-liberal Adjustment, University of Texas-Austin, April.
Dobb, Maurice. 1963. *Studies in the Development of Capitalism.* New York: International Publishers.
Echeverria, Julio. 1994. Gobernabilidad y Crisis de Partidos en el Ecuador. *Nariz del Diablo* 19 (April):14-23.
Evans, Peter. 1989. Predatory, Developmental, and Other Apparatuses: A Comparative Political Economy Perspective on the Third World State. *Sociological Forum* 4:561-87.
———. 1995. *Embedded Autonomy: States and Industrial Transformation.* Princeton, N.J.: Princeton University Press.
Filgueira, Carlos. 1996. Estado y Sociedad Civil: Politicas de Ajuste Estructural y Establización. Paper presented at the Conference on Responses of Civil Society to Neo-liberal Adjustment, University of Texas-Austin, April.
Hopkins, Terence K., and Immanuel Wallerstein. 1977. Patterns of Development in the Modern World-System. *Review* 1:111-45.
Jonas, Suzanne. 1991. *The Battle for Guatemala: Rebels, Death Squads, and U.S. Power.* Boulder, Colo.: Westview.
Landolt, Patricia, Lilian Autler, and Sonia Baires. 1999. From "Hermano Lejano to Hermano Mayor": The Dialectics of Salvadoran Transnationalism. *Ethnic and Racial Studies* 22 (March):290-315.

Paige, Jeffrey M. 1975. *Agrarian Revolution: Social Movements and Export Agriculture in the Underdeveloped World.* New York: Free Press.

Perez-Sainz, Juan Pablo. 1997. Guatemala: The Two Faces of the Metropolitan Area. Pp. 124-52 in *The Urban Caribbean: Transition to the New Global Economy,* edited by A. Portes, C. Dore-Cabral, and P. Landolt. Baltimore: Johns Hopkins University Press.

Popkin, Eric. 1999. Guatemalan Mayan Migration to Los Angeles: Constructing Transnational Linkages in the Context of the Settlement Process. *Ethnic and Racial Studies* 22 (March):267-89.

Portes, Alejandro. 1997. Neoliberalism and the Sociology of Development: Emerging Trends and Unanticipated Facts. *Population and Development Review* 23(June):229-59.

Portes, Alejandro, Luis E. Guarnizo, and Patricia Landolt. 1999. The Study of Transnationalism: Pitfalls and Promise of an Emergent Research Field. *Ethnic and Racial Studies* 22 (March):217-37.

Portes, Alejandro, and Jose Itzigsohn. 1997. Coping with Poverty and Change: The Politics and Economics of Urban Poverty. Pp. 227-52 in *The Urban Caribbean: Transition to the New Global Economy,* edited by A. Portes, C. Dore-Cabral, and P. Landolt. Baltimore: Johns Hopkins University Press.

Portes, Alejandro, and John Walton. 1971. *Labor, Class, and the International System.* New York: Academic Press.

Robinson, William I. 1998. Neoliberalism, the Global Elite, and the Guatemalan Transition: A Critical Macrostructural Analysis. Paper presented at the Seminar on Guatemalan Development and Democratization, Universidad del Valle de Guatemala, March.

Smith, Robert. 1995. *Los Ausentes Siempre Presentes: The Imagining, Making, and Politics of a Transnational Community between Ticuani, Puebla, Mexico, and New York City.* Ph.D. dissertation. Department of Sociology, Columbia University, October.

Stykos, J. Mayone. 1971. *Ideology, Faith, and Family Planning in Latin America.* New York: McGraw-Hill.

Wallerstein, Immanuel. 1974. *The Modern World-System: Capitalist Agriculture and the Origins of the European World-Economy in the Sixteenth Century.* New York: Academic Press.

Wolpe, Harold. 1975. The Theory of Internal Colonialism: The South African Case. Pp. 229-52 in *Beyond the Sociology of Development,* edited by I. Oxaal, T. Barnett, and D. Booth. London: Routledge and Kegan Paul.

Appendix

Summary of the Accord on Identity and the Rights of Indigenous Peoples

The indigenous accord is divided into four parts, a sacred number in Maya cosmology. The tone is constructive, and concrete remedies are suggested for grave social problems. The accord provides a vision of a just society and a measure of the substantial structural and cultural changes necessary to achieve this vision. The first part calls for the *formal recognition* of Guatemala's indigenous people, something denied them when non-Maya *mestizos* were conventionally assumed to be the standard of citizenship. Mayas are defined as the descendants of an ancient people who speak historically related indigenous languages and share common culture, self-identification, and a cosmology that sees the earth as a life-giving mother and corn as a sacred cultural axis. Maya identity is conceived of has having a plurality of sociocultural and linguistic expressions, just as indigenous identity also includes the non-Maya indigenous Xinca and the Afro-Guatemalan Garífuna who also become rights-bearing groups.

The second part of the accords focuses on the struggle against discrimination. Given that racial discrimination must be overcome in order to achieve the peaceful coexistence of all ethnic groups, the accord urges legislative reform to make discrimination a crime, root out discriminatory laws, promote public education, and secure the active defense of rights by providing legal aid for the poor. The rights of indigenous women who receive double discrimination on the basis of ethnicity and gender draw special mention. The accord urges Congress to make sexual harassment a crime and to promote the UN Convention to Eliminate All Forms of Discrimination against Women. It also calls for a reaffirmation of the International Convention for the Elimination of All Racial Discrimination and the ILO Convention 169 on Indigenous and Tribal Peoples, which after being promulgated in 1989 has been sidelined repeatedly in the Guatemalan Congress.

The third section of the accord identifies key cultural rights for indigenous communities. It calls for the recognition and support of indigenous people as the authors of their own cultural development through distinctive institutions. Key to these efforts would be the constitutional recognition of indigenous languages in schools, social services, official communications, and court proceedings. Individuals and communities would gain the right to shed Hispanicized names, as they wished.

Maya spirituality and spiritual guides would be recognized, the distinct spiritual practices of different indigenous groups constitutionally protected. Of great concern is the conservation of temples, ceremonial centers, and archaeological sites of ancient Maya culture as indigenous heritage and national patrimony. The accord asserts that indigenous communities should be involved in the conservation and administration of these centers and archaeological sites. The use of indigenous dress in all arenas would be guaranteed and supported by educational programs.

The accord recognizes the existence and value of Maya scientific and technological knowledge, which, along with the knowledge of other indigenous groups, should be fostered and disseminated through a variety of institutions and media. Increased indigenous access to contemporary knowledge and to opportunities for scientific and technical exchange are to be promoted.

Through the accords, the government commits itself to wide-ranging education reform, including regional decentralization; the inclusion of families in all areas of local education, including the appointment of teachers; the integration of Maya materials and educational methods; the promotion of indigenous languages and bilingual intercultural education; the promotion of national unity and cultural diversity at all educational levels; the development of bilingual teachers and indigenous administrators; and the expansion of educational funding for programs and students. In addition to programs for Maya education, intercultural education would be supported for all children. The Maya schools movement would be fostered along with the development of a Maya university.

Finally, this section of the accords identifies wider access to mass media, especially the radio, for indigenous programming, broadcasts in indigenous languages, and the dissemination of educational programming for the wider public. The fourth section of the accord deals with constitutional reforms in civil, political, social, and economic rights to make possible a multiethnic, pluricultural, and multilingual vision of national society. Decentralization would be promoted through governmentally funded municipal autonomy, which would involve the recognition of localized customary law and community decision-making powers in issues of education, health, culture, and community development. The accord calls for a reform of municipal codes and a regionalization of government structures along the lines of indigenous language communities to facilitate the participation of local communities in wider decision-making bodies. The importance of institutionalizing indigenous representation at all levels so indigenous interests can be actively pursued means that indigenous representatives should be included in all administrative bodies and communities consulted whenever government actions might affect them.

The accords assert the right of communities to use their customary norms to regulate internal affairs as long as local standards are not incompatible with national law or international human rights doctrine. Training programs in customary law are mandated for judges and ministry officials. With subsidized access to legal aid and official interpreters, no one would be judged without access to court proceedings in his or her own language.

Regarding the urgent problem of indigenous land rights, the accords argue for the recognition of communal and individual landholdings, the right of communities to administer communal lands according to local norms, and rights to natural resources in benefit of local communities. In view of the historical vulnerability of local communities to land seizures by those with political connections, financial resources, and fluency in the national language (Spanish), the accords call for legislative and administrative reforms to title, protect, defend, and settle land claims; to provide educational, legal, and linguistic assistance so communities can defend their interests; and to compensate communities that have lost lands. The government is urged to distribute state lands to communities without sufficient land as long as this does not hurt small land owners.

The accords designate commissions, composed of representatives from the government and indigenous groups active in the civil assembly, which were set up over four years to further refine the reform process in each of the areas under discussion. The United Nations Mission to Guatemala (MINUGUA) is the international organization entrusted with the verification of the peace accords.

Note

See Saqb'ichil/COPMAGUA (Coordinación de Organizaciones del Pueblo Maya de Guatemala). 1995. *Acuerdo sobre Identidad y Derechos de los Pueblos Indígenas*. Punto 3 del Acuerdo de Paz Firme y Duradera. Suscrito en la Ciudad de México por el Gobierno de la República de Guatemala y la Unidad Revolucionaria Nacional Guatemalteca. Guatemala: COPMAGUA.

Index

Accord for a Firm and Lasting Peace, 145
Accord on Identity and the Rights of Indigenous Peoples, 5, 14, 53, 57, 67, 149-50, 180-82, 241-43
Accord on Socio-Economic and Agrarian Issues, 54, 58, 70
Accord on the Strengthening of Civilian Power and Role of the Armed Forces in a Democratic Society, 54-55, 58
agrarian reform, 201
agrarian society, 25; and capital, 136, 137; and class structure, 120; and market forces, 124
amnesty, 58
ANACAFE, 139
apartheid, 67
Arbenz, Jacobo, 50, 121
Arzú, Alvaro, 54, 63
Arzú administration, 72, 95, 97, 121
Assembly on Civil Society (ASC), 53, 54, 64, 67, 148
assimilation, 169, 171; and national integration, 170-71
attitudes toward government, 35-40
authoritarian enclaves, 69
authoritarianism, 23, 28-29, 120, 146; and democratic change, 123; and national security, 103-104; and neoliberalism, 126
authoritarian norms, 36-37

bilingual education, 155, 156; and educational reform, 180-86, 242
Bilingual Education Project, 181
budget: and municipal, departmental, and state relations, 88; and *municipios*, 93; and security, 115
Bush administration, 29

camino centroamericano, 64, 71
Carter administration, 29
Catholic Bishop's Conference, 52
Catholic Church, 153, 157; in defense of status quo, 121; and human rights, 112; and Liberation Theology, 30
cattle, 137
Central America, 21, 23, 29, 31, 41, 64, 68, 101, 103, 104, 194-96; and democratization, 123-24; and public security, 114; and transnational processes, 192-94; in world-systems perspective, 216-17
Central American Common Market (CACM), 30, 193, 195, 196
Central American Parliament, 63
Central American Peace Accord, 32, 51
Cerezo, Vinicio, 51, 65, 85, 146
Chile, 64
Christian Democrats, 198
citizen participation, 97, 102
citizen security, 102, 104, 115
citizenship, 114, 123; and free market, 126; and popular participation, 124-25
Civilian Defense Patrols (PACs), 57; and murders, 111
civilian government, 21, 22, 60, 61, 62, 146
civil rights, 122
civil servants, 83; and salaries, 89
civil society, 202
civil war, 50-56, 108-9, 120, 145; and casualties, 3, 146; and population displacement, 146
class, 121-22, 131, 217; and Catholic Church, 121; and ecological degradation, 129; and land use, 129; Maya/Ladino divide, 157; and

political reform, 24-25, 121; and relations with state, 132
coffee 24, 134-35; and indigenous populations, 135; and land use, 136, 139; and national economy, 132-33
Cold War, 4, 5, 28, 29, 32, 69, 104, 116, 121
Colombia and coffee, 135
colonos, 135
comisiones paritarias, 56
comités cívicos, 54, 63, 67
commodities, 11, 132, 133, 137; and coffee, 134; and foreign exchange, 9-10; and price variations, 138
comparative advantage, 131
constitutional reforms, 54
Constitution of 1985, 58, 60, 61, 85; and demilitarization, 109
COPMAGUA, 148
corporatist state, 124
corruption, 124
Costa Rica, 22, 24, 31, 101, 198; and coffee, 135; and GDP, 33; and marginalization of *municipios*, 96; as model of political reform, 104
cotton, 137
counterinsurgency, 57, 64, 69, 145
counterinsurgency state, 61, 199; and end of power 120
coup d'etat, 60, 123, 145
crime, 115, 122; and murders, 107; organized, 110, 114

Dahl, Robert, 65, 66
de León Carpio, Ramiro, 52, 65, 86, 97
death squads, 112, 114
debt peonage, 136
de-centaurization, 50, 57
decentralization, 83, 242; and administration of public security, 115; and biases against the *municipios*, 95-96; and bureaucratic obstacles, 85; and fiscal reform, 88, 93; and regional development, 84-88
delinking, 221, 222
demilitarization, 145; and constitutional reform, 110; and democratization, 115; and peace agreement, 109; and the political left, 129; and security,
102, 115. *See also* El Salvador
democratic norms, 36, 37
democratization, 145; and corruption, 124; and cycles, 122; and free market, 120; and military, 123; theories of, 65-66
denuncias, 53
discrimination, 3, 241; and race, 155
drug trafficking, 112, 114-15. *See also* crime
Dutch disease, 133

ecological diversity, 130
ecological preservation, 130
economic growth, 35; and democratization, 122; and development, 10; and inequality, 13; and political reform, 25; and social mobility, 124
economic reform, 129
Ecuador, 88
educational reform: funding for, 157, 189; and Maya schools, 156; and poverty, 16-17; and use of indigenous languages, 149. *See also* bilingual education
El Quiché, 111
El Salvador, 5, 21, 22-23, 29, 32, 64, 101, 103, 197; and coffee, 135; and demilitarization, 105-8; and GDP, 33; and indigenous resistance 136; and public security in comparison with Guatemala, 112
elections, 60, 62-64, 87-88
embedded autonomy, 234-36
English. *See* language
equitable development, and neoliberalism, 132
environment 129, 216; and class conflict, 131; and economic growth, 12; and foreign actors, 130, 132; and need for managed intervention, 130; and political uses of land and labor, 130
ethnic identity, 154; and globalization, 171, 172; and Maya, 13, 167-68
ethnic relations, 5, 87, 161, 218; historical perspectives, 229; Maya-Ladino, 67, 158, 182

Index

European Economic Community (EEC), 149

Farabundo Martí National Liberation Front (FMLN), 29, 53, 64, 105
farms, small: and coffee, 135, 139; and family labor, 132; and relative inefficiency, 136
feudal serfdom, 230
Figueroa, Carlos, 57
financial reform, 11, 83
flexible accumulation, 214
foreign actors, 25, 26; and educational reform, 157; and investment, 219-21; and pan-Maya movement, 148-49, 157
foreign currencies, 133
Framework Accord, 53
Franja Transversal del Norte, 137
French Revolution, 71

gangs. *See* crime
Garífuna, 149. *See also* language
genocide, 3
Gerardi, Bishop Juan, 4, 112
global economy, 189; and national social classes, 190
globalization defined, 209, 211
globalization from below, 69, 221-24; defined, 207
globalization project, 211-12
governmental structure, 83
grassroots activism, 146, 148; and amnesty, 155; and pan-Maya movement, 156, 158, 161-62
Guatemala City, 83, 91; and gangs, 110
Guatemalan National Revolutionary Front (URNG), 29, 51, 55, 62, 63, 64, 108, 121, 146, 177
Guatemalan Republican Front (FRG), 92, 154
guerillas, 146

Historical Clarification Commission, 110, 111, 153
Honduras, 21, 22-23, 31, 32, 88, 101, 103, 197-98; and GDP, 33
human rights, 4, 13-14, 40, 61, 62-63, 146, 153, 201; and immunity, 112; and transnational linkages, 238. *See also* Historical Clarification Commission
Human Rights Accord, 53, 56

Import Substitution Industrialization (ISI), 232
indigenous political movements, 64, 67, 69
inequality, 9, 12-13, 30, 125, 145, 230; and democratization, 69-71; and distribution of land, 129; and ethnicity, 229; and free market, 126; and language use, 179-80; Maya vs. non-Maya, 169; and transnationalism, 238; in world comparison, 4
inflation, 34
infrastructure development, 10
insurrection, 31, 64, 103
interculturalism, 177, 242; and bilingual education, 180-86; defined, 182; and language, 178-80
international aid, 59
international competitiveness, 10, 133
international constraints, 26, 27, 40, 52, 72, 127; and environmental protection, 130; and globalization, 124
International Monetary Fund (IMF), 4, 218, 219, 223, 231
Ixil, 111

labor: and immiseration, 135; and mobilization, 34; and political coercion, 130, 135; and shortage, 134
Ladino, 67, 158, 160, 218; and pan-Maya movement, 150; and poverty, 157; and racism, 159; response to indigenous rights, 68; and state violence, 153
land use, 129, 131; and fragmentation, 136; and rapid growth of large-scale agriculture, 137
land tenure, 129; and expropriation for coffee growing, 135; and redistribution, 135-36; and rights to land, 243

landlessness, 120
language, 177, 241; and bilingualism, 184; and English, 177, 234; and Garífuna, 152, 177, 179, 183-85; and Kich'ee', 152; and Ladinos, 179; and lingua franca, 152; and Maya, 152, 177, 178-80, 181, 183-85; and officialization of indigenous languages, 151-52, 183-84; and pan-Maya movement, 152; and Spanish, 151, 152, 177, 184, 234, 243; and Xinca, 152, 177, 179, 183-85. *See also* bilingual education
Latin America, 21, 24, 69-70, 88, 219-21; and authoritarianism, 122; compared with Guatemala, 219-21; and democratization, 66; and drug trafficking, 114; and fiscal reform, 88; and GDP, 33; and neoliberalism, 231-32; and public security, 101, 103, 113
Liberation Theology, 30, 67
liberal democracy, 121-22
limpieza de sangre, 157
logging, 137

Man and the Biosphere, 130
mandamientos, 136
market economy, 70, 138; and democratization, 120, 124; and domination of coffee, 132-33; and environment, 131; and inequality, 126, 233; and international capital, 122, 133; and poverty, 121-22
mass media, 242
mass protest, 34
Maya, 13-14, 63, 67, 149, 150-52, 160-61; and community autonomy, 156; and form of local government, 89, 92; and global indigenist movement, 218; and globalization, 174; and insufficient land, 137; and interculturalism, 182; in national government, 154, 158; and state violence, 153, and war casualties, 3. *See also* pan-Maya movement and ethnic identity
mayors. *See municipios*
Menchú, Rigoberta: and Nobel Peace Prize, 146
Mexico, 172, 217
migration, internal, 136, 137; from coerced labor, 135; from political violence, 155
military, 22, 60, 61, 120; and civil-military relations 104, 113; and coercion of labor, 135; and demilitarization, 102, 104; and democratization, 122, 123; and ecological degradation, 130; and militarization, 113; and peacetime mission, 109; and reduction in personnel, 109; and reformism, 28. *See also* death squads
Ministry of Urban and Rural Development, 86
Mobile Military Police, 110
multiculturalism, 3, 13-14, 53, 57, 65, 67, 145, 157, 241-42; and challenges to implementation, 168; and funding of cultural reforms, 155; and pan-Maya movement, 150; and police force, 111; and postmodernism, 171
Municipal Code, 92
municipios, 83, 84, 88-93; and institutional weaknesses, 97; and Maya, 89; and mayors, 89, 91; and support network 91
murders, by the state, 3, 4, 58, 111; and war, 107. *See also* death squads
National Action Party (PAN), 32, 199
National Association of Municipalities (ANAM), 91-93; and public-private partnerships, 92-93
National Civilian Police (PNC), 109, 110-11, 112, 113
National Commission for Reconcialiation, 146
national police force, 103
National Promotion Institute (INFOM), 89-91, 95
National Republican Alliance (ARENA), 32
national security, 102
neoliberalism, 70, 138, 200-201, 231; and Central America, 193; and decline of authoritarianism, 126; and

environment, 131, 132; and global culture, 192; and poverty, 191; and transnational elite, 190-92
New Guatemalan Democratic Front (FDNG), 54, 63, 64, 155, 158
New Right, 194, 195
Nicaragua, 21, 22-23, 29, 31-32, 101, 196-97; and GDP, 33
Nongovernmental organizations (NGOs) and pressure for change, 129; and environmental protection, 132; and pan-Maya movement, 148-49
North American Free Trade Agreement (NAFTA), 193

oil, 133-34
oligarchy, 157, 194, 196, 199; and coffee, 134
Organización del Pueblo en Armas, 55
Organization of American States (OAS), 29, 40, 193

pacted transition, 59-60, 64
Pan-Maya movement, 147, 154, 155, 158; and foreign actors, 148-49; and grassroots activism, 156
path dependencies, 134, 138
peace accords, 3, 4, 59, 101, 120
peace dividend, 34
peace negotiations, 50-56, 119-20, 145, 146
peasantry, 25, 120; and farming, 10; and "post peasants," 161
Peru, 146
Petén, 12; and fragility of soil, 130, and ecology, 132; and in-migration, 137
petrodollars, 133
pluriculturalidad, 50
political culture, 25, 35-39, 68, 145; and democracy, 14-15; and political participation, 235-36; and public welfare, 124
political economy, 33-35
political reform, 15, 22-23; and cycle of democratic change, 122; and demilitarization, 104, 113; and public security, 109, 110; and theories of regime change, 24-28. *See also* corruption

political society, 202
political violence, 30
polyarchy, 65, 114, 224-25; and low-intensity democracy, 132; and transnational processes, 192
popular justice and lynchings, 116
population growth, 12
poverty, 9, 12, 31, 33-34, 125; and formal democracy, 70-71; and Ladinos, 157; and market economy, 121-22; and neoliberalism, 191; and transfer payments, 94-95; in world comparison, 4, 15;
public administration, 83
public policy, and market intervention, 16
public security, 102, 112-15; and demilitarization, 109; and privatization, 114

quetzal, 34
Quetzaltenango, 54, 63, 67
Quezada, Msgr. Rodolfo, 52

Reagan administration, 29, 60
rebellion, 25
reciclados, 111
redistribution, 13, 58, 201
regime change, 21, 22-23; theories of, 24-28
regime types, 23
repression, 3, 31, 36, 61, 120; of labor, 136; of real wages, 10
revenues, 83-84, 88, 134
Ricardo, David, 132
Ríos Montt, Efraín, 63, 154
rural areas, and conflict zones, 61; and marginalization, 93; and policing, 111

Sandinista, 22, 29, 51
Sandinista Front for the Liberation of Nicaragua (FSLN), 29
Schumpeterian model, 59, 65
security forces, 41, 62-63; and bureaucracy 103; and demilitarization, 102
semi-periphery, 208
Serranazo, 52, 53, 57, 65

Serrano, Jorge, 40, 52, 61, 65, 86, 95, 97, 146-47, 199
Sierra de Minas, 132
SINACODUR, 84-88, 95, 97
soils and coffee, 132, 134
Somoza, Anastasio, 31
South Africa, 4, 67, 70, 153, 230
Southern Cone, 59, 64
Spanish. *See* language
spiral of capitalism and socialism, 212-15

taxes, 83-84, 88, 138; in world comparison, 4
Third World, 4
trade, 189
transfer payments and criteria for distribution, 94; and infrastructure development, 97; and state-to-*municipio*, 93-95
transnational elite, 189-92, 219
transnational linkages 237, 238; and pan-Maya movement, 238-39
transnational processes, 192-94, 221, 236-39, 237
Truth Commission, 53, 57-58, 152-53, 155

undermployment, 13, 58
unemployment, 58
United Nations (UN), 5, 29, 52, 55, 148-49, 193, 223, 237; and MINUGUA, 53, 56, 62, 65, 110, 111, 153-54, 155, 223, 243
United States, 32, 40; and the Central Intelligence Agency (CIA), 3, 50, 54, 211, 218; and fight against organized crime, 116; and foreign policy, 28-29; and intervention, 32, 191, 195
United States Agency for International Development (USAID), 193; and environment, 130
urban areas: and institutional bias, 93

vagrancy, 135
Venezuela, 70, 88, 133
violence, by the state. *See* murders
voter participation, 35-40, 62, 63, 125

Western Highlands, 51, 136
women's movements, 69, 154
World Bank, 218, 237; and ecological preservation, 130
world economy, 189
world-systems, 207, 209, 232-34, 237; and Central America, 216-17; cycles and trends, 210; and social change, 208

Xelajú, 63
Xinca, 149. *See also* language

About the Contributors

Nelson Amaro is dean of the social sciences faculty and director of the Master's Degree on Development program at the Universidad del Valle de Guatemala. He has worked with United Nations permanent missions in New York, Rome, and El Salvador, and other missions have taken him to Asia, Middle East, Africa, and Latin America. He was viceminister of Urban and Rural Development in Guatemala from 1987 to 1989. He has published three books: *The Challenge of Development in Guatemala* (1970); *Decentralization and Popular Participation in Guatemala* (1990); and *Decentralization, Local Government and Participation: Latin America-Honduras* (1994). His area of research interest is the axis of decentralization and local government citizen participation.

John A. Booth is Regents' professor of political science at the University of North Texas. He is the author of *The End and the Beginning: The Nicaraguan Revolution* (1985), coauthor of *Understanding Central America* (1993), and coeditor of *Political Participation in Latin America*, vols. 1 and 2 (1978, 1979), *Elections and Democracy in Central America* (1989), *Elections and Democracy in Central America, Revisited* (1995), and *Costa Rica: Quest for Democracy* (1998). He has published numerous journal articles and anthology chapters on political participation, political culture, violence, revolution, and democratization in Central America, Mexico, and Colombia.

Stephen G. Bunker is professor of sociology at the University of Wisconsin-Madison. He is author of *Underdeveloping the Amazon: Extraction, Unequal Exchange, and the Failure of the Modern State* (1988) and of *Peasants against the State* (1991). He studies the social, economic, and environmental consequences of raw materials extraction, processing, and transport on both exporting and importing nations.

Christopher Chase-Dunn is professor of sociology and director of the Institute for Research on World-Systems at the University of California-Riverside. He is author of *Global Formation: Structures of the World-Economy* (2d edition, 1998), editor of *The Future of Global Conflict* (with Volker Bornschier, 1999) and author of *The*

Spiral of Capitalism and Socialism (with Terry Boswell, 2000). He studies urbanization, core/periphery relations and the trajectories of economic and political globalization over the past two hundred years. He also compares the modern world-system with earlier regional intersocietal systems in his book with Tom Hall, *Rise and Demise: Comparing World-Systems* (1997).

Susanne Jonas teaches Latin American and Latino Studies at the University of California, Santa Cruz. She has been an expert on Guatemala and Central America more broadly for more than thirty years, and has written extensively about Guatemala. Her *The Battle for Guatemala: Rebels, Death Squads and U.S. Power* (1991) was published in Spanish in Guatemala in 1994. She also wrote *Of Centaurs and Doves: Guatemala's Peace Process* (2000).

A. Douglas Kincaid is associate professor of sociology and research director of the Latin American and Caribbean Center at Florida International University. He received his Ph.D. in sociology from Johns Hopkins University in 1987. His research interests include public security, civil-military relations, and the relationship between regional and national development dynamics. Professor Kincaid is currently the U.S. coordinator for Central America 2020, a joint U.S./European/Central American project to develop analyses and recommendations for Central American development priorities for the next two decades. His publications include *Comparative National Development: Society and Economy in the New Global Order* (coeditor with A. Portes, 1994).

Susan Manning is writing her Ph.D. thesis on the effects of dependence on portfolio investment on national development. She has done research on the international political economy of Mexican social change and on the rise and demise of ancient cities and empires.

Alejandro Portes is professor of sociology at Princeton University and faculty associate of the Woodrow Wilson School of Public Affairs. He was the President of the American Sociological Association in 1999. His most recent books include *City on the Edge: The Transformation of Miami* (1993) and *The Urban Caribbean* (1997). Portes is a Fellow of the American Academy of Arts and Sciences.

Julia Richards is education specialist for the U.S. Agency for International Development (USAID) in Guatemala. She received her Ph.D. in educational policy studies at the University of Wisconsin-Madison. Her research is focused on education, language, and culture of Mayan peoples of Guatemala.

Michael Richards is an anthropologist who divides his time doing research through the Universidad del Valle de Guatemala's Medical Entomology Department and working as an independent consultant in development. He received a Ph.D. in anthropology from the University of Wisconsin-Madison, and has focused most of his research on education, linguistic, and health aspects of Mayan peoples. In addition to working professionally with the Maya, he spent his childhood in Guatemala.

William I. Robinson is assistant professor of sociology at New Mexico State University and a frequent guest lecturer at the Central American University in Managua, Nicaragua. He is a macrosociologist specializing in globalization, transnational studies, comparative development, social change, and Latin American affairs. His works have appeared in such journals as *Sociological Forum*, *Theory and Society*, *Development and Change*, and *Race and Class*. His most recent book is *Promoting Polyarchy: Globalization, U.S. Intervention, and Hegemony* (1996).

Gert Rosenthal is an economist from Guatemala who has recently served as the Guatemalan representative to the United Nations. He received both his undergraduate and his graduate training in economics at the University of California at Berkeley. He served in the Guatemalan government in various posts (including minister of planning) between 1962 and 1972, and he was appointed a Fellow of the Adlai Stevenson Institute for International Affairs in 1971. He also served in the Secretariat of the Central American Common Market, before joining the United Nations' Economic Commission for Latin America. In this regional organization, he was director of its Mexico City Office, deputy executive secretary, and, between 1989 and 1997, executive secretary. He has taught economic development and public finance at the Universidad Rafael Landivar in Guatemala and has written numerous articles on development issues.

José Serech is a Mayan Kaqchikel, born in Tecpan, Guatemala. He has a B.A. in Philosophy at the Oblate College, Washington D.C.; an M.A. in applied theology at the Graduate Theological Union, Berkeley, California; and an M.A. in social anthropology at the University of Paris VIII—Guatemala Program (pending thesis). His language domain ranges from Mayan Kaqchikel and K'iche' as mother tongues, to Tagalog (Philippines), Spanish, and English. He has working experience in organizing local emergency committees after the 1976 earthquake in the Highlands, and in Kaqchikel missionary programs until 1981. From 1984 to 1990 he taught and did community organization in the Philippines. From 1991 to 1998 he worked as director and cofounder of the Mayan Center of Research and Documentation, CEDIM. In 1998, he became a member of the Consulting Commission of the Ministry of Education for the National Educational Reform as mandated by the peace accords. Serech is the deputy chief of party of the NEXUS Municipal Project, financed by USAID Guatemala and implemented by Development Alternatives, Inc. (DAI).

Edelberto Torres Rivas is a Central American sociologist. He was born in Guatemala, and has served as the secretary general of FLACSO. He is now the director of the Master's Program in International Relations at Landivar University and a human development consultant to the United Nations Development Program. He has written extensively about society and politics in Central America. His most recent book, *Del autoritarismo a la paz* (1998), is coauthored with Gabriel Aguilera Peralta.

Kay B. Warren is professor of anthropology at Harvard University. She is the author of *Indigenous Movements and Their Critics: Pan-Maya Activism in Guatemala* (1998), *Women of the Andes: Patriarchy and Social Change in Two Peruvian Towns* (with Susan Bourque) (1982), *The Symbolism of Subordination: Indian Identity in a Guatemalan Town* (1978/1989), and the editor of *The Violence Within: Culture and Political Opposition in Divided Nations* (1992). Her work specializes in the political anthropology of multicultural societies, public intellectuals and the production of knowledge, and social movements and the state.